CW01401374

MILITARY ARCHAEOLOGY

In memory of my mother, Sheila Jean Heath,
12/11/1941–11/09/2021

MILITARY ARCHAEOLOGY

How Detectorists and Major Finds Improve our Understanding of History

TIM HEATH AND JULIAN EVAN-HART

First published in Great Britain in 2023 by
PEN AND SWORD HISTORY
An imprint of
Pen & Sword Books Ltd
Yorkshire – Philadelphia

ISBN 978 1 39902 323 8

A CIP catalogue record for this book is available from the British Library.

Typeset in Times New Roman 12/16 by
SJmagic DESIGN SERVICES, India.
Printed and bound in the UK by CPI Group (UK) Ltd.

Pen & Sword Books Limited incorporates the imprints of Atlas, Archaeology, Aviation, Discovery, Family History, Fiction, History, Maritime, Military, Military Classics, Politics, Select, Transport, True Crime, Air World, Frontline Publishing, Leo Cooper, Remember When, Seaforth Publishing, The Praetorian Press, Wharncliffe Local History, Wharncliffe Transport, Wharncliffe True Crime and White Owl.

For a complete list of Pen & Sword titles please contact
PEN & SWORD BOOKS LIMITED
George House, Units 12 & 13, Beevor Street, Off Pontefract Road,
Barnsley, South Yorkshire, S71 1HN, England
E-mail: enquiries@pen-and-sword.co.uk
Website: www.pen-and-sword.co.uk

or

PEN AND SWORD BOOKS
1950 Lawrence Rd, Havertown, PA 19083, USA
E-mail: uspen-and-sword@casematepublishers.com
Website: www.penandswordbooks.com

Contents

Introduction

Military archaeology has always been a sub-discipline of traditional historical archaeology. As such, both were once considered the pursuit of learned history professors and their disciples. However, today, military archaeology has flourished and grown into what can only best be described as a hugely popular pastime, and in many instances a multi-million-pound business. With a vast array of technologies available today, even the enthusiast on the most modest of budgets can become an archaeologist – if only in layman's term.

Despite the popularity today in unearthing the answers to the questions of our turbulent past, there are surprisingly few detailed texts available on this fascinating and historically important area of study. By and large the subject of military archaeology found an almost parallel association in the world of militaria collecting. It can be said that the very first individuals to have perhaps inadvertently influenced the craft that is now military archaeology were the relatives of those slain in the various conflicts which have blighted mankind's existence over the centuries – perhaps the finest example being the families of those lost on the battlefields of the First World War. The first pilgrimages to these battlefields began steadily over the years after 1918. Families travelled sometimes considerable distances in order to gain some understanding or perspective on how, where and when their loved ones lost their lives. It was, as it still is, a fairly common practice to collect a cartridge case, piece of shrapnel, a button or a coin; such things were not only collected as a personal memento but as a physical connection to the events that had so catastrophically altered the lives of millions of people around the world. The same can be said for the battlefields of the Second World War where military archaeology began its ascent to the lucrative business proportions of today, in part as a result of the greater awareness that many people have today in their own personal family histories.

The collecting of the relics of war from battlefields had up until the early 1990s been a fairly quiet backwater of the militaria world. At that time, I can vividly recall the flagrant disinterest in the rusty, ground-dug relics often unearthed by enthusiasts with metal detectors. These were the items once viewed by many as the detritus often consigned to boxes beneath dealers' tables at militaria shows. Today it is a very different story, and with the greater awareness of both our ancestry and personal history, there has been a huge resurgence of interest, not only in the battles of more recent times but also those now considered ancient. Some relics can change hands for astronomical prices.

Along with the resurgence of intertest in this area of history comes the inevitable flood of TV programmes and documentaries keen to capitalize on the subject; some are good but most are bad. It would appear today that those once relatively undisturbed backwaters are now crowded with self-appointed experts, some of whom procure a celebrity endorsement to further enhance their product, yet sadly this is the nature of the business today. It is all very demeaning yet typical of the times we now live in.

While it might make great TV, battlefield relics are not 'treasure', as some like to refer them as; these things were not left behind by pirates, thieves or highwaymen – good men very likely lost their lives nearby. The very mention of 'treasure' in this sense is, I believe, an insult as it implies monetary value as opposed to historical. Yes, there are battlefield relics which are extremely valuable, and which many enthusiasts call 'rusty gold'. I have heard this term being used on many occasions in the past, yet in an affectionate context, usually by enthusiasts who have no intention of selling on the items they have recovered. Whilst never entirely agreeing with the term, I understand why many use it and, somehow, it's never seemed as patronizing as that of 'treasure'. The focus in all cases should be firmly on the artefact itself and equally importantly the historical context of the particular item in question as opposed to any monetary value.

The object then of this book is to examine the various equipment available to both beginner and professional, the current laws and regulations as set out by the host countries, including items likely to be classed as prohibited and best left alone, how to go about obtaining permission to either metal-detect or carry out an archaeological exploration on a particular piece of land, then an examination of various military archaeological digs and the various items discovered. We have also endeavoured to cover abandoned military structures such as buildings, POW camps, pillboxes and air raid shelters. Aviation archaeology which has also experienced a resurgence of interest is also covered here. Military archaeology is a vast subject; therefore, it is the hope that with the assistance of some of the leading names in these fields, both Julian and I have produced what will be a valuable reference work for both beginner and professional alike in an up-to-date format. We must stress at this point that this book is by no means an exhaustive study on what is a vast subject. Yet what we have achieved here is not only a useful modern analysis of a fascinating subject but also one where respect for the history of the items covered here is of paramount importance as opposed to any monetary value. You won't find scrotum-hugging, jeans-wearing, tweed-suited Mr Toads swaggering around here trying to convince you they are experts and that what they are pulling out the ground is treasure. All we can hope is that you enjoy this book.

Tim Heath
The Old Inn, Worcestershire
January 2020

1

Eyes on the Ground

The greater part of my youth was spent in the highly popular Cotswolds village of Broadway in Worcestershire, England. Apart from its endearing appeal as a tourist mecca, it was and still is a village surrounded by decades of military history. In fact, the Vale of Evesham still retains much of that history, some of it still clearly visible today. I recall as an 8-year-old lad at Broadway Primary School in the mid-seventies my mate Dave coming to school one morning with pockets full of .303 rifle ammunition which he confided that he had found in an old shed down what we used to call The Sands in Broadway. The ammunition looked as if it had been made yesterday with gleaming brass cases and silver heads. After Dave distributed the contraband items in the playground, the headmaster, Mr McGowan, soon caught wind of things and summoned us boys together where we were forced to hand over the live .303 bullets. I remember him vividly shaking his head in disbelief as he dropped a handful of live .303s into the pocket of his tweed jacket. I, having been slightly more resourceful than my friends, had managed to shove a couple of the rounds down my sock before our dealing came to the attention of the headmaster and I only took them out once safely home. It was after finishing school that afternoon that I had arranged to meet up with Dave to go and have a look in the shed where he had found the ammunition. The shed in question was down a dirt track leading to allotments, known simply to everyone as it is today as The Sands. It was on the left-hand side of the track and was very small, much like a chicken coop. It was a bit of a squeeze to get inside as a piece of wood was nailed across the entrance in a feeble attempt at preventing people from getting in. Being a skinny lad, I was soon inside but it didn't look like there was anything there at all. Dave pointed out what looked like partially buried grain sacking sticking out of the soil; he told me to pull on it and as I did so yards of old sacking came out the ground with bullets falling out all over the place. To me as a lad with an obsession for anything from the wars it was the proverbial goldmine. I filled my pockets with as many bullets as I could and off we went. As we were heading home more lads passed us on the way to the shed to get some bullets for themselves. Of course, these things were quite dangerous if messed about with, but with hindsight what we were doing was no more than what many kids did during the war years. However, our little enterprise was brief as it was not long before our local Mr Plod got to hear about it. Dave and I lay low for a week then decided to go back to the shed but as we walked down the track and rounded the bend, the shed came into view and the entrance had been completely boarded up and there was Mr Plod sitting in his police Mini surveying the scene as we approached. I whispered to Dave, 'If he asks, we've lost our dog' even though neither of us had a dog. Sure enough, as we came within a few feet of Mr Plod, he wound down his window and barked, 'Oi, you two, where are you going and what are you up to?' I told him, 'Oh, the dog got out and it headed this way.' Of course, he knew we were blagging him but with him watching over the shed, there was no way we could get in there again. A few weeks later it was demolished and the ground where it stood was dug up and all the ammunition was taken away. We never did find out how or why that ammunition got there. It may have been a storage unit during the war or maybe even manufactured there as there were small production units dispersed all over the country for such purposes. Much of these things were common knowledge to the old locals of the village, people who are now long gone.

One tale told to us by an old local ex-serviceman soon had us heading out on yet another adventure, this time to the Kites Nest farm up on the hill above the Snowshill Road in Broadway. We were told that during the war a Luftwaffe bomber found itself being chased by American fighters from the Little Rissington airfield and had jettisoned its cargo, a single parachute mine. Apparently, the Luftwaffe bomber's target had been the Gordon Russell factory which at the time was producing wooden parts for RAF Mosquito fighter-bombers. The parachute mine came down and exploded in open farmland, shattering windows of those dwellings nearby and causing quite a stir among the locals. Young lads being young lads, we set off, determined to find where the mine had exploded and hoping to find some shrapnel in the field. We walked the steep drive-up past Kites Nest farm where we bumped into one of the farmworkers who actually gave us some directions as to which field the mine had landed in. Buoyed with this new intelligence, it made the hard slog of negotiating the sheer slope which led up onto a dirt track a little more bearable. We hadn't walked far along the track when we saw this small bungalow to our right. We gathered that this was where the estate gamekeeper lived but as we drew nearer an angry golden retriever came flying out the door, determined to sink its teeth into one of us. It was a miracle that neither of us was bitten as the angry dog was halted just in time by a scruffy, unshaven man wearing green trousers and a well-soiled white shirt who bellowed 'Stop!' at the top of his voice while emerging from the bungalow. Clearly irritated at our intrusion, he roared at us, 'What are you doing up here and what are you looking for?' We explained as coherently as possible that we were looking for where the German mine had exploded in the war, to which he replied, 'Well, you won't find anything there now; the fields all been ploughed and anything that was there won't be there now. Besides, there be crops growing there so you best bugger off.' We sensed that he was not happy having us snooping around so not wishing to provoke his wrath further, we rather disappointedly made our way back down the hill for what was a long walk home.

When we moved house from what was back then often referred to by the Broadway gentry as the 'white trash enclave of Broadway' to that of Cheltenham Road at the other end of the village, I soon discovered that the back garden of the house was a little treasure trove where military relics appeared to be prevalent. When my father began digging a potato patch in the back garden, I would always be by his side just in case something other than the odd silver sixpence and earthworm was uncovered. I recall the one day a silver cross-like badge being unearthed. At the time I was ignorant as to what it was, and it eventually got lost. I later saw that same object in a reference book and discovered that it was a Second World War US Army shooting qualification award. As my father's vegetable gardening progressed, we found wartime-dated cartridge cases, bullet heads and even a Worcestershire Regiment cap badge in very good condition. One of the neighbours, a short stocky man named Brian Holmes, explained that most of the houses around that area were occupied by ex-servicemen returning home from the war and they threw a lot of unwanted stuff out into their gardens; often it was just buried along with other household detritus such as broken crockery.

It was Brian who was out digging in his back garden one afternoon who shouted across to my father, 'Where's your lad?', prompting my father to reply, 'Why, what's he been up to now?' Brian replied, 'Oh, nothing. I've got something for him here, that's all.' So, when I returned home later that afternoon, my father informed me that Brian had been asking for me, and as Brian was still out digging his ground, I went over to see what it was he wanted. Excitedly, he handed me the casing of a British Mills hand grenade which had a slot cut into its top that had turned it into a moneybox which would have contained nothing more harmful than pennies. He explained that he had dug the grenade casing up earlier that afternoon and thought I might appreciate it. I was over the moon and hurried home to show my parents.

It was Brian who advised me to go walking over the fields at the back of the houses once the farmer had finished ploughing as there were probably more items lying in the ground there. The advice Brian gave me was to look carefully for things that were out of place in the landscape. With this in mind, field walking with the view to finding anything military or indeed from the past, became an obsession and over the years a significant bounty of all manner of items was amassed. At the time I never really thought that I might have been the first person to have handled a certain item for a great many years, even less so that this is how many professional archaeologists began their careers. So, to a lesser extent, walking the fields with eyes on the ground is one of the most basic forms of archaeology.

Then there is the researching of a particular item to discover the context of where it was found. From this you can learn the history of a particular item and retain its context for future generations. The research process years ago was not always the easiest of tasks, but it was certainly rewarding in terms of educating oneself to one's surroundings. The technical revolution that was the worldwide web has transformed the research process completely and today most answers can be found at the touch of the keypad, and data on finds can easily be stored and shared with other likewise-minded people and/or institutions all over the world.

Another example of one of the memorable forays of my youth was that of the former Second World War No. 24 OTU (Operational Training Unit) RAF Honeybourne situated some five miles outside the village of Broadway. Whilst today it is a busy industrial park, remnants of its wartime past stand out almost proudly from the sprawling patchwork of agricultural land and coppices which surround it. A few of the five original huge aircraft hangars are still clearly visible from the road today, as are the various air raid shelters, Royal Observer Corps and anti-aircraft gun positions strategically positioned around the surrounding fields. The site ceased operations as an RAF airfield in November 1947 when it was then abandoned and left virtually intact. I recall my first ever visit to this site as a 14-year-old lad with a friend back in early 1979. We made the short journey from my friend's house at Sandscroft Avenue on our rickety old pushbikes. When we arrived at the entrance of the site, the only challenges were a cattle grid and deciding which building we should explore first. We decided to look inside the aircraft hangar nearest the road. There were no locks on any of the doors and soon we were standing inside this vast, empty wartime hangar where Whitleys and Wellingtons were once stored. We looked around in the adjacent offices but as there were no working lights or windows, we decided to go and check some of the other structures. While looking around in one of the old buildings, my friend squealed with delight upon his discovery of an old British 1888 Lee-Metford bayonet minus its leather scabbard lying on one of the old window ledges. Even by Second World War standards it was an ancient weapon, and one wonders how it had originally found its way there. I found a small pile of what at first I thought to be scrap metal outside one of the huts but I soon guessed that what I had found were broken engine parts, in the form of large, toothed cogwheels and pieces of broken aluminium engine casing. Amongst these I made a find I was very happy with when I discovered five 20mm Hispano dummy/ballast rounds still in their links. We were in a sense having a whale of a time and cursing ourselves for not bringing backpacks as we could have taken a lot more back home with us. In fact, the only hinderance to an otherwise exciting search of the abandoned airfield was the herd of rather irate heifers that seemed to delight in ganging together and chasing after us as we tried moving around the site on our pushbikes. They stood eying us rather menacingly through the windows of the final building where we went inside; my last recollection of that visit was that we were feeling slightly uneasy and opting to sneak out of the back door, hoping to fool the heifers which seemed to be waiting for us to come out. We jumped onto our bikes, peddling furiously up the old concrete runway, looking nervously over our shoulders to see thirty or so angry beasts line abreast in hot pursuit. It was a relief to reach the safety of the cattle grid where we then sat down on the grass on the other side, mocking our pursuers while having a crafty fag.

My appreciation for actual battlefield artefacts came a few years later with the purchase of a rusted British .303 Lee-Enfield rifle which had been found on the Somme battlefield in France by a local travel executive who had a business in the local town. I had noticed while walking past his shop that he had this rusted rifle hanging on his wall. I was curious whether it was for sale and what he might want for it if it was. I went inside and asked about the rifle and he took it off the wall and handed it to me, explaining that it had been one of many unearthed during the ploughing on the Somme, and he had brought it back as a souvenir to hang in the shop as he often arranged small battlefield tours to France. He explained that the barrel was slightly bent, possibly as a result of artillery fire which had most likely killed the British soldier who had carried it. The bolt was closed and the safety catch off, indicating it had been ready to fire and likely had a live round in the breech. Back then things like this were not likely to sound alarm bells, with squeals of shock or horror or 'That thing could go off' or 'What if it ever gets struck by lightning or exposed to excessive heat?' etc., etc. Things such as this rusted rifle, with the exception of live ammunition, shells and grenades, were often brought across the Channel without so much as an eyebrow raised by customs on either side. Back then, if basic common sense was adhered to, there were none of the issues that collectors face today, something which will be discussed later. As I handled the rusted Lee-Enfield, I imagined the last moments of the soldier who had carried it into battle: was he killed, was he wounded, did he ever return home to his family? In this sense, to me it was more than just a battlefield relic; it was a physical link to the First World War, and I had to have it. All the woodwork had rotted away but the metalwork was all complete and could be easily cleaned using a bit of oil. Taking the bull by the horns, I then asked if he would sell it and how much he wanted for it. In the event, I walked out of the shop with the relic Lee-Enfield in a black bin bag for £12 which I was very pleased with indeed. When I arrived home, my father was not as enthusiastic and probably thought his son had gone mad paying £12 for what most people at the time referred to as 'that piece of rusty metal'.

The catalyst for the commercial interest in battlefield-dug artefacts, if memory serves me right, came about in the early 1990s when a Worcester-based group made up of experts and ex-services personnel formed Battlefield Archaeology. The group was featured in an edition of *Combat and Survival* magazine with the simple idea of offering genuine battlefield relics of all description and noting the historical context and importance of the artefacts unearthed. The team, who often travelled to the old Western Front battlefields, worked closely with local authorities and landowners in collecting finds, cleaning and preserving them before mounting them in display frames with the history of where the particular items had been found and their historical context. All finds offered for sale in this way were logged in a master register and certificates of authenticity were issued, guaranteeing the item as 'a genuine battlefield relic'. The group produced a mail-order catalogue where the framed relic sets could be purchased directly. Although it had existed before to a much lesser extent, Battlefield Archaeology were, I believe, instrumental in forming what today is an inextricable link between militaria collecting and archaeology. With the arrival of the phenomenon that was the internet revolution, both disciplines of militaria and military archaeology experienced a huge surge in interest. It was a media tool that enabled anyone to either go out there and record their activities and post to the worldwide web or indeed become a seller, or both. The reader may ask at this point what relevance do these reminiscences have in association with this book. Well, the answer is quite simple: this is how a great many people have discovered their passion for unearthing military relics.

2

Getting Started

It is in most cases one of those inevitabilities that the avid military historian or collector of militaria will at some point become involved in some form of associated archaeological activity. I recall the first useful reference work on this fascinating subject in the form of the book written by the respected historian John Laffin, the aptly titled *Battlefield Archaeology* (ISBN 071101602X) published by Ian Allan Ltd. in 1987. I recall this excellent book fresh on the shelf of our local library in Broadway. I wasted little time in borrowing it and soon found myself absorbed in a piece of work clearly written by a man with a passion for his subject and high degree of practical experience. Although the primary focus of John's book was the various kinds of archaeology associated with the First World War, much of the principles discussed could easily be applied to any of the battlefields throughout humankind's brief yet turbulent history.

However, at the time of writing that book, we were living in far different times to those of today. I think if John were here today, he could be forgiven for being more than surprised at the advances that have been made in a discipline he clearly loved. It is obvious to most that things were far less complex back then than today, especially where the legalities of both amateur and professional archaeology are concerned. The technology available today, especially where metal detecting equipment is concerned, is very extensive even for those on the most modest of budgets.

If you asked a group of metal detectorists which piece of equipment they felt was the best in terms of value for money, reliability and performance, I can guarantee that each will give you a different answer based upon his or her personal preference. I say her because yes, today there are as many women involved in the discipline of military archaeology as there are males. As one newly married young man explained to me a few years back, 'I could hardly leave the wife at home every other weekend when I went out detecting, so I bought her a detector and she joined me and got the bug for it too, killing two birds with one stone: maintaining both the hobby and the marital bliss.' In fact, it must be said that an understanding spouse is just as vital as the equipment you are investing your hard-earned money in, as I and countless others have discovered from experience. There is never a guarantee that everyone, even those closest to you, will understand why you enjoy spending long hours sweeping a metal detector from side to side over what appears to be a seemingly barren stretch of landscape in what they perceive as some vain hope of striking 'gold'. If it's 'gold' you're looking for then maybe you'd be better off booking a flight to the Caribbean, as rarely is gold ever unearthed at old military sites, at least not in the form most would understand. Soldiers of the ancient world, much as those of the modern, were unlikely to have carried items of any high value on their person as they went into battle for obvious reasons. So, the attitude one should adopt is one of caution. I have witnessed many excited individuals foaming at the mouth having gained that valuable permission to metal detect on land thought to possess some notable historical significance, only to soon experience the dark clouds of gloom gather under a chorus of moans and groans as pie foils, soft drink cans, bottle tops, tuppence pieces and ring pulls are pulled from the soil in abundance. Yes, it happened to me on many occasions as it undoubtedly has to most who have entered into the fray of a hobby where nothing is guaranteed. My attitude soon adjusted and I endeavoured not to focus too highly on my own personal expectations, but to try and learn something along the way and in this field, there is much to learn, beginner's luck aside of course.

So where do you start, what equipment will you need and how do you get the necessary permission to metal detect on a site that may have some historical significance? Addressing these points requires a degree of balance based upon an individual's available finances and in some cases whom he might know and how well he conducts his research work. With reference to the types of equipment required, this is best explained by Julian in the following paragraphs/

Well, one would suppose that the best starting point for the uninitiated would be the humble spade and scraper/trowel so beloved of the professional archaeologists. This may seem a humble road indeed but can with both time and experience lead all the way to the hiring of a JCB digger. Well, why not? After all, isn't that where *Time Team* started! There is a whole raft of technologically advanced gumpf which one can consider, equipment such as ground-penetrating radar along with all manner of other 'geofizz'-based gadgetry including tape measures, markers, etc. So where does one stop?

Well, perhaps my favourite piece of equipment would naturally be the metal detector. From the late 1960s to early 1970s this tool became available to the general public and was (in most cases) frowned upon by established archaeologists of the era. Thankfully, the relationship between those who wield the coil to unearth our history and heritage and those who rigidly adhere to the benefits of a trowel to do the same thing has now vastly improved with the passing of many years. So, it should be as the metal detector is now responsible for annually finding and recording 95 to 98 per cent of all metallic finds made in the UK (with perhaps similar statistics being achieved worldwide wherever permitted) and therefore the importance to both users and academics or a fusion of the two has now reached a satisfying and undeniable level. Often these days, the metal detector is also responsible for triggering off the initial stimulus that eventually results in larger archaeological excavations. The discipline has evolved greatly over the years and in the UK even has several supportive monthly publications, including *Treasure Hunting* magazine of which I am very proud to be the current editor. Similar metal detecting publications can be found worldwide; *American Digger* is a particularly noteworthy example.

Legal obligations are of course an important factor with the discipline that is both metal detecting and archaeology, particularly where military sites are concerned. Yet the following principles are best adhered to for all.

Although this book largely relates to the UK, it is of course absolutely essential in all cases to establish the legality, local byelaws and additionally any required permissions and procedures applicable for any investigation of battlefields, their surrounding areas or military remains in whatever country where intended research of any similar type is desired to take place. In the UK any investigation of military remains is subject to the Protection of Military Remains Act 1986 and this should be fully appreciated, complied with and understood, with the possession of the appropriate and required licence to undertake any operation that creates disturbance of such remains. Where it is known or suspected that there is the probability of human remains or ordnance being present, such a licence will almost certainly not be issued and will be immediately revoked should either be discovered. It is advisable to be conversant with correct procedures from the point of discovery of both too, which may involve the police, coroner and explosive ordnance disposal (EOD). A good example of the correct procedure when encountering an unexpected occurrence of finding human remains is that of the Northeast England Air Crash Research Group's preliminary dig at the crash site of Hawker Hunter XG236 which crashed at Kielder Forest, Northumberland. The team, led by aviation archaeologists Jim Corbett and Scott McIntosh, encountered what appeared to be perfectly preserved human skin in the peaty soil. Immediately the dig was stopped, and the authorities were called to the scene where the remains were then taken away, preserving the unfortunate pilot's dignity. Despite being given permission by the Ministry of Defence (MOD) to continue their exploration of the crash site, both Jim and Scott felt it more fitting to build a memorial cross at the site and leave it.

Apart from the First World War Zeppelin excavation (covered later in this volume), all other aviation-based archaeological activities covered here were conducted prior to the aforementioned act. There are also Sites of Special Scientific Interest (SSSIs) and Ancient Scheduled Monuments which must also be considered, the latter pursuant to the Ancient Monuments and Archaeological Areas Act 1979. It is important to note that there can also be variations between such relevant laws drawn up in Wales, Scotland, England and Northern Ireland which must also be clarified and complied with in full. During any such investigations evidence of much older archaeological activity might also be encountered and in some cases adherence to policies pursuant to other legal responsibilities including the Treasure Act 1996 may be necessary.

All in all, there is a raft of legal obligations to comply with and strictly observe, of which I am the first to admit I don't always agree with, due to the restrictive complexities caused in being able to access our history and heritage. However, one should be positive with a view to being progressive and organized and having pride in conducting any archaeological activities in the proper manner of which they deserve. I will also be the first to acknowledge that we cannot entertain a free-for-all level of experience. I cannot overstress the importance of 'reading up' and getting it right in the first instance, both legally and morally.

Regarding the actual purchase of a metal detector today there are a great many to choose from. There are of course the starter-grade machines for those just starting out or having to adhere to a tight budget and then there are the very high-spec machines used by the seasoned expert costing thousands of pounds. One of the most popular ranges of metal detecting equipment today offering both versatility and value for money is perhaps the Garrett range which are among the best-selling of beginner models. I have used various Garrett metal detector units over the past few years, most of which belong to a good friend of mine, and all have performed as you'd expect them to. They do the job they were designed for provided they are set up properly beforehand. The three notable models of the Garrett Ace range are the 200, 300 and the more advanced 400 model. The features these machines all have in common is the accuracy in determining target depth whether the target is close to the surface or thirteen inches deep in the ground. All have what is known as target identification numbers 0–99 scale which are very accurate in determining which type of metal you have located plus a target pinpoint mode enabling one to quickly zero in on a target. The coils are waterproof and can actually be immersed in water, but one must note that the machine itself is not waterproof and one should only allow the coil itself to enter water. The shaft of each machine is fully height adjustable which is just as well if you are a short arse! Each model has an easy-to-read digital display and comes with headphone set and environmental covers to protect the unit from rain and soiling. Naturally the starter model is the 200, recommended for beginners both young and old while the 400 is aimed more towards the adult hobbyist. The 300 provides an intermediate choice between the 200 and 400 models. All of these models are designed for ease of use in the field and provided they are used properly will give trouble-free detecting and hopefully assist you in finding whatever floats your boat, whether its ancient archaeology or searching for the relics of war. Prices range from £200 for the Garrett Ace 200i up to £425 for the Garrett Ace 400i model. Compare this to say a Minelab GPZ 7000 at the hefty price of £8,499 and you can see the variation in the prices of the technology despite all the machines functioning on similar principles. It's not our job to tell you which machine you should invest your money in as that is entirely your choice, but you don't have to spend a fortune to excel in the discipline of metal detecting or that of hunting for the relics of war.

What is known as a pinpointer is also a very useful piece of equipment most self-respecting metal detectorists will not be without. The pinpointer is a little more exotic than a manual handheld tubular metal detector used to assist in the searching through soil piles. These units will rapidly detect anything metallic present and help speed up the process of locating a particular find in a hole. Again, the Garrett Pro-Pointer model is as good as anything else out there and, priced from £110, is not too expensive in comparison to other models. Garrett offers package deals where a pinpointer is included with a detector unit and some of these deals are surprisingly affordable.

Once you have the basic equipment it is wise to firstly familiarize yourself with it. The best way to learn how to get the best out of any equipment, practice aside, is to go on a foray with either an expert detectorist or join one of the many detectorist groups. If you are patient, prepared to listen to good advice and are prepared to learn the craft properly, despite finding many of the proverbial ring pulls and pie foils that are the scourge of most beginners, you might just find something very special, something that has lain hidden in the soil for centuries or more.

3

England's Bloody History

For a relatively small island nation England has a rich and vast military history. Many of the conflicts fought on English soil may have been blurred with the passing of time itself, yet even the smallest of the many conflicts has irrevocably helped define us as the nation we are today.

When the Romans under the emperor Claudius invaded Britain in 43 AD, the effect it had upon British society of the time was to further expand upon the already existing divided loyalties between the constituent kingdoms and tribes of our country. There were those who were in fierce opposition to the Roman invaders whilst others assimilated. Those who opposed the Romans were almost certainly condemned to suffer intolerably as a consequence of their resistance, yet some historians argue that the change in Roman policy of repression to that of a more hearts-and-minds approach taking into consideration the feelings and aspirations of their British subjects somehow had a numbing effect on the population.

The Romans began their conquest and occupation of Britain under the command of General Aulus Plautius with a seaborne invasion across the English Channel with the newly formed Classis Britannica fleet which translates to 'the fleet in British waters' or the 'fleet of the province of Britannia'. This fleet as opposed to a fighting naval force was a logistical component, capable of moving large numbers of soldiers and support echelons along with the equipment and supplies required for an invading army. The ships utilized were Mediterranean war galleys, constructed from much thicker wood than commercial seagoing vessels and were sturdier and more suitable for the rough conditions in the English Channel.

When the Romans set foot on the shores of Britain, they rapidly formed into fighting order, forcing their way inland and subsequently becoming involved in numerous battles against the Britons. Among the first battles fought was the Battle of Medway, which in all probability took place in close proximity to the River Medway in lands occupied by the Iron Age tribe of the Cantiaci (in modern-day Kent). Although the invading force was comprised of only 45,000 men compared to the Britons' 150,000, on this occasion it was not numerical superiority that defined the outcome of the battle.* The Romans, although well-equipped and better armed than their adversaries, were unable to secure an immediate victory and the first day of fighting concluded with stalemate. On the second day of the battle the Romans prevailed, defeating what was a significant enemy force. The Britons were forced to fall back to the River Thames which if nothing else afforded them a greater strategic advantage over the Romans. The battles of the Thames, Caer Caradoc in modern-day Shropshire and Mona in Anglesey followed, all resulting in resounding victories for the Romans.

Perhaps the greatest thorn in the side to the Romans came in AD 60 with the rebellion led by the Celtic queen of the Iceni tribe, Boudica. It was this defiant warrior queen who having inflicted heavy casualties upon the Romans almost caused Emperor Nero to withdraw his forces from Britain. Queen Boudica's battles with the forces of the Roman Empire have since passed into folklore and legend. Although much myth and mystery surrounds both the life and death of Boudica today, she is not only regarded as a brave defender of ancient Britain but also a cultural hero to modern British female society. To understand the cause of the Boudican Revolt of AD 60/1 (it seems no one is certain which year), one must go back to the death of Boudica's husband Prasutagus with whom Boudica had two daughters whose names

* We only have Roman historians' figures to go on, which modern historians believe are grossly inflated, perhaps as much by 100 per cent.

remain unknown to this day. Prasutagus had ruled as a nominally independent ally of the Roman Empire, leaving his kingdom jointly to his daughters and the Roman emperor in his will. However, upon his death, the will was ignored, and the kingdom was annexed, and his property taken. According to the texts written by Roman historian and politician Publius Cornelius Tacitus, Boudica was tied to a post and flogged mercilessly while her two young daughters were brutally raped by Roman soldiers within earshot of their distraught mother. When the flogging finally stopped and the rape of Boudica's daughters had been carried out, the Romans were content in having made an example of Boudica, yet all they had created was a tenacious enemy determined to drive them from Britain.

The Roman governor, Gaius Suetonius Paulinus, was spearheading a military campaign against the island of Mona (modern-day Anglesey) off the north-west coast of Wales, which was a refuge for the Celtic rebels and had become a stronghold of the druids. The Iceni tribespeople conspired with their neighbours, the Trinovantes, amongst others, to revolt and Iceni queen Boudica was elected as their leader.

The subsequent revolt was a short and brutal affair as Boudica led the Iceni, the Trinovantes and others into battle against the Romans. They destroyed Camulodunum (modern-day Colchester) which at the time was being used as a colonia, a settlement for discharged Roman troops and which was also the site of a temple dedicated to the former Emperor Claudius. The bloodlust was most certainly at fever pitch and no quarter was given to any Roman captured at the settlement; most were put to the sword, yet a few were held and tortured to death by the rebels and anything of value was pillaged. However, as Boudica's army continued its assault in what is today the St Albans area of London, Suetonius regrouped his forces, amassing an army numbering almost 10,000 men.

The exact location of what would be Boudica's final battle with the Romans remains unknown, yet many historians agree that it took place somewhere along the Roman road now known as Watling Street, a historic route that crosses the Thames at London and was one of the main Roman roads in Britain. What is known is that the battle took place in a narrow pass between some hills, the narrow pass effectively protecting the Roman flanks from attack, while the wooded area behind served to prevent Boudica from mounting any substantial attack on the Roman force. The open plain which lay to the front of the Roman position made any ambush attack unfeasible. Seutonius carefully placed his legionaries in close formation with infantry on the flanks and cavalry in the wings. The stage was set for what would be Boudica's final confrontation with the Roman invader; according to Tacitus, Boudica gave the following pre-battle speech to her amassed warriors:

> It is not as a woman descended from noble ancestry, but as one of the people that I am avenging lost freedom, my scourged body and the outraged chastity of my daughters. Roman lust has gone so far that not our very persons, nor even age or virginity, are left unpolluted. But heaven is on the side of a righteous vengeance; a legion which dared to fight has perished; the rest are hiding themselves in their camp or are thinking anxiously of flight. They will not sustain even the din and the shout of so many thousands, much less our charge and our blows. If you weigh well the strength of the armies, and the causes of the war, you will see that in this battle you must conquer or die, this is a woman's resolve, as for men, they may live and be slaves.

It was to be a battle where tactics would make up for a lack of numbers on the Roman part. Boudica's army numbered some 230,000–300,000 warriors (allegedly) and by all accounts they must have been a pretty intimidating sight as they approached their heavily outnumbered

Roman enemy. Yet Tacitus recalled how Suetonius also made a pre-battle speech to his legionaries where he told them:

> Ignore the racket made by these savages. There are more women than men in their ranks. They are not soldiers – they are not even properly equipped. We've beaten them before and when they see our weapons and feel our spirit, they will crack. Stick together, throw the javelins then push forward: knock them down with your shields and finish them off with your swords. Forget about plunder, just win the battle and you will have everything.

As Tacitus had predicted Boudica led her army forward across the open plain before the Roman position and into the narrowing field in what was a mass frontal attack. As they advanced, they were packed into an ever-tightening mass providing an easy target for the Romans who unleashed their javelins as the warriors approached to close quarters. A portion of the charging warriors were skewered and fell dead to the ground whilst others found they could not remove the javelins which were impaled in their shields and were forced to discard their only protection and were thus vulnerable to the *gladius*, the short stabbing swords the Romans carried. As the javelins were unleashed the Romans rushed forward in a tightly packed wedge formation. This is where the discipline, equipment and armour of the Roman legionaries came to the fore. As the two sides clashed at close quarters, the Roman cavalry, lances extended, entered the fray. Boudica's ranks began to take serious casualties yet as they attempted to retreat, their escape was blocked by an encirclement of wagons, sealing their fate. The Romans hacked and stabbed their way forward killing all Boudica's warriors including the women and children; even the horses were slain in what became a massacre. Tacitus wrote of the battle claiming that 80,000 Britons fell compared with just 400 Roman casualties. However, these statistics have long been regarded as extravagant by modern historians and likely woefully inaccurate.

As for the warrior queen Boudica, what became of her? The truth is nobody knows for sure. Tacitus wrote that she took her own life by swallowing poison, others say she fell ill and died and was subject to a lavish burial fit for a queen. What we do understand today is that although so little is known about Boudica herself, as much of what was written about her was by her enemies, Boudica came closer than anyone else to driving the Romans from British soil. We should remember and celebrate her for that. While Boudica has quite rightly since become a folk hero here in Britain, to the outside world today she is a hero to womanhood. It is a sad irony that today many of the areas where Boudica's people fought and died have since been swallowed up in the scourge of urban development.

While Boudica has since taken her rightful place in British history, the legacy of the rebellion which she led against the Romans is still being discovered. In 2020, Shane Wood literally stumbled upon a hoard of approximately 1,000 Celtic gold coins (known as staters) in a field near Chelmsford in Essex. Initially Shane had been out birdwatching and was busy watching a pair of magpies attacking a buzzard when he took a break at the edge of a field. Watching the aerial affray overhead until all the participants were finally out of sight, he happened to look down at the ground and noticed a disc shape in the soil. He carried on surveying the surrounding countryside having dismissed the disc as probably being a modern plumbing washer or similar artefact blocked with soil.

However, before he departed, he could not resist it. Naturally inquisitive as well as being a metal detectorist, he thought he had better just check it out. Retrieving the disc from the soil, he began rubbing away with his fingers to remove the muck, revealing an ancient buttery, burnished gold colour. Far from being modern detritus, it was in fact a 2,000-year-old Celtic gold stater and as he glanced down, several more could be seen in the recently harrow-disturbed soil.

Shane returned home to collect his Minelab Equinox 800 detector and then began a methodical search where other scattered coins were revealed along with some thin copper sheet which was most likely evidence of some form of ancient container. Nearby lay a mass of gold coins which stood out against the dark soil.

The find was subsequently reported to the landowner and declared pursuant to the Treasure Act 1996. It was a phenomenal discovery not only from the context of our numismatic history but also the fascination and awe attached to such things. The question which needed answering was who buried these coins and for what purpose. The location being Essex, there is the logical tendency to associate some Celtic finds discovered in the east of England with the Boudican Revolt. Such assumptions are often made quickly without any associated evidence or provenance. However, in the case of the Chelmsford Hoard, would it be so unfeasible to suggest that this was an Iceni 'war chest', possibly struck under an emergency situation to make payments to other tribes and/or mercenaries? It is difficult to pinpoint but just maybe the Chelmsford Hoard could have been buried prior to the final battle with the Romans or in the wake of Boudica's defeat to prevent the money from falling into the hands of the hated enemy. Either way, the Chelmsford Hoard remains today the largest of its type to have been found so far but also one of the most important. Julian reflects upon his own personal experiences in this field.

What with 1,600 years having elapsed, we could be forgiven for thinking that discoveries of a Roman military nature would be relatively uncommon. However, with the Roman Empire having been so extensive and the maintenance of such being so reliant on a well-developed and large military model, this is not the case. Even the farthest-flung outpost of Britain has revealed some very interesting military finds ranging from fortifications, shrines and temples to personal burials of individuals who had served in the many operational legions.

Some three decades ago while metal detecting alongside the route of a major Roman road, I discovered a small Roman occupation site. It may have been little more than a crudely built stop-off site, a collection of ramshackle, largely wooden buildings, I assume due to the lack of tile, plaster fragments, nails and large stones evident. It was perhaps a small outpost between the main posting stations, somewhere where soldiers and other travellers could get food and refreshment, maybe even utilize a brothel or change horses. Over the course of several years, I have unearthed a good selection of military fittings, many of which were damaged; perhaps there had been a small smithy or repair workshop on the site. Amongst the finds were strap ends, studs, belt fittings and even copper-alloy hinges from the famous and film-familiar *lorica segmentata* armour. Amazing when you consider that such small discoveries are the only tangible evidence remaining regarding their original owners. You cannot help but wonder what wars they had witnessed, participated in and what fate eventually came of them. Many coins were unearthed too, no doubt the vast majority having a civilian source; however, there was a good selection of early republican and later silver denarii. A denarius equated to roughly one and a half days' pay for a legionary soldier (perhaps lending support to the brothel theory). The early silver coin issues (ranging from 240–10 BC) could be attributed to having been brought over here during the early phases of the occupation by soldiers employed in the frequent theatre of operations. Several coins recovered bore the shaking hands motif on their reverse, symbolizing the friendship of the emperor/empress concerned with the military, which as we know was not in many cases all that successful. One coin in particular, a large later-issue silver didrachm of Trajan, was of particular interest as it had been minted in Syria around 112 AD, the obverse portraying a very worn bust of Hadrian with the reverse depicting the goddess Arabia. Associated research revealed evidence of Syrians in Britain during the Roman occupation, revealed also by the presence of 500 Syrian archers posted at Hadrian's Wall. These factors clearly illustrate the sheer diversity of the components of the legions. There is even a tombstone from South Shields of a female named Regina, bearing carved Western Aramaic text indicating that the mason responsible for creating this work was possibly of Syrian origin. So, 1,900 years later, just how did a Syrian coin end up in a Cambridgeshire field? Perhaps a desperate soldier relieved himself in the thick bushes to the side of the road, perhaps it was a liaison with a local British girl, or did he just wish to leave his mark by leaving a coin behind, an offering of sorts to a country that was so vastly different from his native homeland?

Another curious find here was again a coin which was a large bronze sestertius of Faustina Junior that had a deep iron-filled split in it. It had clearly been hit with some severe impact and it was logical to presume that the lump of corroded ferrous material had been part of the object that had struck it. Had the coin been placed upon a tabletop struck by a soldier demonstrating the sharpness of his sword so violently that a section of the cutting edge of the blade had detached, remaining embedded in the coin which was then tossed away in anger only for me to discover it 1,800 years or so later? How impressive is it that two small coins and a collection of broken artefacts can almost make the tramping of marching legions, gone so very long ago, reverberate in your ears. Of course, in relation to the coins we can never know for certain the factual stories behind them but what delight and educational fun it can be for us all to participate in having a guess at such.

As noted by Julian, Roman settlements were prevalent throughout Britain so it is no surprise that Roman artefacts can be inadvertently unearthed virtually anywhere. My good friend Chris Bayliss has perhaps a good example. For many years Chris had a piece of market-garden ground a short distance outside the village of Badsey near Evesham, Worcestershire, which he had inherited from his father where he grew vegetables for his fruit and vegetable business supplying customers all around the Vale of Evesham and beyond. Chris recalled his father finding lots of Roman coins in the soil every time the ground was ploughed prior to planting. When Chris took over the ground, he too would frequently find evidence of Roman activity. What was perhaps his most significant find was a large slab of Cotswold stone with what appeared to be numerals and odd carvings etched into the stone. When I asked Chris what he did with this, he recalled:

> When it was unearthed one of the local farmers came along and had a look at it and decided it was more use as a balance weight on the back of his old tractor than as a curio, so that's where it went; the farmer took it and used it as a counterweight on the back of his tractor. What happened to it after that I don't know. Maybe at some point it ended up in a museum, but I don't know.

Although many young people today are often wrongly accused of being ignorant of Britain's ancient history, that somehow its rightful place is in the distant realms of antiquity, few could ever be unaware of the next major invader to the shores of Britain which occurred in 1066 following the Battle of Hastings. At this point I reminisce with some fondness and can still hear the now-echoed voice of my sadly deceased middle school history teacher Richard Copper as he introduced the class to the events of 1066 and the Norman conquest of Britain. With his tall, skinny frame in an immaculately fitting pin-striped suit, he paced before the blackboard and made a comment that made me laugh yet exposed our ignorance of what would become a most interesting subject: 'Right, so what do you know of 1066 and the Norman conquest quite apart from the fact that a geezer named Harold ended up with an arrow in his eye socket and the froggies for the first and last time in history would get one over the English?' There was a stunned silence for a moment before he continued, 'Well, there we are then. I shall endeavour to enlighten each and every one of you and further your repertoires with my vast knowledge.'

In brief, the Battle of Hastings was fought on English soil on 14 October 1066 between the Norman-French army of William, the Duke of Normandy, and an English army under the Anglo-Saxon king Harold Godwinson; it was a fateful event which marked the beginning of the Norman conquest of England. The precise location of where the battle was actually fought is still open to debate among historians, yet it is thought to have taken place seven miles northwest of Hastings in East Sussex. The battle itself was a relatively brief yet typically brutal event which would have far-reaching ramifications for England in every respect imaginable. It was the death of the childless king, Edward the Confessor, in January 1066 which effectively set in motion a power vacuum with several claimants to his throne. Harold was crowned king shortly after Edwards's death, yet faced invasion by William, his own sibling, a brother named Tostig, and the Norwegian king, Harald Hardrada (Harold II of Norway). Hardrada and Tostig had previously routed an army of Englishmen at the Battle of Fulford on 20 September 1066, and in turn were defeated by Harold at the Battle of Stamford Bridge some five days later. Both Harold's adversaries, Hardrada and Tostig, were killed in the battle, leaving William as the single most threat and most serious opponent. Whilst Harold and his army were taking some much-needed R&R on 28 September 1066, William landed his French invasion force on the shores of southern England at Pevensey, rapidly establishing a beachhead from which his invasion could be launched. Harold in the meantime had to put the brew on hold and was forced to march south, gathering any available forces as he went. The exact figures of the two opposing sides in terms of manpower is not known and even modern estimates vary considerably. What is known is the overall composition of the two armies: the English army was comprised almost entirely of infantrymen, with few archers, while William's force was the opposite, comprising only a half-infantry force, with the rest split equally between cavalry and archers. To put this into perspective, the archers of the time were the key component to an army; they were the machine guns of the ancient battlefield, capable of causing mass casualties at a distance within a very short space of time. Harold tried a surprise attack on William's forces, but William's scouts had spotted Harold's army, reporting its movements back to William who was then able to make tactical assumptions, moving from Hastings to the battlefield for the main confrontation with Harold's army. The battle began at around 9 a.m. and was fought until dusk. Early efforts to break the battle lines of the English failed; rather sneakily the Normans then applied their tactic of pretending to flee the battlefield in a state of panic and disarray. Believing he had finally routed the Normans, Harold's forces set off in hot pursuit only for the Normans to suddenly turn and fight. It was at some point near the closing stages of the battle that Harold received an arrow that struck him in the eye. This for obvious reasons would have proved fatal; it would have been an injury that even today's medical wonders would have found almost impossible to treat. Harold's death on the battlefield of Hastings led to the English fleeing in retreat.

William's forces began moving inland and along the way a few minor skirmishes with the English broke out, yet resistance was useless. William was crowned King of England on Christmas Day 1066. William's rule was not all doom and gloom for the defeated English. Prior to 1066, it was considered a normal occurrence to murder political opponents; William brought a swift end to this anarchic practice. He also abolished slavery – prior to the Norman invasion it is said that 15–20 per cent of Anglo-Saxon society were slaves. Perhaps the greatest legacy of Norman rule in England is the wonderful architecture that remains today. This alone has created a lucrative tourist trade attracting thousands of visitors from all over the world. Whilst England's relationship with France is today far from what it once was, words from the Norman language such as beef, pork, noble and purchase are part of our everyday vocabulary.

Today where the Battle of Hastings was fought is a site protected under the English Heritage Act. Metal detecting without an officially approved permit is illegal. In 2014, battlefield archaeologist Dr Glenn Foard from the Huddersfield University embarked on a project to unearth some of the last archaeological remnants from the 1066 battle due to the increasing modern contamination at the site. Every year re-enactors act out the Battle of Hastings as part of the English Heritage-run Battle Abbey event which attracts thousands of spectators from all over the world. The problem with these re-enactment events is that often the modern re-enactors deposit materials which can effectively compromise the genuine archaeology which remains buried at the site. In surrounding areas near where the battle was fought, objects have been recovered which include the head of a battleaxe, arrowheads, remains of helmets and pieces of personal armour. Perhaps among the more ominous discoveries made at the Hastings site are the human remains of those slain in the fighting. A skull has been unearthed and clearly visible at the back are six holes made by stabbing blows probably from a sword. The skull is thought to be of an Englishman killed in the 1066 battle due to the location of its finding. The skull alone perfectly illustrates the brutal nature of the fighting experienced in these ancient battles. If Sky News had existed back then and had reported live from the battlefield, you would have witnessed a bloodbath beyond description, with cleaved, smashed bodies strewn across the battlefield with mortally wounded men, sometimes minus arms and a leg, attempting to crawl away whilst being pursued before being hacked to death where they lay. There is nothing romantic in these battles of old and the carnage was sickening.

Perhaps the best example of carnage to have taken place on English soil was that of the infamous Battle of Towton fought during the Wars of the Roses. The Wars of the Roses was a series of fifteenth-century English civil wars fought primarily for the throne of England, between the supporters of two rival cadet branches of the royal House of Plantagenet: the House of Lancaster whose emblem was the red rose, and the House of York whose emblem was a white rose, hence the term Wars of the Roses. The link with green fingers aside, these wars would have both good and bad consequences in equal measure, largely depending on where one's loyalties lay amid all the politics. These wars effectively wiped out the male bloodlines of both the Lancastrian and the Yorkist families which led to the end of the Plantagenet reign and the subsequent rise of the Tudor dynasty in England.

The Battle of Towton was due to the incumbent king of England, Henry V1, who had been in possession of the English throne since 1422. Henry V1 was considered a weak, inept and somewhat mentally unstable leader. The nobles of England exploited Henry's ineptitude and conspired against him for control of the throne. The dissent came to a head in the 1450s when England collapsed into a civil war between the supporters of Henry's queen, Margaret of Anjou, and those of his cousin Richard, the Duke of York. In 1460, the English Parliament decreed an act effectively allowing York to succeed Henry as king. Queen Margaret fiercely objected to this succession instrument which was a flagrant dispossession of her son's birth right to the throne and succeeded in assembling a large army of supporters. The Battle of York followed on 30 December 1460 where the Duke of York was killed and his forces routed by the Lancastrians. Those who supported the late duke were of the view that the Lancastrians had reneged on the parliamentary act of succession which was a legal agreement. The stage was set for the Battle of Towton which it was hoped would settle the dispute between the Duke of York's son and heir Edward who had denounced Henry, declaring himself king. It was a right to rule, effectively through the force of arms. Whoever won the battle would win the right to the English throne. Much was at stake at Towton as the two armies faced off against each other, which would be reflected in the sheer ferocity of the fighting when it began.

The Battle of Towton was fought on 29 March 1461 near the village of Towton in Yorkshire. It was one of the largest and bloodiest battles to have been fought on English soil. On that Palm Sunday an estimated 50,000 soldiers faced each other in a driving snowstorm on a plateau near Towton. The weapons of both sides were a mixture of swords, pikes, lances, daggers, bows, axes, hammers and other everyday implements including farming tools. Again, it would be a good understanding of basic tactics that would secure victory; the army which used both the terrain and the dreadful wintry elements to their best advantage would emerge as the victor.

Upon arriving at the battlefield, the Yorkists found themselves heavily outnumbered by their Lancastrian enemy. A segment of the Yorkist force under the command of John Mowbray, the third Duke of Norfolk, had yet to arrive which added to the already nervous state of the Yorkists. However, the commander of the Yorkist army, Lord Fauconberg looked about the battlefield, sniffing the air like a fox as the winter wind blew heavily to his rear. Fauconberg very cleverly used the driving gale to his advantage when he ordered his archers, positioned with their backs to the wind, to utilize the gale to help drive their arrows into the Lancastrian ranks. The wind also had the effect of carrying the Yorkist archer's arrows to a much greater range than normal. The Lancastrian archers were at the disadvantage of having to launch their arrows into a fierce headwind, and as a result fell well short of the Yorkist ranks. The Lancastrians, frustrated by the lack of effectiveness of their archers, were goaded into abandoning their defensive positions in favour of a full-frontal assault on the Yorkist lines. Volleys of arrows were fired by the Yorkist archers as the Lancastrians advanced across the plateau line abreast, mercilessly falling upon the Lancastrians like stair rods. Men began to fall dead or wounded to the ground which soon turned red with spilled Lancastrian blood. Those soldiers advancing up from the rear, laden with heavy armour and equipment, stumbled over their own dead and the momentum slowed. The Yorkist archers continued to decimate the Lancastrian advance as it closed for hand-to-hand combat, but by the time they reached the Yorkist lines they were already exhausted from the terrible weather conditions and stumbling over their own dead and wounded. As the two sides clashed in a classic hand-to-hand fight the slaughter began. Towton was a slaughterhouse that shocked even contemporaries by the intensity with which the battle was fought. Regional hatreds combined with family vendettas and other personal scores plus the sheer numbers of the combatants involved, almost guaranteed that Towton would live up to its expectation as a bloodbath. Those men who wore armour soon found themselves at a serious disadvantage: wielding maces or swords for any length of time while wearing armour soon became exhausting; they also found it was difficult to get up after being knocked down due to the weight of the very equipment meant to protect them. There were accounts of swords being pushed through the unprotected areas of the armour such as the eyelets of helmets or the neck or groin areas, while axes and hammers were smashed into heads or limbs.

The hand-to-hand fighting had entered deadlock which was only broken upon the arrival of John Mowbray's reinforcements. At this point the Lancastrian line began to collapse. Prior to the battle Edward had ordered that no prisoners should be taken and no mercy shown. The fleeing Lancastrians found themselves being pursued by Yorkist horsemen across difficult terrain; they fled clumsily down the steep slopes of the valley leading to the River Wharfe where many were cut down and butchered. Men were crushed to death underfoot or drowned as they attempted to cross the river, which was said to have been choked with corpses, the water turning red with blood. There are no concrete statistics on how many were slain at Towton. Contemporary sources claimed that 28,000 men were killed that day, yet many modern historians regard these casualty figures as exaggerated. What is certain is that the Battle of Towton, which resulted in a decisive Yorkist victory, was unrivalled in terms of its ferocity and was most certainly one of the largest and bloodiest battles ever to have been fought on English soil.

In August 1996, workmen inadvertently unearthed a section of what was soon discovered to be a mass grave near where the fighting took place at Towton. Osteoarchaeologists and archaeologists were called in from the University of Bradford's Archaeological Sciences department to conduct an analysis of the skeletal remains at the site. Some forty-three sets of individual remains were recovered, some exhibiting hideous injuries. A good example was a skull unearthed bearing a deep slice into the bone from the top of the left jaw travelling just beneath the nasal cavity through the base of the left eye socket to the top of the left temple. This was most likely caused by a blow from a sword that would have almost certainly killed the victim instantly. Again, most of the skeletal remains were discovered with indentations to the bones caused by swords, axes and other weapons.

Interestingly, in 2010, the remains of primitive handheld firearms were discovered at the Towton site near Tadcaster. It was a discovery which would appear to contradict the theory that these rather primitive firearms were only used in that particular period in history to attack fortifications such as castles. The fragments of metal in the form of two pieces of exploded gun barrel, both of which were like that of a miniature cannon, were then examined by experts. It was confirmed that the metallurgical makeup of the material was typical of the period and such a weapon would have probably proved more lethal to the firer than the enemy he was trying to shoot. Even if such a weapon discharged successfully, often its accuracy would have been literally non-existent. Fired into a dense line of advancing infantry at close quarters, the projectile would have almost certainly proved lethal if you happened to be the unlucky soldier to be struck by it, but overall, these weapons proved more of a handicap than lending any tactical advantage. These early, crude black-powder primed weapons were often subject to overload of the propellent charge, due to the lack of understanding of the basic physics involved and the metallurgical factors at the time where the forging process was concerned. If loaded with an excessive black-powder charge, it would likely explode in the user's hands much like a hand grenade, something that would most certainly kill if not inflict grievous injury upon the user and anyone in close proximity. The barrels of all later firearms were subject to proofing, introduced not only as a stringent quality control measure for the metals used in the production of the firearm, but which also brought about the creation of a standard black-powder loading system created to prevent the overpressure of gun barrels which led many early examples to explode.

It is sometimes noted that the Battle of Towton was the last of its kind during the Wars of the Roses, yet the last battle in this brutal saga was that of Stoke Fields which took place in 1487; though Towton will always be regarded as one battle that defined the savagery of warfare through Middle Ages England. Artefacts associated with the Wars of the Roses do come on to the collecting market from time to time. Perhaps one of the most interesting pieces I have seen was one being offered at Stoneleigh Military Convention back in 1997. The item in question was a relic dagger which had been unearthed by an amateur metal detectorist on the Towton battlefield. The piece was in remarkably good condition for its age and had been professionally conserved and mounted for display with all the relevant paperwork on its finding, including photographs etc. The asking price was £250 and while it was an artefact of great interest to me, I passed on it despite the vendor offering to knock off £20 off the price. Looking back, it is perhaps one of those pieces I wished I had bought as I have never seen another one since with such solid provenance.

When handling and viewing such things, one always wonders as to its history: did it draw blood in the battle and did whoever carried it survive to fight another day? These are all the kinds of questions these historical artefacts invoke in the minds of those who seek to both preserve and research them. Private ownership of such items is often a bone of contention among general historians and collectors so maybe these kinds of items should be in the custody of the relevant local museums where they can be enjoyed by all. That said, personally I see no problem with the private ownership of such items or any other artefact associated with past conflicts.

4

England's Battles with Scotland

When one reflects on England's wars with Scotland, one invariably considers images conjured up by big screen dramatizations such as *Rob Roy* or, more infamously, *Braveheart*. Although from a historical context, *Braveheart* is perhaps the least historically accurate, its script having fallen victim to the inevitabilities of cinematographic licence in many areas of its production in order to further the commercial appeal of its main character, William Wallace.

What we know today as the Scottish Wars of Independence were a series of military campaigns fought between the kingdoms of England and Scotland which took place in the latter part of the thirteenth and early fourteenth centuries. Through a considerable proportion of history, the English possessed that nasty habit of wanting a bigger slice of the territorial cake than what was on their plates. During those times the English had no concerns whatsoever about waging unlawful invasions or instigating fierce and bloody wars in order to gain what was seen as precious territory which they viewed was somehow rightfully theirs to conquer. The slavery, rape, violence and general brutality meted out to the Scots by the English was met with fierce resistance, despite the sweeteners thrown to the Scottish nobles in order to make them fall into line.

From 1296 to 1357 a series of twenty-seven battles were fought between the English and the Scots. The most notable battles of the First War of Scottish Independence were those of Stirling Bridge, Falkirk and Happrew. At Stirling Bridge, on 11 September 1297, the Scots under the leadership of William Wallace and Andrew Moray soundly defeated an English army under the command of John de

Warenne, 6th Earl of Surrey, and Hugh de Cressingham in the vicinity of Stirling on the River Forth. The actual fighting took place either side of what was once an earthen causeway leading from the Abbey Craig. The Stirling Bridge that was in existence at the time of the battle is believed to have been some 180 yards upstream from the fifteenth-century stone bridge which spans the River Forth today.

Prior to the commencement of the battle, the Scots who had based themselves on Abbey Craig, made good use of securing and dominating the soft, flat ground to the north of the Forth. The English force, comprised of English, Welsh and Scots knights, bowmen and infantry, had camped to the south of the river. Sir Richard Lundie, a Scots knight who had defected to the English side following the Capitulation of Irvine – an early conflict of the Scottish Wars of Independence which took place on 7 June 1297 due to dissent amongst the Scottish leadership, an event which resulted in a stand-off – suggested that he take a force of cavalry and cross a ford two miles upstream, where sixty horsemen were able to cross at the same time. Cressingham persuaded Warenne to reject the proposal and instead order a direct attack across Stirling Bridge. The thinking behind this was that while the relatively small bridge was broad enough to allow only two horsemen to cross it abreast, it offered the safest means of crossing the Forth, which widened to the east with the marshland of Flanders Moss to the west. The English commanders viewed the bridge crossing as the best tactical solution at the time however flawed that decision may appear today with the advantage of hindsight. For Wallace and Moray watching as the lead elements of the English force began to cross the bridge, it was just the opportunity that both had hoped for. It would have taken several hours for the entire English force to have crossed the bridge and all Wallace and Moray had to do was launch an attack as soon as they had allowed as many enemy troops to cross that they knew they could overcome. It is believed that Wallace and Moray allowed 2,000 soldiers of the English force to cross prior to initiating their attack.

First into the fray were the Scots armed with spears who stormed down upon the English from the high ground, fending off an English heavy cavalry charge before counterattacking the English infantry. The Scots rapidly gained control of the eastern side of the bridge, cutting off any hope of the English being able to send reinforcements across the river. The English found themselves in the very precarious position of being trapped on the low ground and in the loop of the river, allowing no chance of relief or escape, and as a result most of the outnumbered English on the eastern side were massacred. It is believed that a few hundred may have escaped almost certain slaughter by swimming across the river. Sir Marmaduke Thweng, the 1st Baron Thweng, managed to fight his way back across the bridge with a small number of his men. Surrey on the other hand, left with a small contingent of archers, had remained south of the river and was subsequently still in a tactically strong position. The main body of his army remained intact and he could have held the line of the Forth, denying the enemy passage to the south; but his confidence had been bruised, giving his enemy a valuable psychological advantage.

Following Thweng's escape, Surrey ordered the bridge to be destroyed before retreating towards Berwick, leaving the garrison at Stirling Castle isolated and abandoning the lowlands to the Scots. James Stuart, the High Steward of Scotland, and Malcolm, Earl of Lennox, whose forces had been a component of Surrey's army, had observed with horror the carnage which had taken place to the north of the bridge and promptly withdrew. The English supply train was the next objective for the Scots who attacked it at The Pows, a wooded area comprising bog and marshland. The Scots led by James Stuart and other Scots lords plundered the English logistics train, forcing the English to abandon it and flee in terror. Those English not killed in the initial confrontation were pursued through the woods and marshes where many were hunted down and slain.

Stirling Bridge was undoubtedly a great victory for the Scots and a severe mauling for the English. Today the site is still of continued interest to professional archaeologists seeking to learn more about the battle. Following archaeological explorations, particularly in the river around the area, four stone piers have since been discovered underwater just north of the present fifteenth-century structure. Manmade stonework has also been discovered on one bank which is in line with the four piers. Digging and/or metal detecting at this famous site is forbidden as the site today is fully protected by Historic Scotland, an executive agency of the Scottish Office and later the Scottish government from 1991 to 2015, whose task is primarily to protect Scotland's built heritage while promoting its understanding and enjoyment. Historic Scotland has since dissolved, and the site is currently under the protection of Historic Environment Scotland (HES).

The Battle of Falkirk, which took place on 22 July 1298 some ten months after the Scots victory at Stirling Bridge, was a battle where again William Wallace had hoped for another resounding Scottish victory. Wallace's co-victor at Stirling Bridge, Andrew Moray, had during that battle been mortally wounded and was thus absent at Falkirk, a factor which would have a severely detrimental effect upon the outcome of the battle. As with Stirling Bridge, the Scots army consisted largely of spear- or pikemen arranged into four large schiltron formations (dense bodies of troops who formed an almost impenetrable barrier by use of their spears or pikes). The spears and pikes pointed outwards at various heights and lengths; any gaps in this defensive formation were filled by archers. To the rear of the schiltrons were 500 mounted knights. On 22 July at Falkirk, the English cavalry divided into four battles (a battle being a division in medieval terms) then advanced in echelon. The vanguard of the English force, led by the Earl of Lincoln, veered to the left of the Scots ranks in order to avoid an area of marshy ground, followed by the Earl of Surrey's battle. The battle of Anthony Bek, the Bishop of Durham, followed by the king's battle, moved around the area of marshy ground to the right, towards what was the Scottish left flank. Lincoln and Bek's battles charged the Scots and Lincoln was rapidly able to rout the Scottish cavalry. The Scots archers who were under the command of Sir John Stewart (the younger brother of the High Stewart of Scotland) stood their ground in the onslaught but were soon overrun by the English cavalry. Despite this, the Scots schiltrons held firm and the English knights were unable to make any impression upon the dense formations of pikes and spears: 111 horses were speared to death as they charged into the schiltrons, in their riders' vain attempts at breaking them down. The English cavalry began to retreat as the English infantry and archers arrived on the battlefield.

This was the pivotal moment in the battle as the English archers, crossbowmen and slingers sent a hailstorm of projectiles down onto the inexperienced and poorly armoured Scottish pikemen. The one drawback of the men who made up a schiltron was that they had no defence at all and nowhere to hide from the rain of arrows and the projectiles hurled at them by the slings. The schiltrons were effectively sitting ducks, pinned in place by the English cavalry and infantry and unable to either retreat or attack. The battle was lost for the Scots the moment the English archers let loose their arrows. The English army waited patiently for the right moment, observing their king's command. When the Scottish ranks had been significantly thinned out, the English cavalry and infantry attacked and the schiltrons broke with the Scots fleeing for their lives.

The casualties among the Scottish leaders at Falkirk were by no means disastrous, but they included Wallace's second-in-command, Sir John de Graham, along with Sir John Stewart and Macduff of Fife. The defeat of the Scots at Falkirk was due in part to William Wallace's limited military knowledge. Wallace was arguably an outstanding partisan leader, yet he had no real experience on how to train, organize and lead a conventional army. It was said that at Falkirk Wallace simply drew up his army in an open field and froze. Had Andrew Moray been present, the outcome of the battle might have been different. Moray preferred to use the schiltron formations offensively as opposed to a static defensive structure where its effectiveness was severely reduced.

In the wake of the Scots defeat at Falkirk, Wallace resigned his leadership and guardianship. He still had the support and admiration of the masses in Scotland, something which made King Edward more determined to capture the man who had become the embodiment of Scottish defiance to English rule. Wallace managed to evade capture by the English until 5 August 1305 when he was betrayed by John de Menteith, a Scottish knight loyal to King Edward. Wallace was handed over to English soldiers at Robroyston near Glasgow. Following a brief trial, he was sentenced to death by being hanged, drawn and quartered, far from a quick death, Wallace was strangled by way of hanging but released before passing out; he was then emasculated which means his genitals were cut off, then eviscerated – his bowels were pulled out and burned before him. The mercy of death came from the next phase of the proceedings which was beheading by means of an axe. Wallace's body was then cut into four sections and his head dipped in tar then placed on a pike atop London Bridge. His limbs were displayed separately in Newcastle, Berwick, Stirling and Perth. It was a gruesome and inglorious end for one of Scotland's greatest rogue heroes, who like Boudica, has since became a folk hero in Scotland.

This year 2021 also marks the 275th anniversary of the Battle of Culloden, the last major battle to be fought on British soil, a battle which was incidentally the culmination of Scotland's struggle against English rule. This battle was fought on Drummossie Moor, near Inverness in the Scottish Highlands on 16 April 1746 and saw the defeat of the Jacobite army at the hands of the English under the command of Prince William Augustus, Duke of Cumberland. The battle itself, although relatively brief, was certainly an extremely brutal affair where the order was given by the Duke of Cumberland to 'give no quarter' and it appears the soldiers under his command obeyed the order to the letter.

By 1746 the landscape of warfare had undergone considerable change to that of the days where William Wallace routed the English at Stirling Bridge. At Culloden the enemy the Jacobite army was facing were well-disciplined, well-trained soldiers armed with Brown Bess muskets and perhaps even more importantly the socket bayonet on which each man had been specially drilled. The English also had the advantage of artillery in the form of cannon able to discharge either solid ball or canister into the charging Jacobite ranks. The Jacobites had enjoyed the taste of victory over the English at Prestonpans and Falkirk and under the leadership of Charles Edward Stuart, better known as Bonnie Prince Charlie, were confident their Highland charge tactics would overwhelm the superior English government forces sent to quell the uprising.

At 5 a.m. on the bleak, damp and bitterly cold morning of 16 April 1746 Cumberland's army moved out from their overnight camp, leaving the main road to Inverness and marched out across open countryside. At around 10 a.m. the Jacobites on the high ground could clearly see the red-coated English soldiers as they approached from around two miles. As the English closed in around a mile from the Jacobite position, Cumberland ordered his men to form into their line of battle and march forward in full battle order. However,, he realized that his right flank was exposed and so ordered additional cavalry to reinforce it. As the English soldiers advanced the Jacobite's began to mock them in their typical style which courted little response from the English lines. As the English line closed to within 500 metres, Cumberland moved his artillery up through the ranks in preparation. In the Jacobite lines John O'Sullivan, a professional soldier of Irish descent with an understandable hatred of the English who had spent most of his military career in the service of the French and now with the Jacobite army, moved two battalions of Lord Lewis Gordon's regiment to cover the walls at Culwhiniac against a possible flanking attack by English dragoons. Jacobite lieutenant and Scottish nobleman Lord George Murray moved the Jacobite right slightly forward which

O'Sullivan noted had the unintentional effect of skewing the Jacobite line and creating gaps which could be exploited by the English. As a result of this blunder, O'Sullivan ordered a portion of the forces available to him to move from the second line to the first, which depleted the Jacobite reserve and increased the necessity for a strike against the English. At approximately 1 p.m. the Jacobite artillery opened fire, prompting Cumberland's artillery to respond in turn. The exchange of cannonball lasted for only two to three minutes before the Jacobites charged. Observing the advancing Jacobites, the English artillerymen switched to firing canister at the closely packed enemy ranks. Canister was a form of early anti-personnel ammunition where the cannons discharged a hail of shot and/or pieces of scrap metal which gave a shrapnel-type effect, particularly devastating when fired at close range. Accuracy was not a factor and so the rate of fire was significantly increased. Mortars also discharged deadly projectiles from well behind the English front lines meaning the Jacobites were now advancing into very heavy fire. In the event, the battle was won through superior tactics, bravery and the discipline of Cumberland's government troops, who soon routed the Jacobite force, sending them fleeing across the battlefield where they were then murderously pursued.

There is much conjecture as to the effectiveness of the Brown Bess musket. Yet, when discharged into packed ranks of charging enemy at close range, the Brown Bess was every bit as lethal as any modern firearm. The Brown Bess fired a 17.5mm-calibre solid lead ball deliberately undersized to reduce the effects of powder fouling. The bore diameter of the barrel was actually 19mm. The solid lead ball weighed 1.14oz and reached a muzzle velocity of 1,300 feet per second out to a range of 100 yards, but in many cases the enemy were not fired upon until they were just fifty yards distance from the English line. At such close ranges it was the mass of firepower rather than accuracy that was the main consideration. An enemy charging close together in a line were difficult to miss even at 100 yards. The expertly trained government soldiers were taught to fire then immediately reload as fast as possible while the line of soldiers behind them fired and so on. The carnage these large-calibre projectiles caused was terrifying. The government soldiers recorded how their musket balls could take off arms and legs and blow heads clean off shoulders, which were certainly not exaggerated accounts. The English musket balls often created a relatively small entry wound which disguised the massive internal damage wrought in the form of smashed bones and internal organs; the exit holes if they passed through the body were often considerably larger and thus extremely difficult to treat. Those who were wounded often succumbed to infection of the wound path. So, as inaccurate as a musket may have been, being struck by a musket ball was enough to seriously spoil your day.

Culloden was also the battle where the rifle-mounted socket bayonet really proved its worth as a close-quarter weapon. The socket bayonet in use with the British Brown Bess musket at that time consisted of a fullered, triangular-shaped blade. The bayonet was attached by slotting the socket of the weapon over the muzzle, the cut-out slot then slid past the foresight securing it to the muzzle of the weapon. The bayonet in use at the time of Culloden had an overall length of twenty inches yet was minus the locking ring which was fitted to later socket bayonets. As lethal as these early Brown Bess bayonets were as a stabbing weapon, soldiers using them soon discovered they were easily dislodged, particularly during use. There is more than one account where soldiers in that battle stabbed their enemy only to find their bayonet had come off the end of the muzzle and had to be hastily retrieved and reattached, not the easiest of tasks especially with a rank of Highlanders bearing down upon you. Where the bayonet really made a difference at Culloden was how Cumberland's soldiers were trained and drilled to use the weapon. Cumberland's method of bayonet drill questioned the fact that a soldier armed with his musket and bayonet might be at a disadvantage against a Highlander charging directly forwards, that the Highlander might easily deflect a bayonet thrust with his small shield and deliver a counter blow with his sword. Cumberland's suggestion was that the soldier would have a better chance of success by stabbing at the Highlander attacking the soldier to his right. Assuming the Highlander was holding his sword in his right hand would mean that the soldier's bayonet would stab into the area of that Highlander's unprotected side. This was the bayonet drill that Cumberland's men were schooled in, yet it required a great deal of nerve, not to mention faith in the man next to you doing his job properly in order for this technique to work. Yet, despite misgivings, the tactic appeared to work.

The combination of courage, discipline, quality training, the tactically efficient use of artillery support and good leadership were all factors of Cumberland's victory over the Jacobites at Culloden. The moment the Jacobite army began to collapse into disarray, they had little option but to flee for their lives. The government army chased the fugitives down like rabbits for over five miles across the Scottish countryside, leaving a trail of bodies. Most of the fleeing Jacobites were cut down by the government cavalry. Few were spared and wounded and dying Jacobites were either speared, bayoneted or shot where they lay.

The battle had lasted for around an hour yet by its end the Jacobite army had lost around 1,250 killed with almost as many wounded; additionally, 376 prisoners were taken (these being professional soldiers worth a ransom). Cumberland's army suffered very few casualties – fifty killed and 300 wounded. The aftermath must have been a scene of utter carnage, yet for weeks and months afterwards government forces continued the slaughter of the Highland populations, determined that there would be no further uprisings.

Today when one visits the site where the Jacobite uprising was effectively crushed, it is all too easy to be distracted by the beauty and tranquillity of the area. In this piece of heavenly Scottish countryside, the only thing that points to the brutal events that took place there now so many years ago are the visitor centre and the memorials erected to honour the memory of those who fell in the battle. There are several clan memorials at the battlefield today along with the memorial cairn which was erected by Duncan Forbes of Culloden in 1881. This impressive if sombre structure was built to commemorate the Jacobites killed during the fighting and the rout which followed. The battlefield today falls under the protection of the National Trust for Scotland and digging and/or metal detecting on the Culloden battle site is illegal unless special permission is granted by the authorities in charge of the site.

In 2020 a group of amateur archaeologists called Conflict of Interest was granted a permit to metal-detect in the area of a ruined Lochaber croft house. During their investigation a large hoard of musket balls plus some coins and gilt buttons were discovered. This hoard was believed to have been part of an arms shipment from France which landed at Lochaber two weeks after the Jacobite defeat at Culloden. The musket balls were of a size and calibre matching those used in the muskets supplied to the Jacobites. Undoubtedly, much of the physical evidence of the battle still lies buried in the soil of Culloden though occasionally English Brown Bess musket balls have worked their way to the surface where they have been picked up by visitors to the site; considering the numbers that must have been discharged into the Jacobite ranks during the battle, this is hardly surprising. Even items such as these which may be considered minor in terms of battlefield archaeology deserve to be treated with the utmost respect.

5

Waterloo

The mere mention of Waterloo 1815 is likely to cause our friends across the English Channel to *s'étouffant avec leurs cuisses de grenouilles*; even after the passing of so many centuries the Battle of Waterloo is still very much a contentious part of the French historical psyche, especially in the context of its rivalry with England. Britain and France have a long antagonistic history dating back to 1066. Throughout the history of Britain and France our countries have entered military conflict with one another on more occasions than both have had hot dinners. We have fought each other in North America and in Europe, and it seems anywhere was a good place to have a damn good scrap. Perhaps the most notable of all the battles between Britain and France is the Battle of Waterloo, a defining battle which took place in Belgium on Sunday, 18 June 1815. Now, some of the millennial generation may equate Waterloo more with *Mamma Mia* than an actual historical event, yet for this they may well be excused. Yet for my generation Waterloo was discussed in history lessons and was perhaps the most modern conflict we studied at that time. The Battle of Waterloo was the culmination of what were the Napoleonic Wars fought between 18 May 1803 and 20 November 1815. The Napoleonic Wars were a series of major battles between the Empire of France and its allies under Napoleon Bonaparte against what was effectively a coalition formed between fluctuating European powers. The wars were categorized into five conflicts, of which each was termed after the coalition that fought Napoleon: the Third coalition 1805, the Fourth 1806 to 1807, the Fifth 1809, the Sixth 1813 to 1814 and finally the Seventh and final in 1815.

On that Sunday, 18 June 1815, Napoleon led his army of some 72,000 troops against a British-led coalition of 68,000 troops. This was known as the Seventh Coalition, comprising units from the Netherlands, Hanover, Brunswick and Nassau, under the command of Arthur Wellesley the Duke of Wellington, who had risen to prominence in the British army during the fighting against the French in the Peninsular War. The army is often referred to historically as the Anglo-Allied Army or Wellington's Army, and included the powerful Prussian army under the command of Field Marshal Gebhard Leberecht von Blücher. It was Blücher's army which proved to be the crucial component in securing victory over the French.

The battle itself was typical of many of those of its era; fortunes rapidly changed on both sides and casualty figures were typically horrendous. In a critical blunder Napoleon waited until midday to give the command to attack in order to allow time for waterlogged ground to dry out following the rainstorms of the previous evening. This was a serious error of military judgement on Napoleon's part, an error which allowed Blücher's 30,000-strong army the time to march to Waterloo. Blücher arrived late in the day, but his arrival was certainly a huge relief to the British. Napoleon's forces had mounted determined attacks against the British and their allies and for a while there was some anxiety. Yet, Blücher's arrival proved the deciding factor and turned the tide against the French. Napoleon's army had given everything it could under the circumstances but heavily outnumbered, the rout began. The French were pursued by their enemy across a battlefield clogged with the corpses of men and beasts.

The British and Prussian armies suffered more than 22,000 casualties while the French suffered a reported 33,000 casualties, including dead, wounded and those taken prisoner. Napoleon himself was said to have been fatigued and in ill health during the Belgian campaign. This may explain to some degree the reasoning behind his poor tactical decision-making, indecisive actions and the appointing of commanders who were clearly not competent for the job at hand.

The reason for the high casualty rates should be quite clear: the use of artillery had become refined and commonplace in warfare, proving highly effective if correctly positioned on the battlefield. The largest field cannon used by Wellington's force fired 12lb projectiles – just one of these fired into a mass of infantry was enough to cause horrific death and injury. The use of canister was also exploited by both sides. The canister rounds used by Wellington's guns came in two types, light and heavy. The light canister rounds contained 112 metal balls while the heavy canister contained forty-one. The heavy canister round contained heavier metal balls possessing a greater projectile mass. Both were designed to be fired into charging infantry or cavalry with a shotgun-type effect to kill or maim large numbers of men with a single shot.

Cavalry were also utilized to great effect in the battle despite the high casualties suffered in terms of man and beast. The British had also refined the use of the bayonet and each British infantryman had received specific training with the weapon which was put to good use at Waterloo wherever close-quarter actions occurred. The tactically superior use of the infantry both at long and close ranges were also a factor along with good command structure. Under Wellington the Anglo-Allied army had that sound tactician and a firm command structure throughout the battle. By the end of the battle the greatly feared French Imperial Guard, Napoleon's finest fighting men, were said to have fled across the battlefield shouting, 'We are betrayed' as they went. The battlefield was said to have been a scene from hell itself.

Pierre Gauvion, whom I had the pleasure of meeting back in 2001, lived in France and the guesthouse he once ran with his wife was a shrine to the Battle of Waterloo. Within its ancient rooms were walls decorated with oil paintings and prints depicting scenes from the battle. There was also several swords, bayonets and cannonballs which Pierre had inherited from his grandfather which all came from Waterloo. Pierre explained during an interview:

> Waterloo has always been close to my heart as a descendant from my father's side of the family fought there and was wounded in the shoulder by a British musket ball. The musket ball shattered his shoulder, and it is said despite its eventual healing the shoulder was a source of excruciating pain up until his death.

Among other relics in Pierre's possession was a curious large wooden item. Pierre explained that it was a central hub from a gun carriage wheel. This wheel hub had over the years begun to fall apart, and Pierre had to reassemble it and attach a metal strip around its circumference to hold it together. Pierre explained that this was from one of many damaged gun carriage wheels that were taken by locals after the battle and used to make pots or for repairs to farmyard carts and implements. Either way, it was an unusual piece that still sits on a small table in the hallway to the family guesthouse. During the 1980s, Pierre made numerous pilgrimages to the battle site and was able to locate even where field medical posts had been situated. He recalled of his visits back then:

> It was simpler back then. I used to drive there and spend a couple days walking the freshly ploughed fields looking for relics. I struck up a good rapport with the local landowners who were happy to let me search in their fields. The problem was there was a lot of twentieth-century contamination present in the soil, mostly from the two World Wars. Being able to discern lead shrapnel balls from expended First World War artillery shells from musket balls fired during the Battle of Waterloo required knowledge, practice and of course a lot of patience. Over the course of time and many visits, I built up a healthy collection of Waterloo artefacts, things such as coins, buttons, badges, horseshoes, cannon balls and canister

> shot. There was plenty of it present in the soil, but you had to know what you were looking at. Obviously, the laws in Belgium have since changed to protect the cultural heritage of sites such as Waterloo and to prevent illegal activities on these sites. Today you can't just go there with a metal detector and start scanning. In many cases you will require the landowner's written permission and you will have to remain in the boundaries of that land. There are some areas where access will not be granted. Either way, it's complicated and one should always check with the department authorities. A friend of mine had his finds and his vehicle confiscated, not for flouting the rules but being unaware of their complexity. For a hand full of musket balls, it really is not worth it. It is much easier to go to the local flea markets in France and Belgium as there are plenty of old war relics available to buy there. There are many antique shops too where you can buy a Napoleonic bayonet or sword or a mounted display of objects from the battlefield itself. So today there is no need to risk going there and breaking the law.

British soldiers of the Napoleonic War era underwent extremely thorough training in musketry drill prior to their embarkation to the fighting In Europe. Shooting ranges sprang up all over the United Kingdom, usually in isolated rural areas for obvious reasons. The British Army has throughout its existence been trained to a very high standard. The French on the other hand at the time of Waterloo found themselves surrounded by their enemies on all sides and as a result had to raise and train their military forces rapidly. The British had the natural barrier of the English Channel separating them from their enemy, plus the guardianship of the Royal Navy. In short, the British had all the time they required with which to raise a well-trained, high-quality force who would be up to the task asked of them. Of course, these factors, as history has illustrated, are not necessarily a guarantee of victory in war, but they certainly help. On average, it took six months for a British soldier of the Napoleonic era to be fully trained in basic drill, marching, musketry and use of the bayonet. The average French soldier of the time received inadequate training in comparison: many received as little as three weeks' training before being sent into battle. Britain's European allies, Russia, Austria and Prussia, faced much the same problems as the French by way of having to raise their armies quickly, thus producing soldiers who were often below par.

The training of soldiers across the different nations also presented unique problems. For example, a British rifleman received sixty live rounds of ammunition plus sixty blank rounds, a light infantryman received fifty live rounds plus sixty blanks, and a line infantryman received thirty live rounds. When you compare this to say a Prussian *Jäger*** who received sixty live rounds to fire in training in total, while Austrian and Russian soldiers were barely able to fire six to ten live rounds in their musketry training, this exemplifies where the quality of training really became a key factor in many of Britain's military successes.

The volume and high rate of fire by well-trained and disciplined British infantrymen often proved devastating. Analysis has already been provided as to the lethality of the Brown Bess musket in battle in the previous chapter; the specifications of the musket had undergone no further modification by the time of the Napoleonic Wars.

A good example of a Napoleonic-era British firing range is 'Hangman's Hill' located in Worcestershire. Hangman's Hill was first brought to my attention as a military firing range by metal detectorist Ben Davies from Malvern, Worcestershire. It had been used as military shooting range from the Napoleonic Wars through to the Second World War. Its discreet location set in the countryside

** a light infantryman, a skirmisher, lit. hunter

ensured its exclusivity. Ben has visited this site (with permission from the landowner) on numerous occasions and recalled:

> The ground of the whole area is thick with spent munitions. After one metal detecting session there, within a short time I had collected a bucket full of Brown Bess musket balls, some clearly had been discharged in the training while some had obviously been dropped by the soldiers during their training; either way the ground is thick with them, and they are very easy to find. There is also a lot of Second World War-period stuff in the ground there, mostly .303 bullet heads and grenade fragments.

It is clear from this that a variety of military training occurred at the site for a great many decades and despite contamination from modern military activity, it remains an important local site of historic interest.

6

The Anglo-Zulu War 1879

Most of us, particularly those of the authors' generation, would have seen the films *Zulu* (Paramount Pictures 1964) and *Zulu Dawn* (American Cinema Releasing 1979), two epic vintage war movies often screened of a Sunday afternoon back in the 1970s. Although *Zulu* suffered from a very high degree of inaccuracy, especially in its portrayal of some of those who took part in the defence of the mission station at Rorke's Drift, it all made for jolly good cinematographic entertainment which of course was the whole point of both films. Films are made to make money and both *Zulu* and *Zulu Dawn* were no exception.

The British public or at least those who were interested in our military history at that time when such epic movies were created were not the sort of society to take our past colonial military disasters on the chin; that was never a very British thing to do. Yet by analysing our now-fading colonial history, it becomes blatantly apparent that we Brits have very little to be proud of other than maybe the bravery with which some of our colonial forces, who were thrust into campaigns in far-off places they had never even heard of, had fought. Britain's colonial military expeditions to South Africa and involvement in the Zulu War (11 January–14 July 1879), which resulted effectively from unwanted expansions, are perhaps a prime example.

The British Empire had already established colonies in South Africa by 1850, colonies which bordered both native African and Boer territories. Of course, the British Empire had other intentions which were factors towards establishing a firm presence in South Africa. These intentions were other than that of merely subduing the indigenous tribes whom the white colonials had nothing but contempt for yet were hell-bent on enslaving. Southern Africa has always been rich in gold and diamond resources plus exotic luxuries that were unavailable in England itself. The British Empire under Queen Victoria was destined to provoke conflict with the Zulu Kingdom under King Cestshwayo kaMpande, despite Cetshwayo's attempts to avoid confrontation. The British government itself must have been completely divorced of its senses if it thought Zulu chief Cetshwayo would simply submit to the demands laid down by the Crown, something perfectly illustrated by the arrogant terms composed by Sir Henry Bartle Frere under his own initiative with the full support of the British military commander in South Africa, Lord Chelmsford. Frere's 'terms', at least the first five, are not worthy of mention here as they relate to more or less puppet court actions. However, articles 6 to 13 are worthy of note to glean some context of how one man managed to lead the British Empire into a war it could easily have avoided. The terms as dictated to Cetshwayo's representatives by Frere are as follows:

6. The Zulu army be disbanded, and the men allowed to go home.
7. That the Zulu military system be discontinued, and other military regulations adopted, to be decided upon after consultation with the Great Council and British representatives.
8. That every man, when he comes to man's estate, shall be free to marry.
9. All missionaries and their converts, who until 1877 lived in Zululand, shall be allowed to return and reoccupy their stations.
10. All such missionaries shall be allowed to teach and any Zulu, if he chooses, shall be free to listen to their teaching.
11. A British agent shall be allowed to reside in Zululand, who will see that the above Provisions are carried.

12. All disputes in which a missionary or Europeans are concerned, shall be heard by the king in public and in presence of the Resident.
13. No sentence of expulsion from Zululand shall be carried out until it has been approved by the Resident.

Frere ensured that there could be no interference from London as he delayed informing the Colonial Office of his ultimatum to Cetshwayo until it was too late to be countered. The full text of Frere's demands would not reach London until 2 January 1879. Of course, by that date, Chelmsford had assembled an army comprising 18,000 men which included British redcoats, colonial volunteers and Natal African auxiliaries. This army awaited Chelmsford's order to cross the border, effectively invading Zululand. Even at this stage Cetshwayo desperately attempted to avoid a war with the British, yet demanded that if war did break out, that his warriors should only defend their homeland if they were attacked first, and not to carry out any military manoeuvres beyond the Zululand border. He also ordered that his warriors should avoid killing any invaders other than the regular British soldiers in their red coats.

When the Zulu response materialized, it was both swift and savage with no quarter given. Lord Chelmsford, having set up a force at the now-infamous Mount Isandlwana, made perhaps the gravest error of judgement of all, splitting his forces before being fully aware of his enemy's disposition. This is something no professional military commander should ever do, though it is doubtful had Chelmsford not split his forces as to whether the outcome of the battle which took place there between Cetshwayo's warriors and the British redcoats would have been any different.

While Chelmsford left Isandlwana with his main force in pursuit of the Zulus, the entire Zulu army had outmanoeuvred him. Cetshwayo's warriors moved behind the remaining British force with the intention of attacking on the 23rd. Reports of Zulu movements throughout the morning of the 22nd were received by the British from 8 a.m. There was of course much confusion at this stage as to exactly where Cetshwayo's main force was, yet at 11 a.m. Lieutenant Charles Raws's scouting party inadvertently stumbled upon the main force after his men had pursued several Zulus into a valley only to be confronted with 20,000 Zulu warriors all sitting in total quiet. Compromised by the British scouting party, the 20,000 warriors rose and charged at Raw's men who fought a fighting retreat to Isandlwana.

A messenger was dispatched ahead of the scouts to warn the camp of the impending Zulu attack now bearing down upon them. The Zulus formed into their classic horns of the buffalo attack formation, intent on drawing out the British defenders so they would be quickly encircled. Colonel Henry Pulleine who had been left in command of the British camp soon realized he had a major battle upon his hands. He deployed first one then all six companies of the 24th Foot into an extended firing line. The idea was to meet the Zulu attack head on, utilizing firepower to check the enemy advance. The British line was woefully over-extended, and ammunition was not reaching the lines quickly enough which nullified the effectiveness of the British Martini-Henry rifles. It was not only a question of ammunition allocation but the quality of the ammunition itself which also became a factor that affected the outcome of the battle in favour of the Zulus. The spent .577/.450-calibre brass cartridge cases tended to jam in the breech of the weapon, forcing its user to resort to the bayonet. The main cause of jamming with the otherwise excellent Martini-Henry rifle was the fact that the cartridge cases were constructed from rolled brass, and upon firing, these rolled brass cases came apart in a similar fashion to a spring uncoiling in the breech of the weapon. The outnumbered British force could ill afford large numbers of weapons jamming; the firepower diminished as the troops began to fall back on the camp itself.

It soon became clear to the British that the camp would be overrun by the Zulus and that saving the Queen's colour was now a priority.

This unenviable task fell to Lieutenants Nevill Coghill and Teignmouth Melvill, both officers of the 1st Battalion, 24th (2nd Warwickshire) Regiment of Foot. The two fought their way through the camp, ducking spears as they fled and heading for the Buffalo River with the Zulus in hot pursuit. By now the whole area was swarming with Zulu warriors and it must have been nothing short of a nightmare journey to the banks of the Buffalo River. When the two lieutenants arrived at the Buffalo, the river was swollen and impassable due to recent storms. Here the two British officers made their last stand as Zulu warriors closed in on them. Melvill was first to fall. Coghill made a valiant effort before he too was overwhelmed. What became of the Queen's colour remains one of the great mysteries as it was never recovered and remains missing to this day. It is likely it was swept away by the raging Buffalo River. As Isandlwana fell the Zulus took a terrible toll, slaughtering everyone in the camp including the young drummer boys. Nothing was spared and even regimental mascots, horses and livestock were killed. In accordance with Zulu custom all enemy dead were looted of their weapons and stripped naked before being disembowelled to release the spirit from the body. Other savagery was committed where bodies were found with their genitals sliced off and jammed in their mouths.

When Chelmsford's column returned to Isandlwana later on the 22nd, darkness had fallen. A few shots of canister were fired into the camp as a precautionary measure. The darkness concealed many of the horrors yet those that became eerily visible in the dull light of lanterns were enough to shock even the most hardened of the British soldiers. There were no survivors; there were over 1,300 dead. The Zulu force had suffered 1,000 to 3,000 killed in the battle with a further 2,000 wounded. As British commander, Chelmsford's head should surely have rolled following this catastrophic defeat for which he was entirely responsible. He wrote an urgent communication to both Queen and country which simply read, 'I regret to report a disastrous engagement.' Disastrous being something of an understatement,

Isandlwana was the worst defeat ever inflicted on a British army by a native force. (Of course, Chelmsford, far from being disgraced, would have his vengeance and see the defeat of the Zulu nation at Ulundi on 4 July 1879. Following his adventures in Zululand, Chelmsford would fade quietly into comfortable privileged obscurity, unlike many of those who won Victoria Crosses (VCs) in the Zulu War and who ended up broken, ill and destitute on the streets of the country they had fought so valiantly for.)

Isandlwana was by no means the end: the British had received a bloody nose, yet within weeks reinforcements would arrive in their thousands and the British would have their vengeance over what was then termed as the 'ghastly fuzzy wuzzy'.

The Zulu force moved off from Isandlwana yet a portion of the that force which had not taken part in the fighting at Isandlwana advanced six miles to the mission station at Rorke's Drift where 150 British and Colonial troops were stationed. Most of us who have seen the movie *Zulu* have imagined ourselves being at the mission station as the sound of the 3,000 to 4,000 Zulus closing in on the sparsely defended station resounded around the hills and plains of Rorke's Drift. This is of course more cinematographic licence as the Zulu force advanced silently towards their objective wishing to give their enemy no advance warning of their impending attack. There was no sound like a train coming in the distance, no banging of spears against shields.

In fact, the British garrison at Rorke's Drift were only aware of the danger when Lieutenant Gert Adendorff of the 1st/3rd Natal Native Carbineers (NNC) arrived at Rorke's Drift with the news of the massacre at Isandlwana and the news that part of the Zulu force was now advancing on the mission station. A rapid assessment of the situation had to be made and the best course of action decided. To have fled the mission station in wagons burdened with hospital patients out into open, hostile country would easily have been overtaken by the approaching Zulus. It was decided that the best option was to stay and fight, utilizing every available resource with which to turn the mission station into a heavily fortified defensive structure. The two British officers in command of the station were Lieutenants John Chard and Gonville Bromhead, who had around 400 men with which to defend the station – a contingent of around 150 Natal Native Horse (NNH) had arrived, having escaped from Isandlwana – and a defensive perimeter was rapidly established using *mielie* (maize) bags and upturned wagons.

The defensive perimeter at Rorke's Drift incorporated the storehouse, a hospital and a stone kraal cattle enclosure. Firing holes were cut out of the external walls of the buildings and external doors were then barricaded with furniture. As all available defensive measures were nearing completion, Lieutenant Chard believed he had enough resources to fend off the Zulu attack he knew was coming. By the time the Zulu force arrived at Rorke's Drift, they had fast-marched some twenty miles and would spend the next eleven and a half hours continuously storming the Rorke's Drift defences. Cetshwayo had warned his warriors of the difficulties of attacking well-prepared defensive structures, yet the Zulus at Rorke's Drift were keen to bathe their spears in the blood of their enemy and there would be no deterring them. Most of the warriors were armed with the *assegai*, the short stabbing spear, plus cowhide shield. Some of the warriors also carried antiquated muskets and rifles which were generally of poor quality. Despite this and poor Zulu marksmanship, these antiquated weapons would account for seventeen British deaths during the battle.

Prior to Zulu attack Lieutenant Henderson's NNH troopers, low on ammunition and exhausted from their flight from Isandlwana, refused to stay and rode on to Helpmekaar, defying Lieutenant Chard's appeals to help defend the station. If that was not bad enough, Captain Stevenson's NNC company, on seeing Henderson's troop ride off, also decided they didn't have the mettle to stay and fight against what seemed impossible odds. As the NNC fled from the station a few shots were fired after them and a Corporal William Anderson was killed in the process.

The garrison now had just 154 to 156 men. Of these, only Lieutenant Bromhead's company could be considered a thoroughly capable fighting unit. Lieutenant Chard made further defensive arrangements to the post. At 4.30 p.m. the Zulus in almost near silence rushed the southern wall; the British opened fire as they closed to within 500 yards. The fighting at the barricades became close-in, hand-to-hand combat. The defensive wall was too high for the Zulus to scale and many were bayoneted or shot attempting to climb it. The hospital itself soon became the scene of fierce hand-to-hand combat and some valiant actions on the part of British soldiers – Privates Harry Hook, John Williams and Joseph Williams – took place as patients were evacuated room by room. The thatched roof of the hospital was soon set ablaze, but nine of the eleven patients survived.

As darkness fell upon the mission station, the Zulu attacks intensified and only began to diminish after midnight, finally ending by around 2 a.m. Instead, the Zulus harassed the defenders with rifle fire from various positions around and above the post, the light generated by the burning hospital illuminating the post for the Zulu snipers. This harassing rifle fire continued until around 4 a.m. The defenders had lost fourteen men by this point with two mortally wounded and at least eight more seriously wounded. Yet these statistics are nothing short of remarkable when one considers the strength of the attacking Zulu force. The battle had lasted for ten hours, the British garrison were exhausted and running low on ammunition; in fact, of the 20,000 rounds of ammunition in reserve at the station, the defenders were now down to their last 900 rounds.

As dawn broke there was no sign of the Zulu force which had appeared to have gone – all that remained were piles of Zulu dead and wounded. Patrols were sent out to collect rifles from the Zulu dead and to look for any survivors. Most wounded Zulu warriors found alive were bayoneted: possibly 500 were killed in this manner.

It is believed 351 Zulus were killed in the actual battle and possibly as many as 375. There was a sense of elation among the British defenders at having survived the Zulu onslaught until around 7 a.m. when a Zulu force suddenly appeared, and the garrison was ordered to their positions once again.

The expected Zulu attack did not materialize. The Zulus were now exhausted after being on the move for six days prior to the battle and had not eaten properly for two; there were many wounded in their ranks who were several days away from any supplies. They withdrew in the same direction whence they had first appeared.

At around 8 a.m. another force appeared and, startled from their breakfast, the garrison once again manned their positions. This time it was no Zulu force but Lord Chelmsford's relief column. The defenders of Rorke's Drift had survived against extreme odds; had the Zulus attacked once more, it is very likely the British garrison would have expended any remaining ammunition they had and been overwhelmed. Rorke's Drift stands out as one action which continues to typify the gallantry of the British soldier at its best; eleven Victoria Crosses were awarded for this action.

In the wake of the battle souvenirs such as Zulu assegais, clubs and shields were collected by the British, many ending up as the prize exhibits in regimental museums back in England. Many such souvenirs would also later find their way back to Britain as a result of the Boer War which followed the defeat of the Zulu kingdom at Ulundi. The Zulu War had already passed into legend by this time and items such as assegais were prized items for British soldiers stationed in Africa, and were often brought home to grace living room walls as curios in homes all over Britain.

Today, through modern archaeological technology there is a much greater understanding of events, particularly of the Battle of Isandlwana. Through modern archaeological examination and the actual disposition of the archaeology itself discovered at Isandlwana, the scale of unpreparedness and disorganization of the British camp prior to the Zulu attack is emphasized perfectly. Modern analysis has also helped dispel certain myths which plagued accepted historical accounts of the battle. For example, the British firing line sent out to meet the Zulu attack was far more extended than previously thought. This was confirmed by numerous archaeological finds including hundreds of expended Martini-Henry cartridge cases found at the site.

Sadly today, despite being protected as historical monuments, many of the old Zulu War battle sites have been subject to looting on a large scale. Oskar Dippenaar spent a good portion of his life privately researching the Isandlwana, Rorke's Drift and Ulundi battle sites among others. When I last spoke with him about these sites, it was back in 1997 where he expressed a pessimistic view of not only South Africa's future but also the continued protection of the Zulu War battle sites. He recalled:

> Of course, as a man with Boer ancestry and Boer blood in his veins the conflicts between the British, Boers and the Zulus and then the British and the Boers was something I became very interested in, especially after the two films about Isandlwana and Rorke's Drift came out many years ago now. Back then in my youth you could go to these old battlefields and still find fired bullet casings, bullet heads, British tunic buttons, broken bayonets and Zulu spear blades. These things were fairly easy to find, especially after the heavy rains where the mud appeared to give up its secrets to those who visited these sites. Nobody was too concerned back then if you picked up something which many enthusiasts did. Usually, these things were mounted on display boards and donated to exhibitions or sold as souvenirs to visitors or retained by their finders as research material. The finest piece I ever found was a British 24th belt buckle – that was nice – but I later donated it to a

museum in England. I also found an interesting piece reflecting the more mundane aspects of life at the camp before it was attacked. I was walking around the site on this one occasion after some heavy storms and found a huge meat cleaver for cutting up beef or pig carcasses. All that was left was the metal work, the wooden handle parts had rotted but it was in remarkable condition for its age. This had been used by the British field kitchen to prepare meat for the soldiers. It's surprising the Zulu's left it as it would have made an excellent weapon but maybe too heavy to carry in one hand.

Today these old sites are protected and there is a monument to the fallen at Isandlwana yet there is widespread illegal digging and even looting of soldiers' graves. The looters do not realize that no valuables or anything was buried with the bodies, yet they persist in exhuming the remains looking for gold rings, medals or anything of value they might be able to sell on. I have seen the desecration of graves at these sites and it makes me sad that it has come to this; our country faces greater challenges and the protection of old battlefields and the graves of the fallen is sadly low on their agendas. I have heard of people being caught digging on these old sites yet corrupt police officers let the culprits off if they can pay them a few rands. It is also no longer safe for visitors, particularly those from Europe, to go out to these sites unless of course on a properly organized tour with security. South Africa is dangerous country as there are not only bandits operating in certain areas but plenty of wild animals too. I hope the situation improves in the future and the graves of soldiers in our country can be properly protected along with whatever still remains in the ground at these historical sites.

Oskar's pessimism is not without foundation. In 2021, a development proposal was submitted for a twelve-acre visitor complex to include a conference centre, two museums and carparks. These proposals were rather surprisingly submitted by the Zulu monarch, King Goodwill Zwelithini, in association with the KwaZulu-Natal Arts and Culture Trust (Kwa Culture). Excavation work began for the first phase of these works which was to construct an 'affirmation village' with many other structures including chalets and leisure facilities. There are many who argue that such a proposal is in bad taste, that Isandlwana is being turned into a theme park when it should remain a sacred site. I am inclined to agree with the latter, yet common sense and respect rarely prevail in countries with such dire economic issues as South Africa. On one hand the venture might prove a useful component to the South African tourist trade but on the other it may appear as much a desecration as the looting of soldiers' graves. No doubt the arguments for and against will continue for a great many years.

To close this section, it would be interesting to note one of my own most surprising finds with a possible Zulu War connection; whilst not exactly archaeology, it was certainly an oddity within its surroundings and where it was found. It was one Saturday morning shopping trip into the monotony that is our local town of Evesham that my partner Paula and I visited several of the charity shops in the town. Looking through the window of one, I noticed what looked like the blade of a native spear just visible behind a set of drawers where it had fallen. I had already made up my mind that this was a modern tourist wall-hanger piece and quite possibly overpriced into the bargain but thought I would have a look anyway. As the spear was handed to me it was instantly apparent that this was no modern tourist wall hanger. After some careful examination of the blade and the material the rest of the weapon had been constructed from, I soon realized what we had found here was in fact a genuine Zulu assegai and an antique one at that. Inquiring as to the price I was surprised to be told £15, the lady in the shop not having a clue what it was or how old it was. It was a nice find as I had always wanted a genuine Zulu assegai and never imagined I would ever find one in a charity shop in our town. One of my old contacts, Henry Richards Pryce, an antiques dealer and expert in native African weaponry, laughed when I told him about my lucky find over the telephone to which he replied, 'This I have to come and see.' Expecting to see a typical tourist wall hanger, his smirk turned to sheer surprise as he examined the weapon and said, 'Well, what you have here is the real thing and its very old' and he went on to point out the unique features of this Zulu weapon. He was examining the wooden shaft with a magnifier when he noticed something I hadn't spotted, a very faint, tiny inscription written in pencil with part of a date beginning with '18'. Sadly, the inscription was not legible. Henry also noted that the point of the blade had slight rolling, that it must have been used on something pretty hard or got damaged in transit or whenever. Henry also explained that it was not out of the realms of possibility that it could have been carried if not used in any one of the battles fought against the British in South Africa or could have been among the many thousands of Zulu weapons confiscated by the British authorities following the Zulu defeat at Ulundi. Another possibility is it could have been brought home as a souvenir by a British soldier who fought in the Boer War. Many soldiers serving in the Boer War returned home with such weapons so it is really anyone's guess. Either way, it was a lucky find and gave me immense satisfaction when Henry called me that proverbial 'lucky bastard' when I told him where the weapon was found and how much was paid for it.

There is certainly no shortage of relic items from the Zulu War in circulation today for those wishing to collect, yet as always provenance is the key. There are many sites today in the UK where you can find expended Martini-Henry bullets and cartridge case remains, these sites being former military firing ranges or those used by owners of vintage weaponry. I do recall one such individual back in the early 1990s who spent his Sunday mornings digging at an old military firing range now returned to farming and pasture. He would unearth the proverbial bucketfuls of fired Martini-Henry lead bullets then take them home and wash them before mounting four or five in a frame and selling them at £10 to £15 as genuine Zulu War relics found at Isandlwana or Rorke's Drift. Entirely dishonest of course but in his eyes good business with a virtually endless supply with which to meet demand from enthusiasts who didn't stop to think about the sheer volume he was selling and how he had obtained such a lucrative supply all the way from South Africa.

At virtually every militaria show in the UK you will come across framed relic sets from the Zulu War, and these remain popular as historical collectables, particularly if they have been originally obtained through a reputable source. Zulu weaponry from the period 1879 can also be easily sourced but as one might expect these items are not cheap; some start from as little as a couple of hundred pounds up to the thousands mark. The genuine material is often sold through the specialist arms and armour auction sales that take place throughout the year. I recall a Zulu assegai collected after the defence of Rorke's Drift with full provenance selling for many thousands of pounds. Whilst the two movies may in some respects be dreadfully inaccurate in some of their portrayals of the events, the myths they have inadvertently spawned ever since has helped retain the fascination with a series of events which would otherwise have become long forgotten with time.

7

The Second Anglo-Boer War 1899–1902

It was pretty much inevitable that once the Zulu nation in South Africa had been defeated and other tribes brought to heel that the whites would then soon begin fighting amongst themselves. As with many wars fought in far-off exotic locations the catalyst for these conflicts was often greed. The discovery of diamonds and gold in South Africa, primarily in the territories of the two independent Boer states of the South African Republic (Transvaal) and the Orange Free State, became a bone of contention between the British Empire and the Boers. The term *boer* is derived from the Afrikaans word for 'farmer', referring to the Dutch settlers who traced their ancestry to Dutch, German and French Huguenot settlers who had arrived in the Cape of Good Hope from around 1652. The Boers by this time were a well-established presence in southern Africa and had assisted the British in the defeat of the Zulu kingdom, the Zulu traditionally being the blood enemy of the Boers. Yet the Boers did not take kindly to the British exploitation of the wealthy resources which lay beneath the soil of what they termed their lands, thus conflict of sorts was unavoidable. Few could have imagined the long-term political and social consequences of the Second Anglo-Boer War for the whole of South African society, a war fought from 11 October 1899 to 31 May 1902. Unlike the Zulu, the British and Colonial forces in South Africa would find the Boers a far more resilient, adaptable and capable foe. The Boers were natural bush- and horsemen, able to exist and fight anywhere on the South African veld under conditions most westerners would find unbearable. They understood the lie of the land and how best to utilize its geographical features to their own advantage. The Boer forces consisted of primarily irregulars, all of whom were well armed and equipped despite being outnumbered and often outgunned by the British. During the early phases of the war the Boers enjoyed considerable success against the British, this largely due again to the arrogance, overconfidence and unpreparedness displayed particularly by the British command. These factors were continual faults in the structure of the British Army's command ethos of the time. Time and again good soldiers lost their lives due to the ineptitude of both the politicians back in London and officers and commanders on the ground in South Africa itself. There were three phases of the war, the first the Boer offensive from October to December 1899, the second the British offensive from January to September 1900 and the third the guerrilla war waged by the Boers from September 1900 to May 1902. There were over forty notable actions fought during the war. As it dragged on, the Boers, unable to fight the British on equal terms in pitched battle, resorted to a guerrilla campaign which proved so successful that drastic measures were required from the British commanders to redress the situation.

Private Albert Curtiss of the 1st Battalion, South Staffordshire Regiment recalled the way the Boers fought during the guerrilla campaign:

> They wouldn't engage in direct confrontation with any of our forces where they would easily be beaten. Instead, you would be on a patrol where you might have to go through a pass with hills and rocks either side of it. Next thing shots would ring out [and] the man at your side would fall dead to the ground along with others and then they would be gone, they would just melt into the countryside. The Boers were excellent snipers and were the ones who developed the art of sniping into the effective way of fighting it would become later in other wars. It was a simple yet effective tactic that was considered a real nuisance, yet it was an effective nuisance as it put much

> psychological pressure upon us, not knowing where they might attack next. The Boers were expert shots too, they rarely missed their target, and they could shoot very well on the run too, something we were not used to doing.

The British answer to the problem of the Boer guerrilla fighters was both controversial and brutally simple. Kitchener introduced a scorched earth policy and began attacking Boer homesteads and rounding up all of the women and children; the homesteads were burned to the ground and all livestock, crops and any other supplies destroyed. The Boer women and children were then placed in what were essentially concentration camps, vast enclosures filled with tents with armed guards ordered to shoot anyone attempting to escape. Thousands of Boer women and children began to die from disease and starvation and this alone forced those Boer men involved in the guerrilla campaign to the negotiating table. It was in many respects a shameful episode in British military history, yet the commanders of the time may have argued the use of concentration camps brought the war to a satisfactory conclusion. In all, it is believed some 28,000 Boer women and children perished in concentration camps in South Africa. The total figure of all who died in the British camps, including blacks, amounted to some 48,000 people.

British military casualties reported 22,092 dead, 75,430 returned home sick or wounded, 22,828 wounded and 934 missing, amounting to a total of 99,284 casualties. The Boers suffered significantly lesser casualties: 6,189 dead, 24,000 captured or sent overseas, and 21,256 who surrendered at the end of the war, amounting to a total of 51,445 casualties.

Oskar Dippenaar, who has specialized in both the Zulu and Boer wars, gives his perspective on archaeological finds associated with the Second Anglo-Boer War:

> The Second Boer War left a bad taste in the mouths of my people yet many of us metal detect and dig to find

> relics associated with that war which may seem at odds with logic. Where the battles were fought, the ground even today is full of all manner of artefacts and much of it is dug and then sold to collectors all over the world. Generally, I sell in the hope of educating those interested in learning something of the past and about the struggles of my own people against British colonialism. If I find anything significant then I keep it for myself and for my own little museum. I have on occasions found personal items such as gold rings, some even inscribed with the names of their owners, crucifixes, watches and coins. These things are found amongst the piles of horseshoes, bullets and bullet casings, cap badges, shrapnel and other detritus that we generally then sell to collectors outside of our country. It is a lucrative business still, but the authorities have tried to change the rules here as they have all over the world with regard to the ethical principles of metal detecting on old battlefields. The problem is now you can try all you like to protect a certain area and illegal diggers will still come and dig. It is much the same as the Zulu War battlefields, and even graves are being exhumed in the hope these people will find something they can then make money from. Thankfully, we have some great museums here in South Africa specifically dedicated to the Zulu and Boer wars, most formulated from private collecting activities.

One museum which is certainly worth a visit when in South Africa is The Blockhouse. The Blockhouse was created by Doug McMasters and the museum has a fine collection of both Zulu and Boer War artefacts. One such artefact is one of the artillery shells fired at the train of Winston Churchill at Frere during the Boer War. Doug McMasters can be seen with this shell in the illustrations in this book.

As far as I know, viewing of The Blockhouse Museum is by prior appointment only; details can be found locally to enable one to make the most of any planned visit.

The political and social ramifications of the Boer War would be far reaching. Most of us will be aware of South Africa's highly turbulent, racially motivated politics. Despite the end of apartheid, South Africa remains as troubled as ever and change is unlikely to evolve for some considerable time to come.

A licence is not required in order to metal detect in South Africa, yet this does not imply that you can use a metal detector wherever you please. Metal detecting and digging is of course prohibited on heritage and protected sites such as the old Zulu War battlefields. If you intend to metal detect or dig on private land, you will still need to seek permission from the local municipality, and it is wise to get this in writing as verbal agreements count for nothing in most cases.

Oskar Dippenaar also reiterated the importance of joining an organized metal detecting group of which there are a number in South Africa. He also warned that there will be many people you come across who have never seen a metal detector before, and it would be wise not to leave such expensive pieces of equipment unattended as such opulent western goods are understandably high on the shopping list of both petty and career criminals alike. Going out alone is certainly not a good idea for several reasons, apart from the obvious, some of which have been previously mentioned. This is not intended to sound harsh or deter anyone but is sadly the reality. Having made this point clear, I have friends who have visited South Africa on numerous occasions with the intention of metal detecting and carrying out digging for military relics and to date all have found their excursions a very positive and rewarding experience, apart from one who suffered an extremely painful bite from a resident baboon spider. The rule here is never stick your hand down a hole blindly (as my friend did) even if a good signal has been detected as you never know what may be lurking within. Snakes and spiders often inhabit deep holes or burrows in the soil and are another hazard to be aware of when out digging on old battlefields in locations such as South Africa.

My friends also state that it is also easier to securely package and send their finds separately through surface or air mail prior to leaving the country as opposed to taking things back on the flight home. Cartridge cases must be empty of any cordite or other propellant charges, and it is best to always ensure that live primers are fired and oiled to render them completely safe. Empty projectile bodies must also be thoroughly checked and if possible oiled; this applies to fuzes too. Some customs departments automatically dispose of anything such as empty shell bodies and spent detonators, and even relic bayonets can be subject to disposal. It is therefore a wise idea to discuss with the relevant authorities prior to the packing and sending of finds just what is permitted and what is on the prohibited list. All these things will save time, money and a lot of stress so it pays to do your research beforehand to avoid breaking any laws and facing any possible legal action from the host authorities. With the ever-confusing miasma of new regulations coming into effect, the subject of sending military artefacts from source countries to other destinations remains an irritatingly grey area capable of filling a book, and one where much consultation is required if one is not to inadvertently fall foul of the authorities.

8

The First World War 1914–1918

It is difficult to imagine that the actions of a single individual could plunge the world into a war which would last for four long years and claim the lives of nine million fighting men of all nationalities. The Great War of 1914–18 was unique in its ferocity, the first truly industrial war where carnage could be wrought in an instant on a previously unimaginable scale. A war that would leave a further twenty-one million wounded and with civilian casualties quoted at ten million, this equates to the staggering figure of forty million total dead and wounded by the end of the war. When Serbian nationalist Gavrilo Princip aimed his revolver at the Archduke Franz Ferdinand and his wife Sophie on 28 June 1914 in Sarajevo, firing shots at close range and killing both, those shots resonated not just around Europe itself but around the whole world. The assassination set a chain of events in motion which would ultimately lead to the outbreak of what would become known as the Great War for Civilization. Princip's primary target, the Archduke Ferdinand, was heir to the Austro-Hungarian Empire. Princip, along with other nationalists, were violently opposed to Austro-Hungarian rule over Bosnia and Herzegovina in the Balkans. Austria-Hungary as with many other nations around the world, blamed the Serbian government for the attack and quickly exploited the incident in order to justify the settling of the question of Serbian nationalism once and for all. Due to Serbia's reliance on the support of Russia, Austria-Hungary waited until its leaders received assurance from Kaiser Wilhelm II that the German Empire would support the Austro-Hungarian cause. The Austro-Hungarian leaders were fearful of Russian intervention into any conflict as this might bring Russia's ally France, and possibly the British Empire into the conflict too. Either way, the Austro-Hungarian government along with that of Kaiser Wilhelm II of Germany were playing a very dangerous game. Austria-Hungary, assured of the full support of the German Empire, then sent an ultimatum to the Serbian government with such absurd terms as to make them totally unacceptable. Serbia, convinced that Austria-Hungary was preparing for war, appealed to the Russians for military assistance and the Serbian army was ordered to mobilize. On 28 July 1914 Austria-Hungary declared war on Serbia and, in a domino-like effect, Europe's great powers quickly followed suit. Within the timescale of just one week, Russia, Belgium, France, Great Britain and Serbia had faced off against Austria-Hungary and the German Empire, and the First World War had begun.

Few could ever imagine the misery and catastrophic loss of life that were to unfold. Many believed that the war would be over by Christmas, but those romantic notions were soon dispelled. Previously unheard-of locations such as Ypres, Arras, Passchendaele, Verdun, Amiens, the Somme and the Argonne would soon be burned into the collective consciousness of not only Europe but the world itself. By the end of the war in 1918, there would not be a household in Britain that had not been affected by the conflict in some way. It was the sincerest wish of many in the human community around the world that the industrialized slaughter that was the First World War would be the last war of its kind to ever blight humanity. On the first day of the Battle of the Somme, 1 July 1916, Britain suffered 57,470 casualties of which 19,240 were deaths. Following that fateful day, 19,240 households back in Britain would receive the news that a loved one had been killed and would never be returning home. These were fathers, husbands, sons, brothers, uncles and cousins, most of whom before the war were ordinary working-class men from humble backgrounds, men who had answered the British government's call to arms to defend king and empire. The First World War as with any war would leave a bitter taste in the mouths of all of those who had lost loved ones in the conflict. Many attempted to understand both political and social catalysts behind the causes of the war.

As widows all over the country began to receive boxes through the post containing their loved one's service medals, many sought to understand further what their men had fought and died for in places they had never even heard of. This was where the very first pilgrimages were made to the battlefields of the Western Front up until the outbreak of the Second World War when quite understandably all such pilgrimages had to be curtailed. Those who were able to travel across to France and Flanders and gain some understanding of what their loved ones went through and what they had fought for were rightly shocked and dismayed upon surveying the water-filled trenches and dugouts strung out over a shell-cratered landscape.

Martha Smith, a 24-year-old widow from Leicester and mother of three young children, travelled to France in 1921 with her father and father-in-law. Her husband, Charles Smith, was killed somewhere on the Western Front in 1916. What she saw as she looked about the landscape, her eyes staring far into the horizon, were recorded in her notebook:

> There was nothing as far as the eye could see, there were no trees, no hedges, no greenery to be seen anywhere, just shell holes filled with water from the rains. The dugouts remained but from what I saw these were filthy hovels that no human being could possibly have existed in. I can only assume the hell that this place once was when it was under the constant fire from the Huns. To think my dear beloved young Charlie went through this only to die out here and remain entombed in mud. It was a pitiful experience, as we travelled back, we were stopped by a young French woman who handed us a bunch of flowers and gave us her thanks and that all our loved ones would never be forgotten by the people of France. I vowed

> never to return but felt compelled each year to go back as it made me feel closer to Charlie. The sacrifice he and the others who fell with him made for this country and the world should never be forgotten, they gave their lives for heaven's sake, what more could any brave man give than his life?

The landscape of the First World War was and still is littered with the detritus of war. The soil is thick with shrapnel and expended rifle and machine-gun projectiles in what was a vast killing ground, the likes of which had never been witnessed previously. Artillery and machine-gun fire were the two main man killers on the First World War battlefields. The first visitors to these now ageing battlefields were painfully aware of the significance. It was these first visitors who often collected something to take home as a keepsake with which to remember a lost father, son or relative. Of course, at the time, such items as uniform buttons, badges, coins, steel helmets, cartridge and shell casings and shell fragments were not the well-rusted and corroded relics we associate with today in the archaeological or collecting context. These items were often collected as some form of physical connection with which a lost loved one might be remembered and retained out of deeply personal reasons as opposed to merely being a collectable for the future.

A cottage industry of sorts did flourish over the years following the end of the war where items such as shell fuzes, cartridge cases and shell fragments were fashioned into items such as ashtrays, ink wells and dinner gongs, all of which could be put to use in the home. At the same time there were many French farmers who endeavoured to pay homage to the fallen by creating their own memorials, often in the form of museums consisting of interesting items discovered on their land, usually following the ploughing. These little museums were often set up in a barn or other outbuilding where visitors and those wishing to learn more about the various battles that took place there were actively encouraged to visit for free. Sadly, many of these fine early collections were looted by the Germans when they arrived in France following the outbreak of the Second World War, though at the end of that conflict the trend began again amongst many French farmers as is the case today. There are some particularly fine collections residing on farms in France today and providing one can master the language barrier it is always worth visiting a farm in areas of what was the Western Front, where an outstretched hand and friendly greeting of '*Bonjour Monsieur*' and polite request to 'see the scrap pile' will rarely be rebuffed, though I cannot state enough of how important it is to speak the language. Not everyone in France can speak English and there are of course those who will think it rude that you have turned up on their doorstep unable to communicate in even the most basic form. Hand gestures alone will not cut it in such cases.

When visiting farms in France, it is wise to sound your horn first and wait for the farm occupants to come out to you. Dogs often roam freely around French farmyards, and more than one visitor has been attacked over the years. The dogs are there for a purpose and will often react aggressively to intruders suddenly appearing in their backyards. Once you have broken the ice, a request to see the scrap pile will often reveal an Aladdin's cave of items which can often be purchased for a few euros provided the owner is happy to part with them. Much of what you will see has been unearthed during the ploughing season. Empty British 18-pounder shrapnel shell bodies and other such items which are most common, particularly on the Somme, are a menace to ploughing equipment and are often stored in enormous piles in farmyards. Along with these things there are of course extremely dangerous pieces of ordnance such as perfectly live and still potentially lethal high-explosive shells, hand grenades and various calibre munitions containing poison gas such as chlorine or cyanic acid. These dangerous munitions are often stored at roadside collection points where they are collected every month and disposed of by specialist teams. These piles of dangerous munitions can be viewed but they must not under any circumstances be tampered with in the slightest. The reason is of course blatantly obvious: the risk of death or severe injury is very real as the recovery teams, or *démineurs* as they are known, will testify. Many *démineurs* have been killed carrying out the hazardous task of removing and disposing of this lethal harvest unearthed each year during farming activities where fierce battles were once fought. Many of these objects may be well corroded and thus extremely unstable and possibly more lethal than they were when first manufactured.

Today, every year, enthusiasts still flock to the old battlefields in the hope of finding something exciting. Anyone wishing to visit France with the intention of either field walking or metal detecting should be aware of the current rules regarding these activities. The rules have changed enormously over the past ten years alone and are evolving all the time. You should never assume that you can just enter private land looking for relics. You should secure the permission of the landowner first, preferably in writing. Should you not, then you will almost certainly provoke an aggressive response if caught. The benefits of having permission are twofold; firstly, it will make for a more memorable if trouble-free visit and secondly, the landowner will often be able to point you to the best areas where to search. He or she will be aware of any current legislation in-country and may or may not permit the use of a metal detector. In many areas of France today, metal detecting is an activity prohibited even on private land and it is advisable to put in the time and energy into researching this factor prior to any visit; as previously mentioned the laws today are increasingly complicated and it is all too easy to fall foul of the authorities; ignorance will not be an acceptable excuse should you if even inadvertently contravene any of the new legislation regarding the removal of military artefacts. I recall how in years past you could walk the old battlefields quite freely and collect cartridge cases and even live rounds could be picked up and retained provided the heads were pulled out and the cordite emptied from the casings. Most rifle rounds of British, French and German origin were corroded enough that the heads could easily be removed from the cases and the charge inside emptied out. Today such an action would be met with dire consternation and accusations of extreme foolhardiness. Yet, I recall a history teacher taking a group of English schoolchildren on such a jaunt in France many years ago and showing them exactly how one could make one of these live rifle rounds safe in the fashion as described – how the times have changed, eh!

One should also bear in mind that there will be items you discover that you will not be permitted to retain under any circumstances especially in today's nanny-superstate climate. A good friend of mine used to visit the Somme every year from the 1970s to the early 1990s. On the one occasion the French farmer he visited frequently excitedly announced that he had discovered a huge hole in the ground where the soil had collapsed, revealing the remains of a British dugout at the edge of one of his fields. The farmer explained he had pulled helmets, bayonets, gasmasks and personal equipment out of the hole and most of it was in remarkably good condition considering its age. My friendly eagerly set off following the farmer's directions and came upon the huge hole where he immediately began digging with his trusty folding shovel he had bought specially for the task from an army surplus shop here in England. Within just a few minutes he was holding a beautiful condition First World War short-barrelled .455 calibre Webley revolver in his hands. There was barely any corrosion as the weapon had lain in the dry void in the ground in the remains of its leather holster. He was able to break the barrel and empty out the still-live cartridges from the cylinder and the black grips on the handle still looked shiny. The firing hammer of the weapon hung limply in the frame as the spring had rotted away but this was the only part that had appeared to perish. Had the spring still been intact the weapon would have almost certainly still fired. It was a fantastic find yet his elation soon dissolved into despair as he realized his prize find would have to be left where it had been found as by all intents it was a live firearm. Placing the Webley to one side, he continued digging and found a marching compass and silver cigarette case minus its cigarettes. Whoever had been in this dugout all those years previous during the war had left in an awful hurry, the reasons of which were by that time indiscernible, lost in the mists of time itself. Either way, my friend was pretty chuffed with the silver cigarette case, compass and bayonet, all of which returned to England with him in the boot of his Vauxhall and, so far as I know, he is still in possession of them to this day.

The 1960s up until around the mid-1990s were considered a boom time for the collecting of First World War relics. Though it was by no means the hugely commercial enterprise it is today, many collectors and historians travelled from the UK to France, returning with car boots full of bayonets, shells, shell cases and rusty rifles, mostly for their own collections, as back then no one was particularly interested in parting with their hard-earned cash for the privilege of owning a lump of what was often termed rusty metal or junk, even if it did come from Ypres, Arras or Passchendaele. I recall another friend who once supplied a London militaria dealer with some of the items he had acquired in France; perhaps the most outrageous of these items was a pair of field-found but safely diffused British 9.2-inch howitzer shells. He managed, with some assistance, to get both heavy shells into the boot of his car, and he made the journey back through the Somme department and onto the ferry back home without incident. One can just imagine the cursing when the suspension of his car suddenly gave out under the weight just after exiting the ferry at Dover. If this was not bad enough, he was later tasked with the delivery of one of these shells to a customer in the Lambeth area. As the prized collectable was being manhandled up the steps and into the front hallway of the customer's house, it slipped off the sack truck onto the customer's thumb which my friend said, once extricated from the base of the shell, looked like a duck's bill. The customer was adamant he was fine and only when the shell was in its correct place did he then rush off to casualty to get the crushed thumb attended to.

I vividly remember the first battlefield recovered relic I ever purchased. I was 14 years old at the time and every Saturday morning I would join a small team of villagers to assist in mowing the two cemetery lawns in Broadway. For the morning's labour I was paid £15 which to me back then was a useful amount of money, which I then often spent on military items I might have encountered in the once plentiful 'junk' or 'second-hand shops' in Evesham. The first serious First World War battlefield relic I purchased was spotted through the window of a small travel agency at the top of Port Street. I noticed it hanging on the wall of the shop as I glanced through the window as I walked past. I stopped and had a look, gazing longingly at what I knew was the remains of a First World War British .303 Lee-Enfield service rifle. I had seen these battlefield-recovered rifles in museums and books in the past; often all that was left was the metalwork, the wood having rotted away. I decided to go into the shop and ask whether it was for sale or just there for display purposes. The chap who ran the shop told me that being a travel agent, one of his favourite places to visit, particularly in France, was the Somme. He then explained he often picked things up which he came across from field-walking as he often took small organized tours to that region in France as part of his business. Then came the question of this relic rifle. Taking it down from the wall, he explained that the bolt was closed and there was very likely a live round up the spout as the safety catch was off. The barrel was slightly bent to a left angle, possibly caused by a shell burst which may have killed or seriously wounded the soldier who had been carrying it. Of course, these were imaginings, yet perfectly plausible scenarios given the very violent nature of the Somme which served to fuel my imagination further on what to me was a real gem of an item. I then asked if it was for sale and how much it might be if it were. Luckily for me I was told the relic rifle cost £15. Without any hesitation I handed him the £15 I had worked hard for earlier that morning while all my school chums were still sleeping away in their beds and was now the proud owner of what I viewed as a real physical piece of First World War history and an item worthy of the greatest of respect. Before I left the shop, I was also shown a Turkish belt buckle and clip of Turkish Mauser cartridges which the chap had picked up while over in Turkey a year or so previous. I passed on these other items as I had no more money at the time, but like many who have passed on something they know they should have bought, I regretted it later. The relic rifle was wrapped up in a black refuse sack and off I went to meet my dad for a lift back home to Broadway. Once in the car, my dad, Trevor Heath, inquired as to what I had in the bag, and when I proudly announced that I had spent my £15 earnings on a First World War Lee-Enfield which had come out of the ground on the Somme, his face was a picture of horror. He was not happy that I had, in his words, 'wasted £15 on a piece of rusty metal'. At the time I forgave dad for thinking this way as many shared his view, that these things were just pieces of rusty metal with no value whatsoever. Either way, I weathered the storm of my dad's consternation and I had that fine relic rifle for many years after, but like much of what was originally a huge collection it would get lost along life's somewhat unpredictable and bumpy road. The shop where I had purchased that relic rifle all those years ago as a young lad is still there, but it is no longer a travel agency and the chap who sold me the rifle has long since passed away. I only wish with so many of the items I had collected and let go of over the years that I still had that rifle, the sentimentality and importance of which is now only too apparent as I have grown older (and wiser).

Another interesting piece which I still have in a rather reduced collection is a piece discovered at Mametz Wood. Mametz Wood was the objective of the 38th (Welsh) Division during the First Battle of The Somme, 1916. What was initially thought of as a relatively easy objective which would be captured in a matter of hours turned into a slaughter. The German positions in the wood consisted of solid, well-constructed fortifications. Machine-gun and artillery fire killed over 400 Welsh soldiers before they even reached the wood itself. Subsequent attacks by the 17th Division on 8 July also failed. The Germans defending Mametz Wood put up a very stubborn resistance but the wood was finally captured on 12 July following further bloodshed and loss of life. Today Mametz Wood is still standing surrounded by typically picturesque French farmland. If you go walking in the wood, you will find overgrown shell craters everywhere along with the remains of German trenches. There are remains of rusty shell fragments, cartridge cases, bayonets and steel helmets everywhere, which now stand in silent memorial to the savagery of the fighting which took place there back in 1916, much of it at close quarters with fixed bayonets.

One piece found there happens to be one of my favourite items of First World War battlefield-recovered archaeology. It is a blown-off brass base section of a French 155mm (6-inch) howitzer shell casing. The Germans had captured a number of these French 155mm artillery pieces and put them to good use against the Allies. Yet, how does one explain how the brass case which this piece came from ended up like this? It is likely that the ammunition dump for the gun that would have fired this round was hit by counterbattery fire, and a British shell had probably struck the pile of live shell cases, causing an explosion. This would have proved catastrophic for anyone in proximity. The base of the shell casing appears more like a piece of sculpture as its edges were flared out as the charge within exploded and the primer cap was partially pushed out of its hole. This piece was found encased in dry mud, and once the dirt had been chiselled away, it was immediately apparent that the primer cap, although partially dislodged, still contained its initiating charge. With a primer cap almost the size of a .455 Webley pistol cartridge, it was wise to soak it in oil just in case. A primer cap this large is capable of making a pretty big bang and however the unlikelihood of someone actually managing to accidentally detonate it, it is always best to be professional about these things and not take the risk of causing injury either to oneself or other persons. Immersing the piece in some industrial oil also had the effect of removing all the surface mud and grime and when wiped clean, it was discovered that the brass had suffered no oxidization (corrosion) which is very rare for brass material that has lain in the ground for as long as this piece. Either way, it was in my opinion an interesting find even if like so many of these things it has a rather grim history. It represents the fighting that took place in that area and of course the lives that were lost there.

With the recent huge resurgence of interest in our social and ancestral history, there have also been the application of highly innovative methods with which to bring the consciousness of the First World War to a new generation of historians and archaeologists through the physical remnants of that war itself. If you walk anywhere on the Somme, for example, with every bucketful of earth you move you will find shell fragments, cartridge cases, live rounds and maybe even a personal item if you are lucky.

I remember many years back Tony Warrell who briefly ran a small antique stand in the town of Hastings in East Sussex. Tony was a keen amateur archaeologist who felt the context of everything he found was just as important as the price he was selling the items for. He travelled to France regularly, particularly in his retirement years, painstakingly attempting to piece together the individual movements of the various British units who had fought on the Somme and other areas of the front. This was in the days before the internet and the release of many records which would have made such a task so much simpler. Yet, Tony did a commendable job and his Saturday morning stand in what was known as The Arcade always drew a small yet enthusiastic crowd as his engaging manner and knowledge proved a great asset in the sale of relics from the Western Front. He always provided a detailed information sheet with each relic he sold down to the finest of details, all of which he had typed up on his trusty mechanical typewriter. By doing this the historical context of every relic he sold remained with the piece. Sadly, when Tony passed away, much of the hundreds of records, hand-produced maps and documents he had drafted and neatly filed for future reference inexplicably vanished, probably in the fog of bereavement which followed his passing. Tony's wife Mary admitted having little knowledge of her husband's collection and that the 'vultures soon descended on the scene offering to take things off my hands and get a good price etc. Yet, much of it was taken away and I was never to hear anything again'.

I still have a piece of shrapnel in the form of a piece of copper driving band from an exploded 9.2-inch British howitzer shell which had fallen on the German lines which Tony found in the summer of 1994. I still recall when he handed it to me him, looking at it and saying, 'This lump of copper would have been one hell of a lethal projectile' as he bounced it in the palm of his hand. Thanks to the technologies we have at our disposal today, archaeology of all kinds has thrived on the First World War battlefields, not just in France but all over the world. In many cases the remains of the fallen themselves have been located and recovered for proper burial in their respective military cemeteries, one of the commendable assets with modern archaeological techniques. Modern television has also aided the fascination with the First World War with TV documentaries such as *Time Team* and *Battlefield Detectives* where professionals utilize high-tech equipment to answer the questions which have remained mysteries for so long. Today, relics associated with the battlefields of the First World War have become highly collectable as real pieces of history. They grace the display units and dealer tables at all the major militaria shows both here and in Europe and premium specimens today fetch very high prices. Long gone are the days where such objects were called 'rusty crap' and confined to boxes beneath dealers' tables, specifically there for those collecting on a very low budget. I am pleased those days have passed as I never understood the 'rusty crap' attitude of many collectors at the time and why someone would want something which was gleaming and new that had probably come straight out of a factory and had probably never even been used in any action. Those relics dug out of the bloodied soil of the Somme, despite the rust and the dirt (easily cleaned), and other First World War battlefields, were always the 'real' pieces of history which best represented that terrible episode of world history. Tony would advise when out looking for the relics of war that 'one should be mindful, tread carefully, for good men fell upon the ground where you will be walking; they fell thick like wheat being cut down with a scythe, always remember that when you go there, and say a prayer for them before you leave too'.

Perhaps one of the most remarkable of First World War relics I have come across resides not in a museum but in the back garden of a local farm/riding school, run by the Bomford family since well before the First World War. Owner Mrs Joan Bomford, who despite being well into her eighties, still runs both the farm and riding school and can frequently be seen driving a tractor around. Joan is a marvellous character and living archive of memories of not just the old countryside ways but the war years too. She was named BBC *Countryfile*'s Farming Hero 2015. I had known Joan and her late husband Tony for some years as their land contains a Second World War US Army dumping ground of which we will learn more of later in this book. Back to the point: I can always remember locals talking of a 'bomb' that used to reside at the bottom of the drive to the Bomford farm. I heard stories that it had been there for a great many years and that local children used to play on it, yet in all my time in the area I had never seen this 'bomb' and never thought to ask Joan or Tony as to its whereabouts. It was in the summer of 2019 when I visited Joan with a fellow metal detectorist Mark Cheshire and my partner Paula for a sweep of some of the fields at the back of the farm buildings. Although little of any significance was found, I finally asked Joan about this 'bomb' she was said to have had at the bottom of her drive, to which she replied, 'Oh, that; it's in my back garden now. It used to be lying down at the bottom of the drive by the road. It was moved because one night three men in a white van pulled up and tried to lift the thing into the back of their van to steal it for whatever reason. So, we decided it was best to move it closer to our bungalow on the property.' I asked Joan if the 'bomb' was still here and she pointed to her back garden and said, 'Yes, it's over there. You can go and have a look.' What we discovered was no 'bomb' as so many had called it but a rare example of a British First World War 15-inch (381mm) howitzer shell. This huge shell was minus its brass fuze which Joan remarked 'had been stolen off it when it lay near the road at the bottom of the drive'; the copper driving band was also missing probably stolen by a passer-by. These issues did not detract from what was an impressive piece of First World War ordnance weighing in at a colossal 1,450lb (657.7kg). The history of this shell is not fully known but is believed to have been maybe one of a pair that once stood outside Evesham Town Hall, before being relocated to Bretforton Manor before then being moved to Joan and Tony Bomford's farm. I must point out the shell contained no high-explosive filling and was perfectly safe. As we looked at this huge projectile, we could not help but laugh at the story of the three men who had attempted to steal it. Had they managed to get it into the back of their van. the sheer weight would have probably broken the suspension of their vehicle. Either way, it was fascinating to finally see what this elusive 'bomb' was and that it remains at the property as part of the farm's and our local history. I only hope that in future that it goes to the local museum as opposed to ending up at a scrap merchant's.

In respect of the British Empire, the First World War was largely confined to Europe, unlike the Second World War where there was the blitz on British cities with enemy aircraft strafing and bombing targets in British coastal waters along with the real threat of German U-boats starving Britain into submission. One very notable exception in the Great War was that of the German Zeppelin airships. The Zeppelin raids on Britain proved a nuisance yet there were not tactically enough of these airships to inflict any serious damage on the British war effort. Yet, they proved a frightening entity for British civilians who suddenly found themselves on the front line. Methods were quickly devised in an attempt at combatting these night raiders but shooting them down in the dark of night was far from an easy task. Britain's fledgling air force, the Royal Flying Corps, attempted to perfect the art of night interception against these huge and relatively slow-flying dirigibles. Even when located in the air, shooting them down was not as easy as one may think. During the early days of the Zeppelin blitz the German raiders were engaged from the ground by various artillery pieces adapted into the anti-aircraft role. Later the pilots of the Royal Flying Corps would hunt them down in biplanes such as the Royal Aircraft Factory B.E.2 developed for the night-fighter role. The machine guns to shoot the Zeppelins down used specially developed .303-inch (7.7mm) incendiary ammunition. If one of these incendiary rounds penetrated the highly flammable hydrogen gas cells of the Zeppelin, its destruction was almost assured. The first successful night interception and destruction of a Zeppelin airship came on the night of the 2/3 September 1916 over Cuffley, Hertfordshire. The British pilot involved in this action was Lieutenant Leefe Robinson of No. 39 (Home Defence) Squadron, based at Sutton's Farm, Hornchurch, Essex. Although space does not permit relating the actual combat, Leffe fired some three drums' worth of his Lewis gun ammunition at the raider which caught fire and crashed to the ground. Robinson was awarded Britain's highest honour, the Victoria Cross (VC).

Julian had the privilege of conducting an archaeological dig at the crash site of one such raider that was brought down from the night skies over England during the First World War, and this is a rare and exclusive account of a Zeppelin crash site dig previously unpublished. Julian recalls this archaeological survey and dig with great enthusiasm and fondness.

Looking for a lighter-than-air First World War Zeppelin under the earth may seem a somewhat impractical, almost doomed-to-failure task, given that soil is an unnatural habitat for such things, and, especially more so, when combined with the more important factor that no examples of such airships remain in existence today. However, in 2006, I received a phone call saying, 'Jules, could you possibly find us a Zeppelin?' Having been an aviation archaeologist for some forty years now, back then I seized upon the opportunity to look for such a suitable Zeppelin. This was at the request of the BBC who were looking for this type of subject matter for inclusion in a proposed *Timewatch* episode titled *The First Blitz*. After researching the matter further, I then set about the task of looking for a Zeppelin crash site that could be investigated and decided that the most practical would be the crash site of Zeppelin L48 at Theberton, Suffolk. Aerial photography taken at the time of the crash, revealed an isolated rural crash site and therefore I hoped that in the interceding years perhaps not too many people had investigated the site, and more importantly, that the crash site had not been built upon. Over the days following this incident in 1917, pieces of L48 were being snapped up as souvenirs not only by the locals but by others who had travelled some distance in order to be able to grab themselves a war trophy. Most of the the Zeppelin's wreckage lay sprawled upon the surface of the field where it was easily accessible and much of it was later collected up and disposed of, presumably for scrap.

However, we wanted to ascertain as to whether any larger, more deeply buried debris from the crash was present in the ground at the site, particularly from the engines as they impacted the ground. We knew that not every piece of wreckage had been recovered from the site back in 1917 as this would have been impossible, especially with the ongoing war to contend with. All that remained was for the site to be excavated where all would soon be revealed.

Things proceeded rapidly; having visited and checked out the location and gaining the all-important permission for an excavation from the landowner, the next phase was to establish what archaeological evidence might remain intact in the ground.

Several metal detecting surveys were carried out as part of the preliminary exploration, having utilized the photographs taken in 1917 to coordinate our searches. On one such image a hedge could be seen alongside the wreckage, the hedge now long grubbed out; however, evidence of its existence was indicated by a straight line of slightly higher crop growth. Numerous scraps of twisted aluminium airframe, hundreds of tiny copper loops and other artefacts from the crashed German Zeppelin were intact in the sandy Suffolk soil.

Zeppelin L48 had been an example of what was termed the 'Super Zeppelin', a type developed for increased altitude flight; its intended target that night was Harwich. Out of the twenty-four bombs dropped by L48, all of them missed, exploding harmlessly on open pasture. The honour of taking down this night intruder belonged to Royal Flying Corps crew Second Lieutenant Frank Holder and Sergeant Sydney Ashby in an F.E.2b night fighter. Holder and Ashby were not alone in their pursuit of their giant prey and other British pilots were in the night skies pursuing the Zeppelin, all eager to get a 'squirt' in, including Captain Henry Saundby in a DH.2. Holder and Ashby had fired off around three drums of .303-inch ammunition before seeing that the giant airship was by now beginning to burn. Holder glanced at his wristwatch and noted the time was precisely 3:25 a.m. L48 burned with such intensity that it illuminated the surrounding countryside for miles around. As the Zeppelin began to fall in flames, it was fired on again by one of the other British planes determined that there would be no escape for this raider. L48 crashed into the ground in Crofts Field, Theberton Hall Farm. The superstructure collapsed in a telescopic fashion as it hit the ground, until only a portion of the nosecone framework remained, pointing ominously upwards from the ground. Of the sixteen crew of Zeppelin L48 there were only three survivors, Maschinistenmaat Heinrich Ellerkamm, Leutnant zur See Otto Mieth, and Maschinistenmaat Wilhelm Uecker who were then taken prisoner. The crew of Zeppelin L48 who were killed are as follows:

Obermaschinistenmaat Heinrich Ahrens born 22/02/1880 Bremerhaven

Maat Wilhelm Beetz born 04/03/1892 Thalheim

Obersignalmaat Walter Dippmann born 13/09/1880 Frankenberg

Kapitänleutnant Franz Georg Eichler born 29/10/1877 Geibichenstein

Obermaschinistenmaat Wilhelm Glückel born 21/09/1881 Nurnberg

Bootsmannsmaat Paul Hannemann born 21/08/1886 Grub Jlse

Signalmaat Heinrich Herbst born 10/07/1892 Grohn-Blumenthall.

Bootsmannsmaat Franz König biorn 09/09/1892 Magdeberg

Funkeltelegrafiemaat Wilhelm Meier born 25/09/1894 Meitzendorf

Obermaschinistenmaat Karl Milich born 18/08/1880 Striegau

Obermaschinistenmaat Michael Neunzig born 21/01/1882 Cologne

Obermatrose Karl Plöger born 09/10/1880 Hiddesen

Korvettenkapitän Viktor Schütze born 06/03/1878 Hanover

Obermaschinistenmaat Hermann von Stockum born 04/01/1894 Duisburg

Obermatrose Paul Suchlich born 11/05/1888 Niedersalzbrunn

Steurmann der Reserve Paul Westphal born 04/05/1887 Insterburg

The next phase was the actual excavation itself which, like many I have conducted in the past, always seems to begin with the familiar sounds of metal detectors being checked, spades clanging, rucksacks being slung over shoulders and of course the distant sound of an approaching JCB, one of the most vital pieces of equipment for an excavation such as this one.

The rough-sounding engine of the JCB excavator chugged and roared, echoing across the surrounding fields as its wide dinosaur-like scoop began to engage the flint-ridden soil. Initially, six inches of soil were removed over an extensive area. Once removed, this was 'geofizzed' to assess any soil disturbance or perhaps the existence of any noteworthy features from earlier stages of history. Unfortunately, this revealed nothing; however, the following metal detector surveys began to uncover a myriad of small targets, each one marked or investigated immediately and then plotted. Obviously, the exact impact point would reveal the highest density, but a variety of actions might have influenced the distribution of finds over the last nine decades or so, such as agricultural activity as well as both the original official-clearance and less-official souvenir hunting.

Once fully investigated, the site was excavated down to a deeper level and the metal detecting repeated until the entire site had been checked. The whole operation and all associated activities were filmed by the BBC film crew, headed by John Hayes-Fisher. Throughout the excavation little evidence of soil discolouration due to burning was noted; the only evidence of burning having occurred was the presence of several noticeably greyish- and white-coloured heat-subjected fractured flints. We excavated where the large Maybach HS Lu six-cylinder engines had impacted, although this was not specifically definable as no evidence, either engine casing fragments or oil traces, could be identified. We concluded that the sandy nature of the soil had allowed the carbon and oil evidence to simply percolate down to deeper levels or dissipate to an indistinguishable level in the passing ninety years. Overall, no metallic finds were recovered from any depth greater than that the extent of the plough soil.

A wide variety of finds uncovered during the excavation of L48 are held at local museums in Ipswich, Southwold and at Leiston Long Shop Museum which has several related artefacts, including a leather glove that belonged to one of the crew of L48. In addition, there are numerous private collections containing artefacts relating to this incident, which include brooches, rings and other items fashioned from pieces of wreckage taken from L48. It is remarkable that the 2006 excavation of the crash site yielded some 400 recorded metallic finds despite the very evident super-efficient recovery operation of 1917. In all 99.9 per cent of the finds unearthed were directly attributed to L48. Some of the most numerous finds unearthed at the crash site of L48 were the 8mm-diameter loops which had been sewn into the Zeppelins fabric envelope skinning. On these, traces of carbonized fabric material were still present, trapped within the ridges of the small metal loops.

Perhaps of all the finds discovered at the crash site of Zeppelin L48 was a single fired British .303-inch (7.7mm) Mark VII S.A. Ball projectile. This bullet still had traces of molten aluminium attached to it and was one of many rounds that had contributed to the destruction of L48. What perhaps makes this otherwise unremarkable .303-inch projectile is the later research conducted by Ian Castle who featured the artefact in his superb book *The First Blitz in a Hundred Objects*. Through painstaking research into this .303-inch projectile, Ian was able to ascertain that it most likely came from the machine gun of Captain Henry Saundby, as that night his DH.2 was not set up for night flying. The standard .303-inch Mark VII S.A. Ball round was not usually used for such Zeppelin patrols. However, Saundby is recorded as having fired off three drums that night, one of Buckingham incendiary bullets, one of SPG 'Sparklet' tracers and the final one being Mark VII S.A. Ball. Now that really is what I call a truly fine piece of research work, making an otherwise relatively insignificant find into a major part of the story of Zeppelin L48's demise over the British countryside and a highly poignant historical artefact.

As we left the site following the successful excavation of the crash site of Zeppelin L48, I glanced back; a dark-winged marsh harrier banked sharply over the nearby reedbed and a solitary, but very appropriate poppy stood out in the barley crop, fluttering in the gentle breeze. It was in most respects a scene of utmost tranquillity, with nothing whatsoever to indicate the scene of violence that had taken place at the spot all those years ago in 1917. As far as I am aware, this was the very first archaeological excavation of a German First World War Zeppelin airship ever to have been carried out and therefore was an important event. Sometime afterwards I sitting on the edge of the sofa with some of those who had participated in the excavation, as BBC *Timewatch* was finally aired. It was brilliant and we were all very proud, each believing that as privileged, responsible custodians of history, there is little point in researching or being an archaeologist if you do not share what you discover with others. We had done this to the letter in a professional manner and is something we can still be very proud about having taken part in today.

9

The Second World War 1939–1945

With hindsight the rise of fascism in post-First World War Germany should have come as no surprise. Germany had been defeated, and the Allied-brokered Treaty of Versailles was to become a running sore, an additional humiliation that many Germans were soon convinced was specifically intended to destroy Germany's social and economic fabric. Former First World War German army corporal Adolf Hitler seethed with rage at what he saw as the treachery toward not only those who had fought and died for Germany in the First World War but its people. The treachery Hitler was convinced existed in the German political and social system in his mindset had been at least partly orchestrated from within, namely by Germany's Jews. He would exploit the climate of discontent that began to flourish in the Weimar era towards his own political, social and moral ends. The Nazi Party which emerged through all this chaos, with Adolf Hitler as its 'voice of the people', was little more than a band of thugs, who were at least initially few in number, yet with a virulently nationalist racist agenda. What began as a small political force comprised mostly of disgruntled war veterans soon outgrew the smoke-ridden atmosphere of the beerhalls and soapbox-preaching diatribes, injecting itself directly into the veins of Germanys political mainstream. Yet Hitler's rise to power was by no means as rapid or trouble free as many might believe. His path leading to absolute power had been beset with problems and setbacks, including a spell in prison following the failed Beer Hall Putsch in Munich of 8/9 November 1923. Yet it was the failed putsch and Hitler's subsequent incarceration in prison that further fuelled his sense of national purpose. His trial garnered much attention in the German press which far from convincing German society that Hitler's Nazi Party was a proverbial loaded gun, actually served to further support for the Nazi Party. It gave Hitler the tallest soapbox of his fledgling political career to date, and people began to listen. At the time few people really cared that Hitler was being portrayed by much of the outside world as the Pied Piper of doom. Hitler and the Nazi Party had bequeathed the means with which to discard the shackles which bound Germany following the defeat in the Great War, namely in the form of the universally hated Treaty of Versailles.

Hitler was determined that Germany would rearm, and this process was set in motion almost as soon as he came to power in 1933 yet was not made public until 1935. The rearmament programme created jobs for millions of previously unemployed. It all looked as if Hitler and the Nazi Party had performed some kind of an economic and social miracle. The miracle was created in a climate totally geared towards Hitler's desire for war. Most are aware that it was a unique series of events which not only propelled Adolf Hitler to absolute power in Germany but led to the German invasion of Poland and a second declaration of war from France and Britain which was made on 3 September 1939. It is difficult to comprehend even today that just one individual could be capable of causing a world war, a war even more terrible than the first, a war which would last for six long years and result in the deaths of seventy-five million people by its end in September 1945. Just as Gavrilo Princip's revolver plunged the world into conflict in June 1914, it was the nationalistic, racist rhetoric of Adolf Hitler that would sow the seeds not only for his own untimely destruction but that of Germany itself.

There is perhaps a greater focus upon Second World War archaeology today than that of the first which is unsurprising. The Second World War would have a far more direct impact on the population of Britain. Along with the threat of invasion following the fall of France in June 1940, the U-boat menace would return with a vengeance to British offshore waters and the Atlantic and Britain would suffer intense attack from the air by the might of the new German Luftwaffe (air force). The attacks would steadily grow in not only their intensity but by their indiscriminate nature too. The Zeppelin and offshore battleship raids made by Imperial Germany in the First World War would pale into insignificance in comparison to the Luftwaffe's bombing campaign of the Second World War under Adolf Hitler.

The creation of more RAF airfields, well-dispersed cottage industries operating in support of the war, observation posts, Home Guard structures, prisoner of war and refugee camps, and later arrival of American troops and not forgetting US Army dumping sites, means that even today the soil of this once-mighty country is rich in the archaeology of the Second World War in all forms. The British Royal Navy proved the single most formidable obstacle which kept the Kriegsmarine (German navy) at a respectable distance from British shores therefore Nazi attacks upon Britain began more with the offshore harassment of shipping by the Luftwaffe. Each time the Luftwaffe made incursions into British airspace, it was met by the shore defences of the Royal Artillery's Anti-Aircraft command and the Hurricanes and Spitfires of Britain's Royal Air Force. This was a period which many Britons said at the time gave 'a false sense that there was not really a war going on with Germany at all'. Hitler it would appear was rather restrained in the initial attacks upon his British foe across the Channel. There were no attacks on civilian infrastructures or cities, as Hitler felt he could appeal to the British and either force them to 'come on side' with Germany as fellow Anglo-Saxons or simply surrender.

The primary focus of Germany's war against Britain was carried out primarily by the Luftwaffe and of course the U-boats of the Kriegsmarine. While the U-boats targeted shipping from sympathetic nations such as the USA which were supplying Britain with a substantial portion of everyday necessities, the Luftwaffe for the first time would be fighting alone without the support of the Heer

(German Army) which of course had been a vital component in its effectiveness in the conquest of Europe. The two military arms had previously fought together as a single cohesive fighting force honing the Blitzkrieg or Lightning War principle to deadly effect. Hitler's initial hopes were that his Luftwaffe could knock Britain's RAF out of the war, therefore making invasion a more feasible possibility. To do this the Luftwaffe *Kampfgeschwader* (bomber groups) would have to attack RAF airfields in southern England directly, while the German fighters would concentrate on any RAF defences sent up to oppose the bombers. What ensued was the Battle of Britain, fought between 10 July and 31 October 1940, a battle the RAF came very close to losing. It was more down to a stroke of luck where a German bomber crew became disorientated and accidentally dropped bombs on the British capital, London. Britain's Prime Minister Winston Churchill immediately ordered a retaliatory attack on the Nazi capital of Berlin and so in effect a tit-for-tat war of attrition began. While the Luftwaffe began to focus its ferocity on London and other British cities, the RAF was given valuable time to reequip and gather its strength and reserves and come back stronger at the Germans. There have been hundreds of books published on the Battle of Britain and the Blitz and I feel that to explain both campaigns here is unnecessary as most will be aware of the basic history, that Germany failed in its endeavour to bomb Britain into submission and that following the failure to knock Britain out of the war, Hitler then turned his attention east with the invasion of the Soviet Union in 1941.

This invasion of the USSR and the entry of the United States into the war more or less sealed Nazi Germany's fate, ensuring certain victory for the Allies. With the defeat of Nazi Germany in 1945, the geography of Europe changed yet again with the threat of all-out nuclear war between the Western Allies and the Soviet Union. Despite this, many groups of aviation enthusiasts formed and flourished and developed some particularly fine if small museums all over the country. These groups carried out archaeological excavations on the many British, American and German aircraft crash sites which were prevalent and relatively undisturbed. The 1950s to the 1970s were what many recall as a 'boom time' for this form of military archaeology. As aviation historian Peter Halliday recalled:

> Back then it was different to the way it is now. We were interested in the history and the remembrance and preservation of the history of it all. Today it's all about the money you can earn for flogging off a propeller blade or a cockpit instrument of a German plane that so and so shot down in 1940. Most of what is being peddled today as 1940 crash relics are fake and came from other sources such as aircraft accidents and dump sites, but ignorance is bliss, isn't it.

Here in England, unless you happen to live in the far north of the country, you don't have to travel too far to look for signs of the Battle of Britain or the Blitz. In the summer of 1997, I joined a couple of local enthusiasts who were keen on archaeology and the art of field-walking. They had gained permission for a field walk and metal detecting foray on a good stretch of farmland on the outskirts of Folkestone, Kent. The farmer there at the time had found numerous pieces from the Battle of Britain while ploughing his fields and as he had left a large area unplanted and void of crops this one year, he invited my friends to have a good look over the ground to see what was there. It meant an early start of 4 a.m. from our addresses in the Midlands that day to allow for travelling down and being able to spend some useful time out in the fields, but it was well worth the early start and subsequent long hot drive down in the van. It was to be one of the hottest days of the year so far and the conditions perfect for a day out in the beautiful Kent countryside where so much history had been played out in the skies above in those dark, desperate days of 1940.

My two friends had Minelab Explorer metal detectors and were confident of unearthing some interesting finds. We all had cameras and notebooks so as the location of any finds could be fully recorded for their context and future reference. The only obstacle to going out into the fields was a group of seven angry geese which were not happy at such an early intrusion into their farmyard and were thus intent on blocking the path to our intended destination. As we loaded ourselves up with backpacks, shovels and metal detectors, we then made a quick dash for it, closely pursued by the geese with beaks just inches from our arses up the farm track leading to the fields. Owner Bob Marsh stuck his head out of the piggery as we went by to not only laugh hysterically at our predicament but to wish us good luck as he shouted out, 'Them birds be better than dogs, aren't they? Well, good luck and hope you find something.' Bob had drawn a map of the three large fields we were going to explore and noted where he had found things, including the location of several large bomb craters which to his knowledge were undisturbed by way that no one had ever dug them and they had simply been filled in. He also promised that upon our return after the field trip, he had some interesting stuff for us to see stored in a barn. So, in our eyes it should work out to be a perfect day.

Bob's hand-drafted map proved to be remarkably accurate and after just ten minutes of metal detecting, one of my two colleagues found a good signal in the ground and dug out what he thought was a cannon shell casing, but it looked too short. Handing it to me I knew straightaway that it was indeed a 20mm cannon shell case of the type used by Luftwaffe fighters such as the Messerschmitt Bf 109 and Bf 110. It was a fired 20mmx80RB (rebated rim) shell casing from a German Oerlikon MG FF cannon which had been fired in anger by either a Bf 109, Bf 110, Heinkel He III or possibly Dornier Do 17z, as these were the only Luftwaffe aircraft in service equipped with this weapon during the Battle of Britain. Bob did mention that the old locals talked of low-flying German fighters and bombers strafing targets in the area. Pretty soon more such finds were being unearthed including many fired British .303-inch Browning machine-gun cartridges, fired .303-inch bullet heads and some fired German 7.92mm MG 17 bullet heads. The fields were pretty much thick with the stuff, and we were all in our element. I had my first ever go with a Minelab Explorer metal detector which was my friend's pride and joy, so I was very conscious of not breaking it. I found a few pieces of well-corroded aircraft aluminium scattered over the field. As there were no large concentrations of 'Daz' – the nickname given to the presence of large areas of rotting aluminium in soil which breaks down to the appearance of the brand washing powder – no aircraft could be assumed to have crashed there. Later research confirmed this along with the fact that maybe these pieces of metal had fallen away from either British or German aircraft shot up during the dogfights which took place above. It was difficult to comprehend the violence which had visited the skies above these now-tranquil fields all those years ago and we imagined what it might have been like to witness those events as they occurred. The things which we had found that day were the tangible physical links to those events now confined to an ever-distancing history.

Before we left the fields, we did a quick scan over one of the large bomb craters which was naturally quite overgrown with stinging nettles which did not bode well for three guys wearing shorts. I had brought a good-sized knife with me to hack away any unwanted foliage and the bomb crater was soon cleared enough for the detector to do its work. Sure enough, metal was detected in the ground at one edge of the crater at a depth of around two feet. After a few shovelfuls we pulled out two good-sized bomb fragments. Both were lumps of metal around an inch thick, over eight inches long by around five wide and weighing approximately ten pounds. These were good pieces and would not take much effort in cleaning up either, but it was a pain having to carry them back to the van at the end of the day.

We packed up and made our way back to the farmhouse at around 4 p.m. eager to see what Bob had got in his barn before we had to leave for the journey home. As we arrived in the farmyard it was to our relief that we found Bob just locking up the geese to prevent them from becoming fox fodder in the night. He smiled and told us to follow him into one of his old barns. It was typical of many old barns back home. Rusty old gin traps hung from the walls on nails and parts of old farm machinery were scattered around in a state of half-repair. In the room that Bob showed us it was a different story: an aircraft propeller blade stood in one corner, an aircraft wheel in another and a table piled with various rusted metal items. Bob told us the propeller blade had been recovered from his land during the war but no sign of a crashed aircraft anywhere nearby. After looking closely at the propeller blade, we could see it had come from a German aircraft but what type could not be ascertained at the time. The propeller blade had bullet or shrapnel strikes on it and appeared to have been severed from the propeller boss. I was not so sure that even eight .303-inch Browning machine guns were capable of severing a metal propeller blade from its boss and it was likely due to damage caused by an anti-aircraft shell that was the likely culprit. A few shards of rusted shrapnel had been discovered on Bob's property, so our prognosis fell into the realms of feasibility.

On the table were various lumps of aluminium including a good-sized section which Bob said had come from a Bf 110 shot down locally. Another interesting item was part of a Spigot Mortar which had been in use with the local Home Guard. Bob said his father had found it discarded in a hedge bordering one of his fields. The only question left after looking at these items was if any of it was for sale. Bob explained that he'd let the propeller blade go for £300, the Spigot Mortar part for £80 and the other miscellaneous bits as a bundle for £20. My two friends were both married to spouses who would have gone mad at them for spending such a sum on their hobby, and reluctant to become divorcees, they declined to buy anything, so I took the lot off Bob; the prices were very cheap indeed for the time where these things were starting to become expensive as collectables, yet Bob explained he was no dealer and didn't like dealers too much, as in his own words, 'They tend to be sly, smarmy bastards.' Bob wasn't a fan of big-shot historians either and was very particular about whom he allowed on his property, so we felt somewhat honoured. After shaking hands and loading up the van, we set off home promising to return for another foray. Sadly, I never had the chance to go back and Bob has since passed away and the farm has changed hands numerous times. It was, however, a window of opportunity that I am glad I took when I did.

The Luftwaffe air campaign known as the Blitz, which began on 7 September 1940 through to 11 May 1941, was an intense and protracted bombing campaign which brough the civilian population of Britain directly into the front lines of the Second World War. While remnants of this now-infamous period remain in the form of shrapnel dings on old city buildings and long overgrown bomb craters in the surrounding countryside, the ruins of Coventry Cathedral stand as perhaps the most visible reminder of this period of Luftwaffe terror. In London's East End it is even possible today to find rusted pieces of shrapnel from exploded anti-aircraft shells and fragments of German bombs buried in the back gardens of many of the houses there, testimony to the fury vented by both sides in what was yet another battle of wills between Nazi Germany and the British Empire. John Stills from Kent recalls buying his first house along the Devonshire Road in Walthamstow in London's East End in 1985. He had renovated the terraced property yet was plagued by an incessant leak in the roof which could not be initially explained. John recalled:

> I had been up in the loft countless times looking for any holes and signs of daylight coming through the roofing tiles but saw nothing. I had spent most of my cash on buying the house and its subsequent renovation and was dreading facing the prospect of having to take out a loan to sort out any major roof work. There was this persistent leak when

> it rained heavily and the loft space became damp, yet I'd shine a torch around and couldn't see any issues with the roof or anything. It was only when I called a mate in who was a roofing expert to take a look that the problem was found to have been there since the Second World War. My mate got a ladder up there right under the tiles and said, 'You'll never guess what's been causing your leak, mate.' So, I replied, 'Well, what is it?' He took a pair of pliers out of his toolbelt and began wrenching away at something lodged in the tiles, something I had been unable to see previously until he pointed it out. After a bit of grunting and cursing, he finally pulled the offending object out and chucked it down to me. It turned out to be a 5-inch-long piece of shrapnel from an exploded British 4.5-inch high-explosive anti-aircraft shell. These guns were used to fire at German aircraft when they came to bomb London at night during the Blitz. This piece of shell was in remarkably well-preserved condition seeing that it had been up there all those years. My mate fixed the hole and replaced a few tiles, and I had a little conversation piece I intended to get mounted in a frame or something as part of the history of the house. Speaking to some of the elderly locals, they told me the guttering of the houses around here got clogged with shrapnel during the air raids and often these steel splinters would pierce tiles and the roofs of garden sheds and Anderson shelters too sometimes.

British comedy actor and musician Reg Varney of *On the Buses* fame recalled being caught up in an air raid while travelling on a London double-decker bus. Reg recalled:

> I was sat there on the upper deck on my way home when the sirens began to sound, and the conductor came and

> informed me that a raid was coming in. All I remember of it was that suddenly something came through the roof of the bus and landed down between my feet. It was a piece of shrapnel from a shell that had exploded high up in the sky above. It was a miracle it didn't hit me on the head, as if it had of done, I might not be here now telling you this story. The shrapnel was about four inches long, it was red hot and you could see it glowing for a minute or so just like a piece of coal in the hearth. As you can imagine I exited the bus pretty sharp and made my way to the nearest air raid shelter to wait for the all clear to sound. These raids by the German planes were just something we all became accustomed to. You'd see young kids afterwards looking around collecting up the shrapnel and there was lots of it all over the place.

Another former East End resident, Charles Courteney, recalled how one night a large German bomb exploded nearby and the solid steel-pointed nose section of the bomb landed in his parents' back garden. Charles recalled:

> We – me, my mother and sister – had gone into the shelter early that one night in anticipation of a raid coming in. They were hitting us every night from 7 September all through that winter. It was mum who insisted we leave the house for the big communal shelter that night; we couldn't argue so off we went. Sure enough, the bombers came and the usual commotion of whistling sounds and bangs which would shake the ground could be heard above us. By dawn the planes had gone, having done their work. As the all clear was sounded we made our way home. Apart from a few shattered windowpanes there was no damage to our house at all. I went out into the

> back garden and saw this huge lump of metal just lying there amongst the cabbages we had grown. My mother was alarmed and reported it to the police, but when the local copper came and had a look he said, 'It's harmless, it's just the solid metal nose end' and then made his excuse that he had better things to attend to than this, so off he went. That bomb nose section remained where it was until dad returned home from the army after the war. Dad dug a dirty great hole and rolled this piece of bomb into the hole and covered it over; he just buried it and it's probably still there today.

Intrigued by the story, I carried out some brief research to discover a) if that house where Charles lived as a boy during the war was still there and b) whether the current occupants of the property would allow a scan-over with a metal detector to see if the bomb nose was still there. After hearing Charles's story, the current occupants agreed to let two friends based down in the London area carry out a scan and recovery of the bomb nose provided it was still there of course. Since Charles's boyhood days, a brick wall had been built and Charles himself admitted the garden looked so much smaller than during the war. Having got the trusty Minelab Explorer out, it was decided to scan the garden, moving from the back door to where the brick wall had been built in a parallel sweep. My friends had almost reached the brick wall without so much as a single squeak from the Minelab Explorer when bingo! The Minelab Explorer began to alert the guys to a large metal signal at a depth of approximately three and a half feet down. So, out came the shovel and after what seemed an eternity of digging the rust-coasted nosecone of a 1,000lb Second World War German bomb was seeing the light of day again. Moving the heavy piece of metal would be a different story and a sack truck had to be borrowed from a local pub to get the piece out of the back garden and around the front of the house. The lump of metal had to be left where it was for the time being until proper logistics could be arranged to collect it. Three days later before the bomb nose could be collected and taken to a museum where it was to be put on display, it had vanished. Someone had stolen it from out of the front garden of the house, but how, when and why remains a mystery. It has never been seen since and one can only imagine it has ended up in someone's private collection somewhere.

This is by no means the first time such things have been 'half inched' (pinched/stolen) from outside a house. I once knew a guy whose pride and joy was a deactivated Soviet missile which he had positioned in the middle of his back garden. The missile stood there for many years where it proved something of a curiosity to passers-by, until one evening it vanished under the cover of darkness. Nobody saw or heard a thing despite the proximity of other houses. To say the guy was gutted would be rather an understatement as he had invested over £2,000 in his now-lost missile which had had to be specially shipped over from Russia where it had been purchased from defence surplus.

I also recall many years back the remains of a Junkers Ju 87 Stuka cockpit being shipped over from a crash site in Russia. The cockpit remains were left outside a house and promptly vanished off the back of the truck it had been left on. No number of appeals where its brief owner squeaked of it being worth just a few pounds in scrap metal through the local media made any difference. Whoever stole it wasn't that dumb and understood that it was a very rare lump of wreckage and worth a lot of money to the right people, thus worth all the effort in stealing it. The moral of the story here is that there are few morals and even less honour amongst thieves even where military archaeology is concerned.

Further down the coast of southern England in certain areas the fields are littered with shrapnel, not from exploded German bombs but from exploded British anti- aircraft shells fired at the raiders as they came in across the Channel. During the war both the heavy-

and medium-calibre (3.5- to 4.5-inch) anti-aircraft guns had been strategically positioned to meet the threat of German air attack. The guns themselves were often some considerable distance from where the shells exploded, sometimes as far as twelve miles from the actual gun emplacements. The idea was to fill the sky with as much high explosive as possible, generally at the same altitude as the enemy bombers. The time-fuzed high-explosive shells were pre-set to detonate after so many seconds. When they exploded, they sprayed a wide area with lethal, razor-sharp, red-hot steel splinters. These splinters travelling at high velocity were more than capable of piercing the engines, crew compartments and fuel tanks of a bomber. An anti-aircraft shell exploding near a bomber could easily bring it down in flames. Yet surprisingly few German bombers were successfully shot down by anti-aircraft guns. Sometimes thousands of high-explosive shells had to be expended to bring just one or two raiders down.

There is a section of privately owned farmland in Dover near the coast where every year after ploughing, bucket loads of British anti-aircraft shell fragments can be found. The ground is so thick with the stuff that a metal detector is not required. The tenant of this piece of land back when I last visited it was a Thomas Wyatt. Thomas had studied a little of the wartime history of the land himself as he had been puzzled as to why so much shrapnel lay in some of his fields while others were barren of such detritus. After conducting some research, he discovered the positions of the anti-aircraft batteries responsible for firing the shells, finding that their fire converged exactly over the fields where every year thousands of pieces of metal of all sizes are recovered. Thomas saved some of the best pieces which could be seen on top of walls around his farm courtyard or used as doorstops either in his house or outbuildings.

One of his notable finds was an almost complete half-section of a 4.5-inch shell that he had pulled out of one of his fields. Normally these shells exploded into hundreds of smaller fragments so why didn't this one? Looking at the actual metallurgy is the key here. Instead of a jagged edge much like the serrated blade of a steak knife, the piece had separated with an almost clean, flat edge. This is normally indicative of a faulty shell where there may have been a hairline crack in the metal itself, something which had occurred during the manufacturing process and which would only have become apparent after the round was fired, literally exploding into larger, lower-velocity and less-lethal fragments. At the time such large pieces as these would have been highly prized souvenirs for young lads, most of whom were avid collectors of shrapnel. The most coveted items were the nose fuzes of the exploded shells. On the window ledges of Thomas's barn where most of his machinery is kept there are lines of aluminium time fuzes from anti-aircraft shells which he has found over the years. In all I must have counted over 150 and most were in surprisingly good condition having been soaked in diesel and cleaned. Thomas admitted he has sold a fair few to the odd visitor over the years, normally for a fiver a piece.

Yet, he saved the best for last, as in one of his fields was a very large crater obviously made by something other than a conventional bomb. In winter the crater is often full of water, doubling up as a duckpond but as it was summer it was perfectly dry. Thomas explained it was where a V-1'Doodlebug' (V-1 flying bomb) had fallen well short of its intended target of London. As far as Thomas was aware, the crater had never been dug, so there could still be something buried in there. If this was a hint that he was as curious as me, I arranged to come back with a couple of pals, Mark Bainsworth and Roger Coulson, around a month later. Again, a Minelab Explorer model was the main tool for the job but Roger, with links to a professional archaeology group who normally sought out Roman remains, brought with him a ground surveying unit, the likes of which I had never seen before. He told me with the confidence of a man who clearly understood his craft that 'this piece of equipment will save us much time and if there's anything there, even down to the smallest lump, this thing will find it'. Back then in the 1990s, this was pretty much cutting-edge technology only normally used on 'big digs', certainly not the type of kit amateurs such as Mark and I were acquainted with. Either way, setting it up looked a complicated business so Mark and I were more than happy to let him get on with it while we sat watching smoking cigarettes and drinking tea from our flasks whilst admiring the stunning views around us. Roger's contraption looked like a supermarket trolley gone wrong once assembled and it was no easy task for him trying to push the thing over the rough ground of the crater. He scanned the crater itself and an area twenty feet around it before studying the data on a screen which had to be plugged into it after scanning was complete. By the time he had finished there was a stack of silver-black, foam-lined metal flight cases piled at the side of the crater and I recall thinking, 'This is a lot of trouble just to find what may be just a few bits of metal.' Once Roger had finished his work he indicated where we should dig and how deep we should be digging and, while he packed his equipment away, it was the turn of the Minelab Explorer and our spades to do the rest. Sure enough, some good-sized rusty pieces of the V-1 were soon extricated from the ground. Most of the pieces recovered were sections of the sheet-metal skinning, none of which was in the best of condition and which were badly corroded, but these pieces were collected up and later donated to a local museum where they were properly cleaned in order to prevent further deterioration.

Speaking to some of the locals, one of them, Tony Green, recalled how he used to work on the land at that spot back in the war; he explained that the engine of that actual V-1 had lain at the side of the crater for a good few years before it was removed. He said it was all squashed into a half-size lump as if it had impacted the ground very hard. When asked about who had removed this part, he said it was a local scrapman that took it away and that his fee was a drop of cider. I guess that would have been fair enough during those times when there were the greater concerns of growing crops and feeding the country as opposed to preserving things for the future. Tony recalled that the patch of ground where the engine had lain remained 'bald' for many years as if it had leaked something toxic into the ground. Tony also recalled:

> After that V-1 explosion there was shrapnel all over the place, all over the field there were pieces of green painted metal and internal bits and things. We had kids from the nearby village coming over the fences looking for bits for souvenirs. The local bobby [policeman] had a field day with these young rascals. He was a big stern type, an ex-First World War army sergeant with big moustache and he didn't take any nonsense from anyone, man or woman. He would peddle down the lane and leave his pushbike at the gate and be on the lookout for kids 'up to no good' as he would say in his own words. If he caught any of them, he'd give them a right thick ear and tell them to 'bugger off' or he'd be 'down to speak with your parents'. He'd tell them to empty their pockets too, taking anything they'd found off them and once he'd sent them packing, he would throw any confiscated bits into the stream by the gate, shake his head and he'd get on his bike and off he'd go cycling back up the lane. He'd do this several times a day. It didn't endear him to the local lads who saw him as a bit of a killjoy, nicknaming him 'PC Piggy' and 'Badger' to name a few of the more repeatable ones.

These are the sometimes-amusing anecdotes that make an otherwise serious subject a real pleasure to work on; they are so typical of their times, yet priceless pieces of our social history today.

10

France & Belgium

Following its second invasion by the Germans, in May 1940, and subsequent five years of occupation, France was probably left in a far worse situation than at the end of the First World War. Strewn with the debris of war from the fierce fighting, especially that which ensued following the Allied invasion of 1944, much of its infrastructure was in ruin and a second plague of danger from all manner of live ordnance and weaponry that lay all over the countryside was added to that of the previous war and occupation. The occupation of the Nazi era in France is today without doubt one of the most hotly pursued in terms of military archaeology. Remnants of the Second World War can be seen all over the French countryside and again there are many private museums set up by military history enthusiasts and ordinary French farmers where visitors are often welcomed. If you go to France with the intention of searching for the relics of the Second World War, the same rules apply to those explained earlier in this book. You must firstly understand the rules of what can and cannot be collected. This has become somewhat confusing in recent years as I know of enthusiasts who have travelled to France obtaining the full permission of the landowner to either field-walk or metal-detect for Second World War relics and complying with the common-sense law that no live ordnance should be tampered with or collected, only to fall foul of the French customs on their way out of the country. One enthusiast I was friendly with during the mid-1990s regularly visited France to specifically search for Second World War battlefield relics. On one occasion he had a car-boot full of rusty bayonets, shell fragments, German helmets and some empty hand grenade casings. Prior to embarking on the boat back to 'Blighty' (England), he decided to visit a French flea market, one of many he had visited over the years to legitimately buy some extra bits of militaria. To his haul of battlefield relics, he added a few Iron Cross Second Class medals, a Nazi dress dagger and Nazi-era armband. All was fine until he arrived at the French customs prior to leaving the country. He was flagged on the hand grenade casings and the Nazi items because they had Swastikas on them. These he was told would be confiscated and no amount of debate on the current law which he was familiar with and had adhered to was of any use in this case. The threat of having to return to France to face a possible court appearance and receive a fine were also put to my friend and for a few weeks this otherwise innocent trip for war relics hung over him, causing him no end of stress and sleepless nights. In the event, after several appeals no charges were brought yet the damage had been done. My friend lost £800 worth of goods he had legitimately purchased plus the items he had found, and due to the stresses this debacle placed upon him and his wife, it also almost destroyed his marriage. He never returned to France again as he was too fearful of a repeat of the previous trip.

Similar things have happened to others doing the same, so while France is an area rich in this particular area of military history, one should be very wary indeed of what one decides to bring back to the UK as it seems even the French customs are at times a law unto themselves. Yes, they have a difficult job to do, and one must have an understanding of this, but the laws have been very confusing along the way which doesn't help the situation. I know of other enthusiasts who have even had innocent items such as trench art pieces confiscated from them. One should be aware that things are not always as clear cut as they may appear. Gone are the days where schoolkids went on trips to France and were sometimes inadvertently sold live shell detonators as in one such case covered by the national press a few years ago. Yet in many gift shops in France you will see shelves stocked with pepper spray and knuckle dusters which of course are illegal in the UK; it can take considerable restraint to not be tempted to buy and take a chance at getting them through customs the other end. So again, it is up to you to use your common sense, find out and understand the rules and the possible consequences of breaking them.

Another consideration is the geographical area of France. France is a vast country; thus it would be wise to focus upon a certain area or particular battle in order to get the most out of any visit there. Going there without a plan can lead to all kinds of problems, especially if you are unfamiliar with the various departments which constitute France and/or do not speak the lingo.

We have all seen either in the flesh or through books or television the kinds of Second World War militaria that can be found in France and in the territories of her nearest neighbours: bullet casings, shrapnel, shell cases, helmets, water bottles, bayonets, all manner of personal items plus rusted weapons of various types. Perhaps one unusual find was that turned up purely by accident in 2005 by a French farmworker who discovered a small cache of buried weapons and ammunition. The weapons, in the form of several Lee-Enfield rifles, pistols plus some knives, were found at the edge of a ditch in a wooden box. The mystery was how did these things get there and why had they been buried. Naturally having been in the ground next to a ditch for some sixty-odd years, the weapons, ammunition and accompanying knives had suffered from corrosion, but they would turn out to be some surprisingly important war relics. After some research carried out by local historians, it was soon ascertained that this cache of weapons had been amongst those airdropped by British aircraft specifically for use by the French resistance. One of the old locals who had been active in the resistance confirmed the weapons would have most certainly been dropped by the British specially for them. He explained they were dropped by parachute from RAF Halifax bombers at prearranged destinations. The local resistance groups would then hide the weapons until they were needed. It seemed this cache for whatever reason was forgotten, only to be discovered sixty years later. The cache was made safe before being offered to several local museums. Sadly, the museums explained they were already inundated with such items and had no room for more of the same. So, where this cache ended up remains a mystery, but the contents are very likely on display in a barn somewhere in France.

Normandy has long been one of the focal points for enthusiasts of Second World War history and its associated archaeology, the reasons for which are quite simple: Normandy was where the liberation of Nazi-occupied Europe began following the Allied landings there on D-Day, 6 June 1944. Though the Allies gained that valuable if tentative foothold in Normandy on 6 June, it by no means meant that the Germans were beaten or that they would simply surrender. D-Day was costly in lives for both Allied and German soldiers yet many fierce battles, tactical blunders and near misses lay ahead before the outcome of the war would finally be decided. Normandy is an attractive prospect, not only due to its soil being rich in the archaeology of war but also the associated structures which constitute the infamous Atlantic Wall built by the Germans (rather German slaves), the construction of which began in 1942. Many of the concrete pillboxes and artillery casements are still intact and attract thousands of visitors each year. The structures associated with the Atlantic Wall will be looked at in the appropriate chapter.

When one thinks of Normandy and the D-Day landings, one cannot help but imagine the death and destruction that took place at Omaha Beach, for example. Omaha quickly became a slaughterhouse for the Americans who landed there and to say it was a close-run thing would have been the mother of all understatements. Omaha Beach attracts huge numbers of visitors, particularly through the summer months. Today Omaha Beach is serenely peaceful and it is difficult to imagine that this place was once a scene of hell itself. The German pillboxes that once housed the machine guns which wrought such havoc upon the American troops that day still stand, and although now silent monuments, they still possess an air of menace about them. Beyond the beach itself remains of the landings are still very evident. It is very easy to find fired US .30-calibre Garand rifle cartridges which are thick in the ground in certain areas. I have a few found in varying states, some very good, some badly corroded. A nice lump found by my friend Shane Willett during one of his pilgrimages to the Normandy battlefields was a substantial lump of shrapnel, very likely a segment of exploded 88mm shell. The German 88mm artillery gun was one of the deadliest and most versatile weapons of its kind, therefore 88mm shell fragments are pretty thick on the ground in Normandy as they are on the Eastern Front. Signs of the intense Allied bombing and offshore shelling by the Allied navies are also prevalent along the Normandy coastline. Ex-pat Mike Armstrong, who moved to France in 1985 to take over a small farm and vineyard in the Normandy area, recalled how one object in the ground damaged one of his ploughs the one year:

> I was working the fields and just heard this right loud bang at the back end of the plough, and I felt the sudden resistance of something caught by the plough blades. I switched off the engine and very sheepishly went to see what the problem was or rather what I'd hit. I was wary as I'd been warned not to mess around with anything in the ground unless I was sure of what it was, as it could be dangerous. As I looked, I saw this big lump of rusty metal which had actually broken one of the blades of the plough. I managed to free it and raise the plough and move it clear of the object. I called the local authorities to come and check on it to see if it was dangerous or not. They sent two guys wearing black uniforms out to the farm and I took them to where this thing was in the ground. They cleared the soil from around it and told me it was a very large fragment of shell from an Allied ship which had bombarded the area during the Normandy landings. They

> said it was probably from a round with a calibre of 12 to 15 inches, so it would have been a big one. As it was just a piece of solid metal, they shook my hand and wished me luck if I wanted to move it [he laughs]. I couldn't move the bloody thing, and, in the end, I had to get some help to get it off the field out of the way. I dumped it in the shallow ditch which runs alongside the field. It lay there for around a couple of years before some chap I had mentioned the story to came and bought it off me. He gave me £100 for it which I was more than happy with.

The Falaise Gap, sometimes also referred to as the 'Corridor of Death', is another infamous location in France. Falaise (12–21 August 1944) was the decisive battle of the Normandy campaign and where German Army Group B, with the 7th Army and 5th Panzer Army were encircled by the Allied forces. The Germans trapped in the Falaise pocket were subject to a merciless bombardment from the ground and the air. Falaise became a slaughterhouse for the Germans and those who managed to escape could count themselves lucky indeed. The result was a decisive victory for the Allies and paved the way for the liberation of Paris.

The Falaise Gap today is littered with a substantial amount of dangerous, unexploded ordnance of all kinds, and it is now prohibited to dig or metal-detect in certain areas, even on private land. Even the collecting of Second World War artefacts lying on the surface in the Falaise area is yet again a grey area and frowned upon by the French authorities who appear unwilling to add any clarification to this rule. You certainly don't need a metal detector to find basic evidence of the fighting which took place here. If you have a stroll around the quiet lanes and fields keeping your eyes to the ground, you will almost certainly find various relics. What you might find is purely down to luck really. I have in my own collection a piece from the Falaise battle which is a curious-looking object that at the time I had no idea what it was or what it had been used for. This is where the local expertise comes in as a visit to one of the nearby museums confirmed that it was a bracket from either a German machine gun or mortar carrying/stowage rack which the Germans often strapped to horses or mules for transport. Many of the photographs of the aftermath of the Falaise battle clearly show the carcasses of horses and mules killed in the fighting, and it is sad to think these gentle harmless creatures had to endure this hell in the name of man and his mania for conquest. So, to me this rather unremarkable piece has much significance as an animal lover, something which often gets overlooked.

During our four-day stay in Paris in 2017, Paula and I did a fair bit of travelling around while there. One place I wanted to visit was Cinthaux, which was a four-hour drive from where we were staying. What was of particular interest to me at Cinthaux was the death of German panzer ace Michael Wittmann. The field where Wittmann met his end in a Tiger I tank was one I felt worth a walk over and I had intended to find the landowner to ask permission. However, the weather was particularly dreadful that day with freezing wind and rain, so our sightseeing had to sadly remain strictly on the tourist trail. The good thing is a nearby museum contains a number of relics from Wittmann's Tiger tank including a section of turret floor where Wittmann would have once stood. Such things are iconic items to Second World War tank buffs and one wonders what Michael Wittmann himself would have made of his legendary status amongst modern-day historians.

Just across the French border into Belgium is another popular area for archaeologists and Second World War historians. This is the area known as the Ardennes Forest, which was the main invasion route for German armour in the Second World War as the Blitzkrieg rolled towards France. In previous years the Ardennes has been well picked over, as one enthusiast joked, 'much like a Welsh coal mine'. Some particularly fine war relics have been unearthed in Belgium, some of which are considered of high value, both financially and culturally.

I was lucky to have made a connection with a Belgian national some years ago by the name of Dirk. Dirk lived in a place called Dillingerbrück (in Luxembourg) with a forest nearby where he would take his dogs out every morning. One morning as he walked through the forest, he stubbed his boot on something partially sticking out of the ground and almost tripped over it. Scraping some of the soil away, he could see whatever it was, it was metal and pretty large. He took out his penknife and began scrapping away more soil out of curiosity more than anything else. He guessed that this partially buried lump of metal was something from the Second World War, but what was it? After exposing the mystery piece, Dirk noticed traces of paintwork; he tried to lift it but found that it was too heavy. He decided to leave the object where it was and come back later with his son. In the event Dirk and his son returned to collect the object and it was taken to Dirk's house and cleaned up. He put it on his bathroom scales where the weight was recorded at almost 80lb, not surprising for a solid lump of Krupp's finest steel. Dirk then set about the task of restoring the paintwork as close to the original as possible. The paintwork was typical of that used by the Germans in Normandy which gave a clue as to the nationality of the piece, yet this did not answer the question of what it was and how it came to be where it was found. A trip to a local museum supplied the answer. After being examined by one of the curators, it was identified as part of the forward breech block from a Panzer Sd.Kfz. 138/1 s.IG.33 'Grille' (Cricket). Quite a mouthful that, but to put things into basic terms translates to a 15cm (150mm) s.IG3,3 heavy artillery gun mounted onto a Panzer chassis and used as a self-propelled artillery piece. These self-propelled guns (SPGs) were used to great effect by the Germans in the infantry support role where their firepower proved very effective against the American forces. The Grille was not produced in huge numbers, making this relic a rare find. The inner section of the piece has large threads where the gun barrel would have been screwed into the breech block. How this piece ended up where it did was explained by the museum curator who told Dirk:

> Dillingerbrück was part of the Sauer River frontline from September 1944 to January 1945 during the Battle of the Bulge. The weapon that this came from had most likely belonged to one of the support units of the German 7th Army. As the 7th Army retreated, they were attacked heavily from the air and the ground. Either the weapon this came from was hit by a bomb from an aircraft or maybe destroyed by its crew to prevent it falling into the hands of the Allied forces. To have blown this section away like this, it is likely a direct hit from a bomb as the most plausible cause of its destruction.

This piece was shipped to the UK along with a consignment of machinery from the WMF company in Belgium where Dirk's wife was working at the time. So, it was sent to the UK where it was delivered direct and completely free of charge, a story in itself.

Some of the more remarkable finds unearthed in Belgium were those associated with the colossus that was the German 80cm 'Dora' railway gun. At the 2007 War & Peace Show held at Beltring, a Dutch militaria dealer turned up with what must have been one of the biggest showstoppers of that event. A year previous, in 2006, the Dutchman had been out in some fields when he encountered three 'water butts' which had been buried in the ground and were being used to water the farmer's cattle. The 'water butts' were buried up to their rims and most would have thought nothing of them and walked on. The Dutchman sought permission from the landowner to excavate them more on instinct than anything else and discovered that they were very rare and very special indeed. Once unearthed these three 'water butts' turned out to be three giant steel shell cases fired by the infamous 80cm (800mm) Schwerer Gustav railway gun

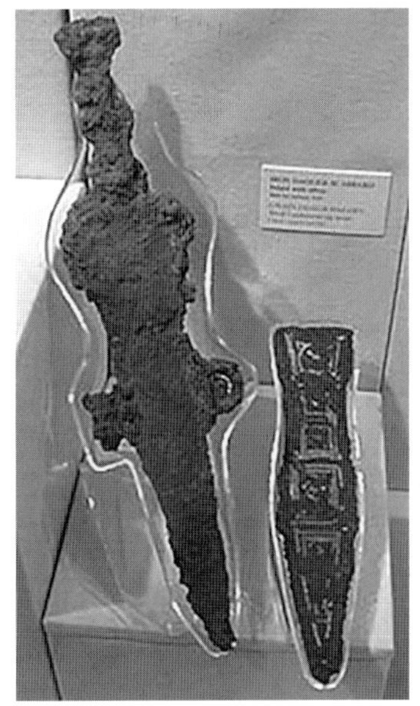

Above left: Iron dagger dating to the Boudican Rebellion of 60 AD. (Courtesy RLM)

Above right: The Chelmsford Hoard as it became known. (Julian Evan-Hart)

Below left: Obverse of one of the Chelmsford Hoard gold coins. (Julian Evan-Hart)

Below right: Reverse of Chelmsford Hoard gold coin (Julian Evan-Hart)

Above left: Anglo-Saxon battleaxe head possibly used at the Battle of Hastings, 1066.

Above right: Coins from the Chewiston Hoard. (Julian Evan-Hart)

Below left: A broadsword likely to have been used at the Battle of Hastings.

Below right: The skull of an Englishman killed in the Battle of Hastings. The skull was discovered with six stab wounds.

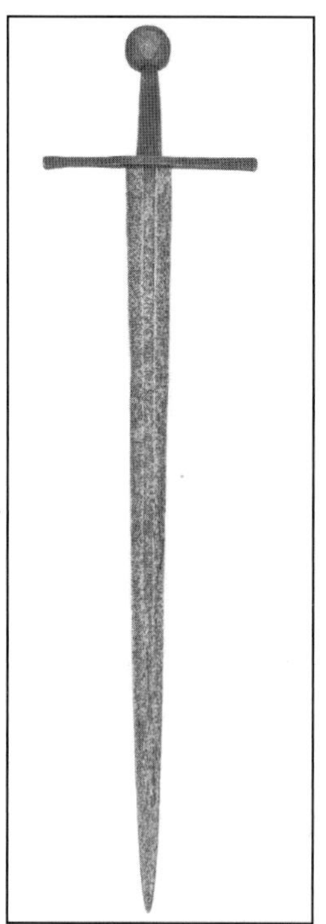

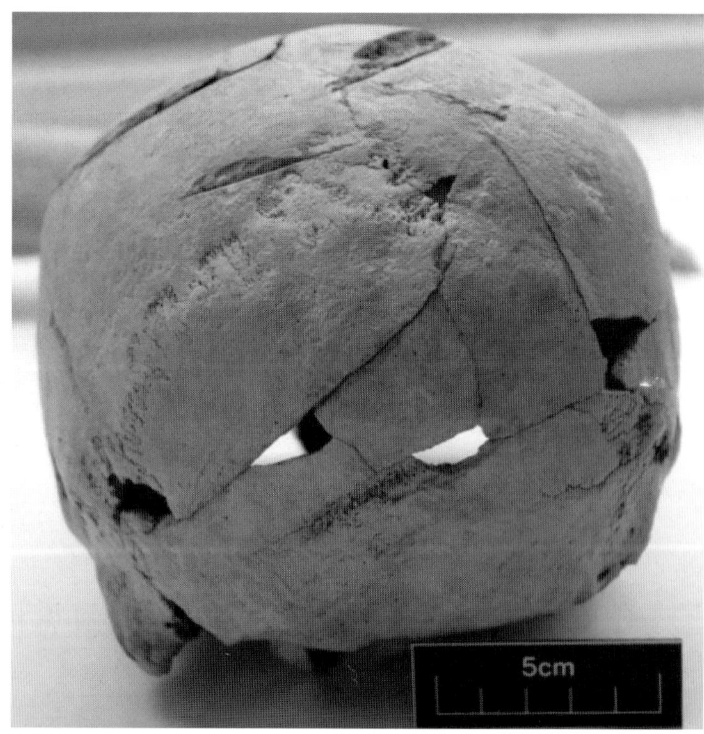

Above: An artist's depiction of the Battle of Hastings.

Right: A memorial cairn at Culloden.

Above left: The memorial to the Zulu dead at Isandlwana, South Africa.

Above right: Doug McMasters outside his Blockhouse Museum in South Africa. The shell to his left was one fired at Winston Churchill's train during the Boer War. (Courtesy *The Armourer*)

Below: First World War battlefield relics on display in the barn of a French farm on the Somme.

Piece of British 9.2-inch howitzer shell shrapnel found by Tony Warrell on the Somme battlefield. (Tim Heath)

Joan Bomford's unusual garden ornament – a First World War 15-inch howitzer shell. (Tim Heath)

German Zeppelin L48 before her destruction over the English countryside in the First World War. (Julian Evan-Hart)

An aerial photograph showing the wreckage of Zeppelin L48. (Julian Evan-Hart)

The excavation of Zeppelin L48 gets underway. (Julian Evan-Hart)

Above left: Julian Evan-Hart briefs the BBC film crew as the excavation of Zeppelin L48 progresses. (Julian Evan-Hart)

Above right: Some of the archaeological finds unearthed during the excavation of Zeppelin L48. (Julian Evan-Hart)

Below left: The .303-inch bullet found during the excavation of Zeppelin L48, discharged by one of the British aircraft that attacked the giant airship. (Julian Evan-Hart)

Below right: The British anti-aircraft shell fragment found lodged in the attic of John Stills's house. (Tim Heath)

Above left: Some of the archaeological finds unearthed from Thomas Wyatt's fields, including a British 4.5-inch anti-aircraft shell fuze and three pieces of shrapnel. (Tim Heath)

Above right: Group of archaeological finds recovered from a field behind Omaha Beach, Normandy. Items include a German helmet, large fragment of German 88mm shell and two US .30-calibre Garand cartridge cases. (Tim Heath)

Below left: German Panzer Sd.Kfz 138 s.IG33 breach part found by Dirk while out walking his dogs in the Belgian Ardennes. (Tim Heath)

Below right: One of three very rare German 80cm 'Dora' railway gun steel shell casings found being used as water butts for cattle in a field in Belgium. This one was sold for £5,000 at Beltring. (Courtesy *The Armourer*)

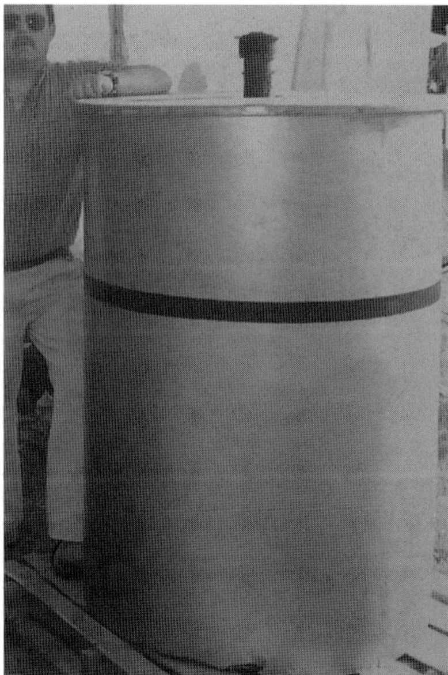

Above left: A relic Soviet 7.62-mm Maxim heavy machine gun unearthed by a metal detectorist in Poland. (Courtesy Janek Nowak)

Above right: What must be the mother of all finds! A Second World War artillery piece emerges from the ground at a location somewhere in Russia. (Courtesy Janek Nowak)

Below: A well-preserved German MG 42 machine gun and K98 rifle remains found in woods outside Aachen, Germany. (Courtesy Anton Riebel)

One of the buildings at the former Second World War German/Italian prisoner of war camp situated at the top of Fish Hill, Broadway, Worcestershire. (Tim Heath)

Another photograph of buildings at the prisoner of war camp at Fish Hill. (Tim Heath)

The runway at former Second World War RAF Honeybourne airfield pictured in 2001. (Tim Heath)

The control tower still standing at the old RAF Honeybourne airfield. This photograph was taken in 2001. Today the building is used as a dwelling. (Tim Heath)

One of the air raid shelters at former RAF Honeybourne, taken in 2018. (Tim Heath)

This red-brick structure at former RAF Honeybourne may have been either an observation or gun post. (Tim Heath)

Above: One of the remaining aircraft hangars still intact at former RAF Honeybourne, taken in 2013. (Courtesy of Andrew Smith)

Left: The US 'pineapple' hand grenade casing found wedged into an opening in one of the corridor walls inside one of the original buildings at former RAF Honeybourne, 18 November 2018. Although corroded, the casing could not be removed. (Tim Heath)

Above left: A .50-calibre (12.7mm) Browning machine-gun projectile found in a field at former RAF Honeybourne on 15 June 2020. It has a silver-painted tip, indicating it to be an incendiary type. (Tim Heath)

Above right: A fragment of exploded 40mm Bofors shell found in a field to the south of RAF Honeybourne, 10 June 2020. The airfield was equipped with these rapid-firing 40mm guns which were specifically designed for the anti-aircraft role. (Tim Heath)

This heavy lump of what appears to be steel plate from an armoured vehicle was discovered atop a spoil pile to the east of the old runway at RAF Honeybourne, 20 July 2020. The piece is heavily damaged by what looks like 20mm/30mm and .50-cal projectile strikes. How it got there is a mystery. (Tim Heath)

The former Polish camp at North Littleton, in 2013. (Tim Heath)

The memorial stone and plaque to Aleksander Wolski at the former Polish camp at North Littleton. (Tim Heath)

One of the Brixham Battery bunkers photographed in 2019. (Tim Heath)

Above left: Entrance to one of the Brixham Battery bunkers, 2019. (Tim Heath)

Above right: Pilgrim House at Westerham, Kent, scene of the crash of the KG 2 Dornier 217E4U5+MR 5591. (Tim Heath)

Below: Relics recovered from the crash site of Dornier 217E4 U5+MR 5591. Items include two oxygen bottles, radiator coolant veins and pieces of airframe structure. (Tim Heath)

Above left: Two fired German 20mm MG FF shell casings. Due to the location where they were found, these probably relate to the incident of 18 July 1941 where RAF Wellington X3169 was fired upon. (Julian Evan-Hart)

Above right: Albert Schultz pictured here in the back of a staff car. (Courtesy Melvyn Brownless)

Below left: The damaged German wound badge found at the crash site of Volkers' aircraft.

Below right: US ferry pilot Second Officer Mary Webb Nicholson who lost her life on 22 May 1943 at Littleworth, Worcestershire. (Courtesy Jim Corbett)

Above: The site where Mary Webb Nicholson's Miles Master aircraft crashed in 1943. (Courtesy Jim Corbett)

Below left: Second Lieutenant Jack Tuggle Jamison. (Courtesy Andy 'Badger' Long)

Below right: The Hymac excavator at work during the dig on Second Lieutenant Jack Jamison's Lockheed P-38 Lightning. (Courtesy Andy 'Badger' Long)

Above left: Ian 'Mole' McRae with one of the propeller blades recovered from Jamison's P-38. (Courtesy Andy 'Badger' Long)

Above right: Remains of the Jamison P-38 during the dig which terminated at a depth of twenty-nine feet. (Courtesy Andy 'Badger' Long)

Below left: The discovery of the piece of RAF Hunting Percival Jet Provost XM423 in an abandoned plum orchard at Norton, Evesham, 21 February 2021. The photograph shows the piece as it was discovered wedged beneath a fence. (Tim Heath)

Below right: The large piece of wreckage from XM423 after it was extricated from beneath fencing showing the yellow paintwork on the outer side. (Tim Heath)

Above left: A photograph of Hunting Percival Jet Provost from the RAF Little Rissington Central Flying School before her loss on a night-flying exercise. (Courtesy RAF Little Rissington photo archives)

Above right: The water-filled bomb crater at Warrens Green. (Julian Evan-Hart)

Below left: Second Lieutenant Paul Bellamy USAAF. (Via Julian Evan-Hart)

Below right: Sergeant Richard McAteer USAAF. (Via Julian Evan-Hart)

Boeing B-17 Flying Fortress named *Ding Dong Daddy*. (Via Julian Evan-Hart)

Second Lieutenant Carlton Sacco USAAF. (Via Julian Evan-Hart)

An Argentine Pucará light attack aircraft put out of action by the SAS during the raid on Pebble Island in the 1982 Falklands War.

The tail unit of Fleet Air Arm Sea Harrier XZ450 which was shot down by Argentine 35mm anti-aircraft guns during an attack on Goose Green.

An undercarriage leg from Sea Harrier XZ450.

The Tank Farm located in the desert outside of Kuwait City. (Courtesy Tim Crockett United States Navy)

Another view of the Tank Farm. Note the unexploded shell lying on ground to the left. (Courtesy Tim Crockett United States Navy)

An Iraqi 57mm anti-aircraft projectile which failed to explode. (Courtesy Tim Crockett United States Navy)

An abandoned steel ammunition box of 27mm Mauser BK27 cannon shells left behind by the RAF at the end of the Gulf War, Operation Desert Storm, 1991. (Courtesy Tim Crockett United States Navy)

Hundreds of pieces of ordnance litter the desert outside Kuwait City, 1991. (Courtesy Tim Crockett United States Navy)

'No place for the faint of heart!' US Explosive Ordnance Disposal range at Ali Al Salem airbase after the 1991 Gulf War. (Courtesy Tim Crockett United States Navy)

A 1,000lb bomb is blown up in a controlled explosion at Ali Al Salem. (Courtesy Tim Crockett United States Navy)

Above left: The torn metal entrails of an Iraqi vehicle destroyed on the 'Highway of Death', the Basra Road, at the end of the 1991 Gulf War. The desert outside Kuwait City is still littered with the debris of this infamous action. (Courtesy Tim Crockett United States Navy)

Above right: The breech of an Iraqi 23mm ZU-23 anti-aircraft autocannon lying amongst other destroyed and discarded weapons somewhere outside Kuwait City in 2000. (Courtesy Tim Crockett United States Navy)

Below left: The Second World War Soviet Ilyushin IL-2 tailplane shortly before its purchase at the Plymouth Militaria Show. (Courtesy Mark Bentley/Tiger Collectibles)

Below right: The group of German Second World War Focke Wolf Fw 190 relics unearthed from the crash site of Unteroffizier Horst Gabel's' 'Yellow 10'. Items here are three 20mm Mauser MG 151 cannon shells, plus links and MG 151/20 firing bolt. These artefacts were sold by Relics from The Front in 2022. (Tim Heath)

used by the Germans in the Second World War and eventually named 'Dora'. The shell casings were transported from the field where they were found before undergoing restoration work. One of these huge shell cases was then transported from Belgium to the UK Beltring War & Peace show, carrying with it a £5,000 price tag. One can only imagine the logistics involved in moving one of these shell cases, as being constructed from steel, the weight would have been immense. These are seldom ever seen outside museums and rarely if ever do they come onto the collecting market and are most certainly as rare as the proverbial hen's teeth in every respect.

Perhaps of all the archaeological finds encountered on battlefields, personal effects of the soldiers themselves are certainly amongst the most evocative items. A particularly treasured item of mine is a German silver Saint Christopher medallion found in the Ardennes in 1999. It was found in what was once a foxhole along the route that the 1st SS Panzer Regiment of the Leibstandarte SS-Adolf Hitler took to Stavelot in the Ardennes battle. The 1st SS Panzer Regiment was part of Kampfgruppe Peiper (Battlegroup Peiper) so named after its commanding officer, Joachim Peiper. The medallion was discovered while scanning the foxhole with a Minelab Explorer. The Saint Christopher was in remarkably good condition and on its reverse were inscribed the words '*Gott Schutze Dich*' which translate to 'God Bless You'. It's not of any great value yet its context is priceless. Was it a gift from a girlfriend or wife back in Germany? Did the soldier who once wore it around his neck make it back home? The questions are endless with these things and the saying 'if only the piece could talk' often comes to mind.

The Battle of the Bulge, being the last German offensive of the war, has long been a source of fascination amongst archaeologists and historians. The freezing weather conditions, ferocity of the fighting coupled with the heroic stand made by the American forces defending Bastogne, and the Malmedy Massacre (committed by Peiper's troops) have all since passed into military folklore.

The Belgian Ardennes has also provided a rich source of military artefacts over the years and has proved a highly profitable venture for many relic hunters. Ardennes battle artefacts are among the most sought after amongst collectors today; some areas have been systematically pillaged of their heritage over the years according to sources in the Belgian government. The activities of 'black diggers' or 'nighthawkers' as they are often known has proved to be a serious irritation to the Belgian authorities, especially where the digging for German military relics is concerned. There was a time not so many years ago where you could have travelled to the Ardennes and provided you received the necessary permits from landowners, you could have indulged in what had become a free for all in the harvest of German war relics. The high prices being realized, particularly for anything Waffen-SS-related, of which much still lay in the soil of the Ardennes, attracted the attention of the less scrupulous. These illegal diggers often went onto private or protected land under the cover of darkness to illegally metal-detect and dig for relics. The most prized items, such as SS skull badges, belt buckles and helmets, could then be sold on to collectors via word of mouth or on internet auction sites for a premium. Many historic locations in the Ardennes were subject to these illegal activities which became so prevalent that the Belgian government was forced to act. The Luxembourg website Wort.lu reported that Belgium was suffering from a 'veritable plague' of amateur treasure hunters pillaging precious artefacts by the use of metal detectors. The report was submitted to the CNRA (Centre national de recherche archéologique) after police had caught a number of Dutch men in a forest near Wiltz. A CNRA spokesman said:

> Hunting for military memorabilia over the last fifteen years has degenerated into what can only best be described as a veritable plague. Quite apart from the disturbing of the remains of fallen soldiers which has now occurred on numerous occasions, there is the danger posed by

> unexploded ordnance which still litters the area. Locally there is also the loss of our heritage. The CNRA believe that artefacts should only be removed by officially sanctioned archaeological associations who have the actual interest of the public in mind and not profit.

As a result of the increased activity in illegal digging in the Ardennes, the Belgian police released their own statement regarding the issue which read:

> We warn anyone regardless of nationality if you are thinking of coming here to partake in any illegal metal-detecting activity in the region, you will now face a fine of up to 25,000 euros, a six-month prison sentence and confiscation of all goods and any vehicles the offender may be in possession of at the time of the offence.

Does this sound a little draconian? Not really, as these are the actions of a country trying to retain its heritage from those who would steal it merely to make a quick buck. The Belgian government has since tightened the rules on both metal detecting and digging in the country. In places blanket bans have been imposed on both metal detecting and digging and visitors are asked that if they do see something, even if it is on the surface, to leave it alone, as it is not their history to take. More on illegal digging of Second World War relics will be discussed later in the book as there are arguments for and against and it is interesting to examine both sides.

11

Poland, Ukraine, Russia & Germany

Poland was of course once a lucrative source of military relics of all kinds. Throughout her existence Poland has been subject to a more or less constant struggle against oppression, quite apart from the devastation wrought by the Nazi invasion of 1939. Poland herself is a symbol of defiance against tyranny thus her soil is rich in the blood of those who have fought for freedom and who gave their lives for it. Yet it is Poland's Second World War history that stands much above many others. Poland became infamous for the murder factories such as Auschwitz, Treblinka, Belzec and Sobibor. The Poles are well aware of their own history; in fact they are fiercely proud of it and if you talk to them, it will be very hard for you to find one Polish national whose family was not affected in some way by either the German invasion of 1939, the Holocaust which followed or the Soviet occupation of their country at the end of the war. I have met many Polish nationals as a result of both daily work and through my militaria collecting activities.

One named Janek whom I met at a car boot sale in 2008, was a young man from Kraków in Poland. He was a regular at our local car boot sale and his stall was always full of mostly Second World War German ground-dug relics being offered at very sensible prices. I was curious to speak to him about his metal detecting in Poland and what it was like to detect there. He invited me to come back at the end of the day when he would have more time to talk. Good to his word, at the end of the day I met up with Janek in a bar in Cheltenham to talk about his digging work in Poland. At the time it was still relatively easy to go out and metal-detect but again, provided you had the landowner's permission, etc. Janek recalled:

> My friend over in Poland has a farm of many acres of land and he allows me to metal-detect and dig for German war relics on his land. The ground is heavy with German stuff especially and I have discovered some truly amazing finds. For example, I once found a German Luger pistol and it was in beautiful condition and it could be easily made to fire again, I have found German helmets, some with the SS decals still visible on them, also medals, buttons and personal effects such as gold rings and stuff. Poland is very good for this stuff and the English buyers like it a lot and I can sell it easy over here.

Janek initially built up a large collection of Second World War relics and items that he intended to keep in his own little museum at his parents' home in Kraków. The other items he did not want to keep were then packaged up by his family and sent over to him in England so as he could sell on at car boots to make extra money for his family which included his wife Maria and their little daughter. Janek continued:

> The kind of stuff I get my father to send over here are mostly helmets, rusty bayonets, belt buckles plus anything of interest he might find cheap at flea markets in Kraków city. I have regular buyers who purchase items from me; they tell me what they want, and I will do my best to source it for them when I go back to Kraków on visits. Of course, I cannot bring weapons over here as restrictions have become severe regarding even relic weapons, so I must leave those sadly but anything else is good mostly.

I asked Janek what his most valuable find to date was and he replied:

> I have found a lot of gold rings and these all mount up in price if you keep them all. The single most valuable item

> I have found was a Nazi German Cross in Gold which I found within the remains of a rotten German tunic. The cloth although rotted had protected it from the elements and it was in beautiful condition … I would sell it, yes, but I would want at least £2,000 for it.

Further east in the Ukraine lies a veritable deluge of not only military archaeology but that of the ancient world too. In fact, the eastern territories of the Ukraine and Russia are where perhaps the finest of the ancient historical archaeological record can be found along with a seemingly endless abundance of Second World War militaria. For the Ukrainian metal detectorist/archaeologist there are virtually no legal constraints placed on anyone wishing to go out detecting and digging. In some ways, the east has been a free for all for many years and provided you have permission to go onto the land where you intend to detect and dig over, you have no further obligations or restrictions, unlike the UK and many other places in Europe today. There are also huge swathes of sometimes very remote land where there is no specific ownership where one can freely metal-detect and dig. With regards to the Ukraine, one must consider certain factors if planning to visit the country. The time of the year is perhaps one crucial consideration. There would be no point in visiting during the savage Ukrainian winter for obvious reasons; another is it would be wise to have a guide as some areas can be very remote and the environment very challenging if dangerous to the uninitiated. Another factor to consider would be the current political tensions with her neighbour Russia. This became all too apparent in February 2022 when Russian dictator Vladimir Putin launched an invasion of the Ukraine.

I have a good friend who lives in the Ukraine who has been a metal detectorist and military archaeologist for some years now. There is a room in his home which is crammed with the artefacts of war which he has discovered over the years. Andrej Smirnov, a German national living in the Ukraine, is a devoted family man with a wife and two young children and one of those people you just immediately warm to. His passion and enthusiasm for the relics of the Second World War and his vast knowledge of the subject is as exemplary as his mastery of the English language. It was my intention that Andrej would write this chapter for this book, but Putin's invasion meant my dear friend had to put himself and his family first and move out of his city into safer zones in the countryside. In his absence I can only endeavour to write this section as best as I can with the knowledge already gleaned from Andrej.

Andrej noted that the Ukraine is regarded as a veritable inventory of historic material from as far back as the ancient world to that of the modern. If you intend to go metal detecting, while there are no rules as such as where you are allowed to actually detect and dig, one thing, apart from the having the right equipment, is to obtain the landowner's permission in writing. Verbal agreements are all very well but if anything of high value is discovered and you cannot produce a letter of written permission from the landowner stating that he or she he has given you permission to be there for the purpose of metal detecting for whatever may be buried there, it can open a can of worms more detrimental to you than the landowner, who can claim ownership of what you have found, regardless of any verbal agreements made beforehand. So, this rule is imperative in all cases of metal detecting and digging on private land in much the same way as it is here in the UK. Of course, there are those who do not bother to seek permission and take the risk of losing anything they find but most do adhere to the rules. Any other land other than privately owned is as I have already explained a kind of free for all in many aspects.

Andrej has been out metal detecting and has sometimes discovered the remains of the fallen, mostly from the Second World War battles. Remains of fallen soldiers are something Andrej has very strong views about. In all cases, if he discovers remains, he ensures that the relevant authorities are contacted so arrangements can be made for the proper burial of these fallen soldiers. Their personal effects, if still present with their remains, are treated with the respect they deserve. If any of the remains can be identified, Andrej then takes steps along with the authorities to return personal items to the families of the fallen. In Andrej's view it is not merely learning about and trying to preserve the tumultuous history of the country he lives in but the respect one should give to those who gave their lives. Andrej himself has accumulated a fine collection of Second World War battlefield-recovered artefacts which include helmets, dog tags, badges, buttons, medals, shells and shell cases, bayonets and weapons of various types. He explained there are areas of the Ukraine where he has unearthed German Luger pistols in near perfect condition and you are allowed to retain ownership of them unlike here in the UK where there are severe restrictions placed upon even the ownership of non-working, deactivated weapons. Through his metal detecting and archaeological activities, Andrej has unearthed thousands of weapons over the years and there are still many thousands if not millions still buried in the soil of the Ukraine.

As mentioned, rare artefacts from the Ukraine's distant past can often be unearthed along with those of its more recent history. Some detectorists searching for relics of the Second World War have inadvertently stumbled upon gold rings, brooches and coins dating from the Middle Ages. Even weapons from the Middle Ages have been unearthed, much in good condition considering how long it has lain undiscovered in the ground. These include spear and arrow heads, swords and battle-axes. Sadly, with the Ukraine currently fighting for its very existence, it may be some time before detectorist/historians like Andrej can return to their homes and normality.

Russia itself like the Ukraine places very little to no restrictions on metal detecting, though the same above rules apply about metal detecting on private land. Many years back I contacted a Russian metal detectorist named Lev Ivanovich. Lev had a real passion for military history especially that of Nazi Germany. He was the kind of man willing to share his experiences and as a result he made many friends from the west over the years following the fall of the Berlin Wall. He sometimes took groups of enthusiasts out into the wastelands of Russia on detecting forays as he used to say that the best military artefacts are generally in the remotest areas. Lev explained:

> You can find military objects from the Second World War fighting virtually anywhere in Russia, the ground is heavy with these artefacts and some of them are in as new condition as you could get. To find the best items you must be prepared to put up with some discomfort which means sometimes having to travel a long distance on foot, in either very cold or very hot conditions where you also have clouds of biting insects to contend with, but if you can handle that, these places are where you will find the best items buried in the ground. Sometimes you don't even have to dig for them; they can sometimes be just sitting on the surface exactly where they were left back in the Second World War.

I asked Lev what his best German find was and after some momentary reflection he smiled and replied:

> Ah, that's an easy one. I took some guys out to a marsh area once; it was early summertime, so the ground was boggy but not too difficult to negotiate. Within a few minutes of scanning the ground I pulled out a German MG 42 machine gun from the peaty soil and it still had an ammunition belt attached to it and the condition was immaculate, the weapon had been perfectly preserved by the peaty ground, so much so that with a good clean, I could have probably got it working again. You can find lots of German weapons including machine guns like the MG 42, but many are not in as good condition.

> You must consider these factors, what type of ground is likely to produce the best states of preservation, things like that. Archaeology is more than just swinging a metal detector about; it's about studying the geography of the ground itself and the types of soil and effect upon old metal objects which may be buried in it. Over the years I have found hundreds of gold rings, some have names written inside them. I have found German combat awards and perhaps my best find was a Knights Cross which I discovered in the remains of a rotten tunic which I also pulled out of a bog. The metal of the Knights Cross was perfectly preserved – you wouldn't believe its condition – and all I had to do was wipe the dirt off it. Because I never had a lot of money back then I sold most of these things to wealthy collectors in Europe and beyond. They used to send me a wish list of items they were happy to pay big money for and most weekends I would go out and look for these things; it didn't take me long to find them either in many cases.

Asked if he had any particularly hair-raising moments while out engaging in his hobby, Lev replied:

> Only the once. I took four American guys out into the tundra area as one of them was interested in aircraft wrecks and I happened to know of a pretty good one I could show them. It was quite a long drive followed by an eight-mile slog on foot; when we got there these American guys were like kids in a sweetshop. One of them was busy cramming his pockets with 20mm Shvak cannon shells which lay all over the site. I had to insist they put them down right away as they were high explosives and still deadly dangerous. I also pointed out

> to them that the pilot of this aircraft was also said to haunt the wreck site and maybe they should be just content to take photographs. Finally, they listened to me, but many people forget their common sense with these things. Live ammunition, mines and grenades still lie thick in the ground and if you don't show caution, they can still kill you after all these years.

My last contact with Lev was back in 2008 following another one of his trips where he took some enthusiasts out to detect over some Red Army trench lines on what had been the Eastern Front. He had found something partially sticking out of the ground and when he unearthed it, discovered it was a German Nebelwerfer rocket nosecone. Lev found several more of these nosecones which often separated as the rocket exploded. It seems the Soviet soldiers in this area had been subject to a Nebelwerfer bombardment. As the group continued their search, some bones were found. The position was marked with a GPS device for later referral and a red-coloured marker flag was also left at the spot. Hopefully the site would be properly investigated and any remains removed for proper burial by the authorities.

Lev very kindly sent me one of the Nebelwerfer nosecones completely free of charge. This particular relic was from one of the German 150mm weapons and was designed to kill more through blast than fragmentation. Either way, it is still one of my most treasured Second World War relic items. It is a sad fact that in recent years there have been those diggers in Russia who have little respect for the fallen, those whose graves they are unearthing. I recall one such video where the culprits' faces were conveniently blurred out where they had unearthed the skull of a German soldier and had proceeded to place a helmet on top of the skull and then a lit cigarette between the teeth. Photographs were then taken, purely because they believed that some people might find it amusing. This ghoulish activity continues to this day and, as I have noted, there currently appears to be no such controls over this activity. The dead are simply stripped of any valuables that might be on their person and their bones discarded without any consideration whatsoever.

While Germany today is trying hard to put the unhappier aspects of her history behind her, interest in the Third Reich has reached fever pitch. There are more collectors today of Nazi material than there have ever been, yet at the same time there are forces at work who are attempting to be our moral consciousness where Third Reich artefacts and archaeology are concerned. In Germany today the sale of Nazi memorabilia is banned and considered illegal. Many antique and curio shops in Germany do not openly display Nazi-era memorabilia, though some have an 'under-the-counter' policy for those they consider trustworthy enough and this certainly existed up until the 1990s. Some German dealers have managed to circumvent what they consider overtly draconian rules regarding the acquisition and sale of Nazi-era material, but as a rule in Germany, it is considered in bad taste to ask about Nazi memorabilia in the many antique shops and flea markets there.

Archaeology on the other hand appears to have flourished in Germany and while there is no such blanket ban on metal-detecting activities like those imposed in some areas of Europe today, most metal detecting for Second World War relics is often conducted strictly on private land where permission again must be obtained in writing from the landowner and not the tenant of any particular land. In most areas of Germany today metal detecting is banned. Of course, there are alternative methods of conducting a search of an area of interest such as that of 'eyes on the ground'. That said, great care should be taken when venturing onto any former Second World War battlegrounds as the dangers are obvious. At the end of the day the risk is entirely your own, but it is always worth hooking up with local Second World War enthusiasts who will often be more than happy to show you around.

One example is that of the Seelow Heights; if you take a hike into the woods around the Seelow Heights which once formed part of Berlin's last-ditch defence against the Soviet Red Army you will find all manner of relics. It is where some of the most bitter fighting of the war was fought, and the ground is still littered with dangerous live ordnance and thus metal detecting is expressly forbidden there. There are those who flout the regulations and carry out illegal digging and metal detecting and the evidence of these activities is clearly visible, but it really is not worth being caught as the penalties can be severe and again no excuses will be accepted by the German police.

A good friend of mine, Phil Turnstall, had a particular interest in the Seelow Heights battle and visited the area back in 2018. Phil hooked up with a couple of local German enthusiasts who were happy to show him around the area and what material still lies on the surface and to point out why you must be very careful when visiting the area. In one part of some woods the area was littered with the remains of Soviet Katyusha rockets. The rusted remains of these rockets were perfectly safe having exploded, yet some had very sharp edges to them. These objects, being surface finds, were permitted to be taken as souvenir material, but Phil was advised if he wished to keep any they should be packed and mailed before he left Germany, as at the time some customs departments were not allowing material like this to pass through their checks despite being harmless relics. The two German enthusiasts explained that if a Second World War relic such as a piece of shrapnel or Katyusha rocket casing has sharp edges, the authorities were in their rights to consider it dangerous and confiscate it on the spot. Before departing the old battlefield, Phil's two German companions were anxious to show him why it is wise to be very careful when visiting the area. Wedged at the base of a tree was a very live and still very dangerous large-calibre Russian mortar bomb. Such an object would not have been made any safer with the passing of time and should be avoided at all costs. Old, corroded munitions can be every bit as deadly as they were the day they were made and can explode if tampered with. As Phil explained after his visit, 'The Seelow Heights is a place of ghosts, it felt eerie there and despite my enthusiasm I'm not sure I could ever go back again.'

I was speaking to my friend Andrej Smirnov just prior to the Russian invasion of Ukraine about his relic-hunting activities in Germany and he told me of a stretch of woods he often visits when in Germany where the ground is literally inches thick with American .50-calibre heavy machine-gun shell cases. The reason for this is that the woods in question lie along the route to the German city of Schweinfurt which was heavily bombed by the American daylight raiders. All the cartridge casings are from the defensive machine guns of the American bombers as they tried to fend off the attacking Luftwaffe fighters. Andrej explained the shell casings were in very good condition with no rot or oxidization which you normally encounter with brass cases exposed to the elements for many years. When I asked Andrej how many of these fired cases he has collected over the years, he replied: 'There is a box of them in the basement of my parents' house containing around fourteen kilos of these .50-calibre casings. Yet, there are hundreds more still lying on the ground in those woods.'

It illustrates the fact perfectly that you do not always have to metal-detect or dig to find a piece of Second World War history in Germany.

12

Second World War Structures, Airfields & Dumping Grounds

The evidence of Second World War activity is spread across the whole of the United Kingdom. In my locality alone there is a wealth of Second World War dumping grounds, structures and at least three former RAF airfields, all within a twenty-mile radius. My locality is also rich in the structural side of the Second World War. The Cotswold countryside is littered with prisoner of war and refugee camps, pillboxes, anti-aircraft gun emplacements plus former military observations posts. I recall when growing up in the village of Broadway the old locals talking of a former prisoner of war camp situated on top of the Fish Hill just outside the village, 'in the sticks' as they used to say. These camps were often situated in what were once considered remote areas, away from the villages and towns for obvious reasons.

The prisoner of war camp on top of Fish Hill housed largely Germans and I would imagine either airmen shot down over the UK or soldiers captured during the fighting overseas. Many were brought back to the UK as there was little provision for such camps at the battlefront. I remember talking about the Fish Hill camp with a schoolmate back in 1979 as a 14-year-old and we decided we should go and pay it a visit on the Saturday morning. It was not the easiest of journeys as Fish Hill was akin to climbing Everest even on foot to us back then, and we set off on our old 'grandad bicycles' as we called them which had no gears at all to assist the burning muscles in our legs. When we arrived at the camp, I recall seeing all the brick huts still intact through the trees which surrounded them; a dirt track ran up through the middle of the two rows of huts disappearing over a hill. We left our bikes near the entrance and rather stupidly did not bother to attempt to conceal them in any way, something we would regret later. Starting at the bottom building we went inside and despite the buildings being just empty shells, they seemed to reek of history in a way that only old buildings do. We looked around in all the rooms and my mate took some photos with his Polaroid Instamatic that he always carried with him on our forays. We were hoping that maybe we might find something good. My friend's father had been working up at the site a year or two previous and had found a trench art letter knife fashioned out of a cartridge case and piece of brass lodged beneath the roofing of one of the buildings; we imagined ourselves finding something like it and went through each of the huts but in vain. We had got about halfway up the dirt track when a car suddenly appeared and began to speed up the dirt track towards us; we beat a hasty retreat into the woods which luckily for us were conveniently close. After a cat and mouse game which lasted for about ten minutes, whoever had been in the car gave up and drove off but not before removing the saddles of our bicycles and casting them off into the woods somewhere where we'd never be able to find them. In the event we decided we'd better head home as it was obvious we were not welcome even though we were doing no wrong. The ride back down Fish Hill without saddles was an experience we could both laugh and brag about at school on the Monday.

I returned to that same camp in 2000 with a friend from South Africa and we approached the owner who was using it for vehicle storage at the time. He let us have a wander around on the condition we did not enter any of the buildings which had vehicles in them. Of course, we agreed to the rules and spent an afternoon looking around what was quite an extensive camp at one point. We did ask the owner if he had ever found anything, and he said that he had found Second World War German coins mostly but had never metal-detected the area to see what else there might be buried there. After looking over the old camp the probability of modern contamination was high as we did notice lots of nuts, bolts and nails lying around the site, detritus of the activities going on there at that time. The camp so far as I know is still there, along with all the original buildings, but I was told it has since changed hands again.

Perhaps a lesser-known former camp is a small one situated in the village of North Littleton, Evesham, in a now-overgrown orchard on the Offenham Road leading to the Fish & Anchor public house. This one was not a camp as such for the housing of German or Italian prisoners of war but constructed as a resettlement camp for refugees who had fled from Poland as the Germans began their invasion in 1939. Unless you knew about this camp, you would never know it was there. Today, the camp known to locals simply as 'the Polish Camp', is largely overgrown with tall grass, thornbushes and fruit trees. The fruit trees would have been there during the war years and no doubt provided some welcome seasonal extras for the refugees. There are several well-worn pathways around the camp and during the time it was inhabited there would have been numerous small huts around the site. Today only one of these remains as a bare structure with a corrugated roof yet evidence of wartime activity can be found.

Up until the 1990s, one of the Polish refugees who had lived in the camp, a man named Aleksander Josef Wolski, used to go back there during the summer months and a wooden hut was constructed for him and a few family members to stay over. I met Aleksander only once and I wished I had taken his story down. He explained that rather than stay in Poland and face possible enslavement or death under the Nazis, he and his family fled to England and came to North Littleton where they set up a camp in a farmer's orchard. For a living they often worked the land, and, in the summer, they picked plums, pears and apples in the orchard. There was always a surplus of fruit for them. Life could be hard and in the winter the huts were very cold with just a single coal-fired stove to provide heat and cook on, but Aleksander explained it was a far better life than what it would have been under the Nazis or the Russians after 1945. Aleksander passed away on 30 September 1993 and since then the family visits to the old camp are few and far between. In the centre of the camp is a small stone memorial which was constructed during the war years. Last time I was there it was very overgrown, so I cleared it as best as I could. Near the wooden hut used by Aleksander and his family is a plaque attached to a stone obelisk which reads: 'Cherishing the memory of our beloved Aleksander Josef Wolski 1 September 1922–30 September 1993. Always present among his favourite places where his cheer and warmth still abound'. This camp has always intrigued me and it is my belief that it was larger, stretching out beyond the main area of the orchard as there were numerous well-worn pathways in the nearby woods by the roadside and it was there I discovered numerous spent wartime-dated British .303 cartridge cases, while a friend of mine found a large silver Second World War-dated coin which he (sacrilegiously) turned into a ring before I could have a proper look at it to ascertain its origin. It is possible there are more artefacts buried in the old camp grounds but gaining permission to carry out a metal-detecting survey may be difficult as it is likely the land has been sold since my last visit there. Either way, it is a possible project for the future.

Worthy of note is the UK database of such camps pointed out to me by my friend Donald 'Yocker' Yarnold. Having sent me the link to this online resource, I began cross-referencing and noticed one such camp listed as number 665. 665 was a Polish camp but location stated as unknown yet somewhere in South Littleton. It is possible that this camp, Aleksander's, could be number 665 and the South Littleton location given is a possible error. Donald Yarnold has some unique perspective in this case as back in the 1960s as a 17-year-old construction worker he recalled a former camp which he helped demolish for the small housing estate down the Shinehill Lane. He recalled that lots of live ammunition, some of it still in boxes, were unearthed as they were digging the footings. He also recalled finding many badges and buttons at the site and an old Polish chap who was with them spent the day knocking the bullet heads out of the brass cases. Imagine this happening today, how it would send health and safety into an uncontrollable frenzy. I asked Donald if he took any of the artefacts that he dug out of the ground, and he answered:

> I was 17 and not really interested in things like that at that time apart from girls and motorcycles. I believe the camp started with the US Air Force, and a small POW camp which is now the recreation ground at South Littleton. There was a military vehicle park almost opposite the HM Long Lartin prison too and next door to the governor's house was a large storage facility for munitions. As far as I know most of it has now been built on.

At Weston Subedge just outside Willersey in Broadway were the satellite units for the Second World War No. 24 Operational Training Unit (OTU) RAF Honeybourne airfield. This airfield was in operation from 15 March 1942 to July 1948 and formed part of No. 7 Group RAF Bomber Command. The airfield and its satellite installations including the railway were targeted by Luftwaffe bombers on numerous occasions. In my early teens I helped during the haymaking at Saintbury Farm which had a staff of just two, Jack and Ted Smith, two brothers from Willersey. In the summer holidays I worked with Jack and Ted back when the owner of the farm was an elderly Mr Bennet who had served as an officer with the Royal Artillery in the First World War. Mr Bennet who was confined to his bed at the time explained that the Luftwaffe once dropped incendiary bombs that fell all around the farm and into the fields, luckily causing no damage to property or livestock. He recalled that near the bottom of Saintbury Hill on his land was the bomb storage area where bombs for the RAF aircraft were stored. He also mentioned the large, elongated brick structure in one of the fields close to the Long Marston Road just out of Weston

Subedge, which was where the armourers at the RAF airfield tested the .303 Browning machine guns for the aircraft stationed there. This would make sense as in the event of any round going astray, where it was positioned in the middle of the field would not pose a threat to the public. Mr Bennet recalled piles of spent .303 cartridge cases which the RAF armourers had dumped in the corner of the field after doing their testing work. Access to this structure was easy enough and I investigated it a couple of times as a young lad. On the first investigation there were remains of sand partly filling the structure and I found a handful of fired and rather squashed .303 Browning machine-gun bullet heads embedded deep in the sand. I also checked the corners of the field for any trace of any .303 cartridge cases as mentioned by Mr Bennet. I found a few badly corroded bullet casings in the ditch but none worthy of keeping so I left them there. Sadly, that structure was bulldozed and removed and today there is no sign that it was ever there. I only wish I had taken some photographs of it before it vanished from the field and local memory.

For many years in a field along the Cleeve Prior Road to Bidford-on-Avon was a fuselage section of an RAF bomber which was at the time being used a shed. I recall my father Trevor mentioning it every time we passed by the field where it once rested. No RAF aircraft was listed as crashing in that particular location so how that fuselage section came to be there remains one of those mysteries. With many of the old locals who would have known all about it now long gone, I doubt whether the mystery of how it came to be in that field will ever be solved. My father said the fuselage shed had the green and brown RAF camouflage paintwork on it and it was pretty large and easily spotted from the road. What type of aircraft it came from is also unknown. It was apparently removed sometime in the 1960s but what happened to it is a mystery. In all probability it was sent to one of the many local scrap merchants and melted down. Having visited the field and scanned it with a metal detector, I could find no physical evidence of it.

The old Second World War RAF Honeybourne airfield is still in existence today (just about) but is now a shadow of its former self as a retail/business park. Two of the original and quite huge aircraft hangars where Whitley and Wellington bombers were once stored are still standing but are now in use as business premises. Most of the old runway has been taken up over the years and today only a small section remains along with the concrete taxiways. Sadly, few of the old buildings which once stood on the site when I first visited it as a young lad remain today. That said, it is nice to see that many of the anti-aircraft emplacements, observation posts and air raid shelters are still standing in the surrounding fields. Some look as if they have been filled in with soil, others are covered with dense thornbushes but one or two are still accessible.

The last visit I made to the airfield was in 2020 with my partner Paula. We went inside one of the bunkers in the field near the road and noticed a name the name 'Len' followed by '1941' had been etched onto one of the bricks inside with what appeared to be black ink or chalk. 1941 pre-dates the official operational period of the airfield but shows there was activity there prior to March 1942. There were even the remains of a rusted single bed in one of the bunkers. One of the old blocks was also still accessible despite the windows being bricked up. Paula and I went inside to find a maze of passageways and rooms which mirrored the lair of the psychopath Buffalo Bill in *Silence of the Lambs*. If it were not for our torches, it would have been pitch black. In a wall along one of the passages we found an American pineapple hand grenade body lodged in the end of a section of piping. The grenade was stuck fast, and one wonders why it was put there and by whom. The old, abandoned RAF buildings and indeed those in use today on the business park it is said are also home to one or more resident ghosts, one of which is frequently seen around the office of one of the units and described as a male wearing a khaki uniform. This is an intriguing subject as there were many deaths associated with RAF Honeybourne, particularly from crashes during local training flights.

A local man was out walking in the field in front of one of the old aircraft hangars one afternoon with his 6-year-old daughter. The child was a few yards ahead of her father when she suddenly stopped and began waving at the aircraft hangar. Her father asked, 'Sweetheart, what are you waving at?' A chill went down his spine when the little girl replied, 'I'm waving at that man over there sitting on the wing of that aeroplane, daddy.' The child had no idea as to the history of the place or the surrounding buildings and her father, who could see nothing but an aircraft hangar with its doors closed, was convinced his daughter had seen one of the resident ghosts. When asked again later at home, she repeated, 'The nice man sat on the aeroplane wing waved at me, so I wanted to wave back at him, daddy.' Paula and I have been to the site on many occasions and have experienced nothing of a paranormal nature but this does not imply that it does not exist.

The fields around the old control tower, which is also still intact and now a dwelling, are littered with the airfield's wartime past. I have walked around the fields often after ploughing and found .303 cartridge cases plus the odd live round (which was incidentally left in situ), coins and lots of US .50-calibre heavy machine-gun bullet heads. The last one I found was lying on the surface between the rows of crops and in good condition. The projectile was marked with a silver tip indicating that it was an incendiary bullet. These .50-calibre incendiary rounds were not filled with highly dangerous phosphorus as used by the British and Germans, instead they contained a magnesium pellet in the tip of the bullet that upon impact would create sparks capable of igniting fuel and oil in an enemy aircraft or vehicle. It is the kind of place where at certain times the fields are barren with nothing of interest coming to light while at other times you can be picking up relics using just eyes on the ground all day long.

During one perimeter walk with our dog along some bulldozed spoil banks near the road, I saw what I first thought was a metal drain cover sticking out of the top of the soil. I almost passed on investigating it, but my magpie instinct got the better of me and I climbed up just to check what it was. Having pulled it out the soil, I thought maybe it was a section of girder cut from one of the aircraft hangars. Removing the dirt, I could clearly see holes and strikes on the metal made by either 20mm or 30mm cannon rounds and heavy machine-gun bullets. The 30lb lump of steel had traces of a whitish paintwork and appears to have been cut from an armoured vehicle. Was this a souvenir from the Second World War or maybe a part of a larger test firing plate? Once I had got this piece back home, I was able to take a closer look at it. First task was to clean the soil from the metalwork then spray a coating of WD40 over the metal before removing what was only some light surface rust with oiled wire wool then wiping it all clean with a rag. With this done it was much easier to see the metal and its condition. The metal showed no signs of pitting through age and there was a noticeable lack of deep corrosion one normally encounters with Second World War relic metal pieces. If this piece had been from the war, then it could have been left inside one of the buildings where it was less exposed to the elements before the building was demolished and the piece discarded along with the debris. Another possible theory is that this piece may have been a trophy brought back from the 1991 Gulf War (Operation Desert Storm), the reasoning behind this being the later concern and paranoia expressed about the widespread use of depleted uranium munitions against Iraqi armoured vehicles. It is possible that this piece was taken as a souvenir and later dumped by its original owner due to these concerns. If this was the case, why dump it at the old airfield?

Before finding this piece, I did find an empty mortar bomb fuze storage box dating to the mid-1980s and my first thoughts were, 'What the hell is this doing here?' I left it where it was and went back for it a few days later but it had gone. Either way the piece of armour plate was one of my most interesting eyes-on-the-ground finds to date yet – carrying it the quarter of a mile or so back home was not much fun. A word of warning: the former RAF Honeybourne site and the fields surrounding it are not a free for all. The business park is protected by twenty-four-hour security, and you cannot just turn up and wander around. Richard Appleby, the farmer whose fields surround the old RAF site, will not be pleased if he catches you stomping around his fields without his permission; you must remember his land is his livelihood and this must be always respected. Paula and I inadvertently found ourselves on the receiving end of his wrath on one occasion whilst out walking the dog along the perimeter of the old base. After a few minutes of talking with him, the atmosphere calmed and before we left, he gave us his card and told us if we wanted to look over his fields to give him a call first so as he could ensure we did not go over fields with seed or young crops planted in them.

Anyone doubting that the threat of German invasion in Second World War England was not being taken seriously enough should simply look about, as evidence to the contrary is everywhere, much of it hidden in plain sight. As a lad I recall these odd circular concrete structures often at the edges of the local roads, most of them in the middle of nowhere and often wondered what these things were and their original purpose. Of course, later I learned these were the mounts for Spigot Mortars which in the case of invasion would have been used by the local Home Guard. In the village of Bretforton just outside Evesham there is one such Spigot mount with a plaque attached to it and another such mount on the opposite side of the road. These Spigot mounts were all strategically placed around RAF airfields and army installations for obvious reasons. The Spigot Mortar was designed primarily as an anti-tank weapon in the event of a German invasion. It fired two types of bombs, one weighing 14lb, the other 20lb, to a range of 100 yards at a muzzle velocity of 245 feet per second. The weapon was universally despised by those tasked with using it as it suffered reliability issues and was heavy and cumbersome to transport. Either way, some 22,000 were produced and issued in the war. An interesting example of a Spigot emplacement is that situated at the weir at the Fish & Anchor pub at Offenham. There is a pillbox on the opposite side of the riverbank to the pub with a small viewing slot where a light machine gun or rifle could be fired from. The Spigot Mortar mount is on the pub side alongside a public footpath which leads to the village of Offenham. Had the German invasion of England gone ahead as Hitler had planned, Britain's waterways would have been as invaluable as the road networks themselves to the Germans. Therefore, pillboxes and Spigot Mortar mounts can be found situated along strategic points of Britain's waterways.

Perhaps one of the finest remaining military structures I have seen in the UK is that of the Second World War Royal Artillery 378 Battery (Southern Command) complex at the popular holiday town of Brixham, Devon. Although manned by the Royal Artillery, it was strongly supported by members of the 10th (Torbay) Battalion of the Devonshire Home Guard. The complex is situated on the cliffs above Brixham harbour overlooking the whole of Torbay. Had the Germans attempted an invasion, this fort and its guns would have played a major part in shelling the invasion force. Some of the rooms of the complex are accessible to the public as it is now the Battery Gardens, part of the South West Coast Path. The only downside to visiting this wonderful example of our wartime heritage is that some dirty individuals persist in using this fine complex as a public toilet, subsequently it is littered with human excrement and toilet paper and care should be taken where you tread. I have found this a continuing trend with the various pillboxes and bunkers all over the country; they are not public toilets, they are historical monuments yet clearly some people have no such respect for the history which they are relieving themselves upon.

There are also numerous Second World War military dumping grounds scattered across the length of the UK. I inadvertently stumbled upon one such dump containing equipment disposed of after the war by the American forces stationed here in England during the war. It was in 1942 that the first of over 1.5 million US service personnel arrived on British soil in preparation for the Allied offensives against Nazi Germany. There are currently no specific databases recording locations of either British or American military dumping grounds; many were only known to the locals who lived nearby and who witnessed the activities of the post-war disposal process. Some of these old dumping grounds have since come to light through urban development programmes or farming activity. The US Army dumping ground I discovered quite by accident was known to many of the old locals whom I would later consult to try and ascertain what had been buried at the location in question.

It was while I was out walking in the fields near HM Prison Long Lartin at South Littleton that I noticed several shiny objects in a small stream in one of the fields. These silvery metal objects had been brought to the surface by the hooves of the cattle which had been drinking from the stream. Curious as to what these objects were, I decided to take a closer look and when I did, I discovered that they were unstamped Second World War US Army-issue dog tags. The term dog tag refers to the metal identity tag each soldier is issued with, usually bearing his number, name, unit, blood group and religious denomination. There were four of these silver metal dog tags in the stream and I took them back home, deciding I would carry out some research as to how these things got to be where they were found.

Speaking again with some of the old locals, I was told that at the war's end in 1945, the American forces had a storage facility up near where Long Lartin prison is now situated and all the equipment there was dumped in a large pit and filled in. Inquiring as to what type of equipment was disposed of at the site, I was told everything from medical supplies to Jeeps and other stores. The Jeep aspect seemed a bit of a tall story to me, and I thought surely not. Then another elderly local I spoke with said there were also tank parts buried up there, mostly brand new. This was certainly enough to arouse my curiosity and I then set about the task of finding where the actual dumping ground was located. This was not a difficult task as one of the locals pointed to one part of a large field and said, 'It's over there somewhere.' Nothing was immediately obvious until you looked at the actual geography of the land itself and the fact that there was an area of ground which appeared out of place with the rest of the field. Upon closer inspection, it soon became clear that most of the field was well-established grass pasture while the area of interest appeared rough and unnatural compared to the rest of the field, due to the topsoil which had been placed over the pit. The easiest way to find out was to carry out a preliminary dig with a spade and see if any clues could be found. Sure enough, after removing some six inches of topsoil, there was a soft peaty kind of soil and as I dug further all manner of things began to surface. I was finding knives, forks and spoons all stamped with the USAMD stamp (United States Army Medical Department), surgical instruments, brass tunic buttons, bottles which still contained much of their contents including lotions and tablets, and all these things, despite having been buried for many years, were in beautiful condition. There was also what must have been tons of broken USAMD porcelain in the ground and I pulled out a complete shaving mug with the USAMD stamp on its side. Moving a few yards off, I again began digging but this time found a bundle of 150 unstamped brass dog tags, .30-calibre cartridge casings plus some other objects which I could not identify at the time. It was clear that this was most certainly a major dumping ground and further investigation would be required to understand its full context.

I contacted the landowner who gave me permission to go onto the site whenever I wished, so I took a group of friends along and we spent a whole day digging there in the summer of 1990; we found literally hundreds of objects which included aircraft engine valves, some of which I found during my earlier digging but had cast aside as I had no idea what they were. Then we began to find many glass phials containing a clear liquid which we thought might be either a saline solution or quite possibly morphine. At this point, we felt it best to contact the authorities as the main area of the dump bordered a play area for young children. The local council came out and I took them to where the glass phials had been found plus an area near a stream where many unused old medical syringe needles had been unearthed. The council, rather than bring in specialists to conduct a proper full-scale archaeological dig on the site, opted to erect a fence around it instead to keep people out. This was disappointing as who knows what history is buried at the bottom of that pit. With the fence erected, access to that part of the field was cut off, yet over the years people have cut holes in it and climbed over it, to the point where it no longer serves the purpose of keeping anyone out and is back to being part of the playing field once again. I have over the years taken many individuals and groups of enthusiasts onto the site. The last group I took there were members of the War Relics Forum. Sadly, it was during this dig that certain members took it upon themselves to ignore the basic safety rules and the wishes of the landowner. While digging along the edge of the field, one of the members called out that he had found something. I went to see what it was and he was busy tugging away at a cylindrical object which thankfully turned out to be nothing more than a very old fire extinguisher. His response was, 'Damn, I thought it was an artillery shell.' I replied, 'And what did we say in the pre-dig brief about finding any suspected live ordnance?' Had that old fire extinguisher turned out to have been a live artillery round, it could easily have gone off the way the person in question was wrenching it out of the ground, and had it done so it would have probably killed us all in one go. Of course, the individual concerned laughed the warning off as overreaction, but I know of more than one fool who has caused injury to himself or others through ignorance of the basic rules. On that same dig another person decided, despite being told twice, that he would not fill in any holes he had made or dispose of any broken glass he had dug up. It was at the landowner's request that any glass be bagged up and put in the skip at the farmhouse and not left on the surface where livestock might injure themselves. The same individual also took live ammunition off the site after being told not to, a direct contravention of the Firearms Act. No number of attempts at reasoning with him could compete with his arrogance and he was never invited back to the site at the request of the landowner. This is just an example of why one should be careful who you invite along to your digging activities. As all it takes is that one rotten apple to undermine the faith and trust the landowner has placed in you. There will always be those who think they know better than everyone else and that the laws and principles involved do not apply to them.

Having had an excellent relationship with the landowner for many years, she was prepared to overlook this one blot on an otherwise clean copybook and put it down to experience. I had hoped to organize a proper excavation of the dumping ground but the outbreak of COVID-19 meant that all plans had to be put on hold. I am hoping that with the restrictions now lifted, I can tie up a few loose ends and conduct a long overdue archaeological dig at the site, hopefully within the next two years.

One of the questions most asked about these military dump sites is why these items were dumped there in the first place. At the end of the war when the American forces began returning home, there was little desire to take back the tons of supplies they had brought with them. It was easier in many cases that this unwanted surplus be thrown into large pits and burned or disposed of mid-Atlantic on the journey back home. At my site there is evidence of burning to some of the glass bottles and the peat-like soil beneath the top layer is more ash than peat. Either way, it is a dumping ground very rich in a wide variety of militaria relating to US forces on British soil in the Second World War.

There are also many munitions dumps situated around the country which originated in some cases well before the Second World War. Some of these have been forgotten and are accidentally discovered during urban development or farming activities. One such dump at a location I have been asked to keep confidential yielded ammunition dating as far back as the 1800s. All manner of ammunition types has been unearthed there from Martini-Henry rounds to .303 Lee-Enfield rounds and dummy drill ammunition. Most was in the form of unfired projectiles and their separate cartridge casings, most of which appear to have been deliberately cut in half, plus the ammunition storage boxes. Digging work over the years has unearthed hundreds of metal ammunition storage boxes in varying states; the last time I was there the landowner mentioned that the site is now as good as cleared which he was quite relieved about. Apparently, it has been a hot spot for nighthawkers. The dump has since been made into a large wildlife pond and the landowner has erected a warning sign which states, 'Danger Crocodiles!' At least the nighthawking menace has not dulled his sense of humour.

13

Second World War Aircraft Recovery

Second World War aircraft recovery in its infancy was nowhere near the technological art that it is today. Back in the 1950s and 1960s when various groups of enthusiasts formed with the serious intention of recovering aircraft wrecks buried in the ground in locations spanning the whole of the United Kingdom, there was little in the way of high-tech equipment with which to aid the process. With virtually all the official wartime reports on crashed Luftwaffe aircraft still unavailable to the general public, these small yet dedicated archaeological groups, many of which formed their own museums, had to put in much painstaking local research, relying as much on eyewitnesses as their own knowledge of the aircraft and various incidents involved.

The most active in the early years of aviation archaeology were names such as Alan Brown, Chris Elliott, Roger Freeman, Steven John Hall, Peter Halliday, Ron Buxton, Stewart Evans and Peter Foote, to name a few. One must also note the emergence in 1973 of the now-world-renowned *After the Battle* publications. At a time when official data was somewhat thin on the ground, these superbly researched quarterly editions proved invaluable as a resource to not only historians but those in the archaeology field in general. The relationship many of the aviation archaeology groups had with one another was not always a harmonious one. Peter Halliday recalled that rivalry did exist within the discipline and groups often strived to beat one another to what were considered the most lucrative crash sites in terms of not just the history but the archaeological material still present in the ground.

Naturally, Battle of Britain period crash sites have always been viewed as the most desirable. Subsequently, today there are few Battle of Britain-period crash sites that have not been investigated on multiple occasions. It was seen as a logical progression that many of these aviation groups would form their own aviation museums, often relying on the small entry fees to keep them active. Sadly, many began to vanish as the years went by for various reasons, most down to finances and some down to wrangles over the rents of buildings being used, etc. Peter Halliday recalled the demise of many of the once-thriving aviation groups and museums and recalls witnessing the sometimes-physical disputes over who would get what as they were being dissolved. It is true that much has changed over the years, yet the basic principles of aviation archaeology have remained much the same. Today, should you wish to carry out an investigative excavation of a Second World War military aircraft crash site on UK soil or in UK territorial waters, whether it be British, German or American, you firstly have to apply for a dig licence through the Ministry of Defence Joint Casualty and Compassionate Centre (JCCC). You can under no circumstances interfere with or remove artefacts even if lying on the surface of any aircraft crash site without going through the correct legal procedures as set out in the Protection of Military Remains Act 1986 and the JCCC guidelines. This Act was introduced to protect military aircraft wreck sites both above and below ground and under water from unscrupulous wreck hunters who were only ever interested in making a profit from whatever material they could recover. Prior to the introduction of this Act, it was something of a free for all with no respect given to the fact that human remains might also be present at the sites.

The process of applying for a dig licence to excavate an aircraft crash site is straightforward and today, like so many things, it can be done online. Before applying for any dig licence, it is wise to firstly approach the landowner in order to obtain written permission as a dig licence does not cover this and is a separate consideration. In the application for a dig licence, you will be asked to provide as much information as possible, giving location, date, aircraft type, serial number, unit, casualty lists (where applicable), grid co-ordinates of the crash site and whether human remains are likely to be present. If you have established that no human remains should be present at the crash site, you will be asked to indicate dates and places of burial and the like to satisfy the relevant authority that should you be granted a permit to dig, there will be no disturbance of any human remains. If human remains are likely to be present a permit to dig will not be granted, as such sites are considered war graves and are protected by law, and rightfully so. If the authority is happy with the information you have provided, it can take up to three months for a licence to be granted and this also must be a consideration when planning any excavation work. Once a licence is granted you will be given a deadline by which to complete your work.

You also must bear in mind that in many cases you may have to hire heavy digging machinery. Some crash site material may be embedded very deep in the ground, sometimes up to thirty feet deep, and that access to the proposed site also allows for any heavy machinery that may be required. Then there is the question of a qualified driver/operator for any digging machinery. Most of us know someone who can do this, but it is worth bearing in mind that this does not always come cheap even with mates' rates. Basic site safety equipment such as high-visibility clothing, gloves and hard hats are also a requirement and must always be worn during any excavation work.

There are of course unique hazards with crashed aircraft recovery. Some crash sites can be heavily contaminated with aviation fuel and oil residues. With the obvious dangers of the risk of fire aside, aviation fuel and oil can be extremely hazardous to health and the appropriate protective clothing and equipment should always be used. This is particularly important at crash sites where the impact craters have filled with water or are situated on boggy ground. Then there is the issue of any live ammunition which may still be present. No matter how thorough the original clear-up operation may have been, it is impossible to account for every live round and preparations should be made beforehand to cater for any live ammunition discovered at a site. Where machine-gun ammunition is concerned, any live rounds unearthed can be safely deposited in a bucket filled with an industrial oil placed at a safe distance away from the digging area. These can be disposed of by the relevant local police authority. No live ammunition should be taken away as souvenirs no matter how tempting it may be. I have been present at digs where certain individuals have chosen to defy this rule and carried live ammunition off the site in their pockets; despite attempts at appealing to their common sense, some simply do not have common sense in the first place. The possession of live ammunition without an appropriate licence is a serious offence in the UK. Again, ignorance of the law is not considered an acceptable excuse before a court of law. Cannon shells are a very different story. In wartime cannon shells were either fitted with solid/armour-piercing projectiles or were high-explosive/incendiary types. The projectiles were always colour coded, so an understanding of Second World War British and German ammunition colour codes is always useful. Some Luftwaffe cannon shells of 20mm to 30mm calibre were fitted with projectiles containing a phosphorus chemical. Such ammunition is extremely dangerous and should not be tampered with under any circumstances. Even a basic Second World War 20mm high-explosive cannon shell will have a blast and incendiary effect much like that of a hand grenade. If one were to go off in your hand, the result does not bear thinking about. It is always a good idea where possible to have someone present with experience in EOD (explosive ordnance disposal) who can advise on a situation should it arise. It is always better to be prepared and be safe than sorry; I have been on a few well-organized digs where at least two ex-army people were present.

The rest of the digging activity should be carried out, again with a common-sense approach and being aware of any moving machinery and standing well clear. A spoil pile should be subject to thorough examination for anything small such as personal possessions and all material recovered from the crash site must be recorded in the relevant documentation and submitted to the MOD at the close of any excavation work. It will then be decided whether you can retain the recovered items as your own property or whether they be considered the property of the MOD. This applies largely to those artefacts that may be considered of special historical interest. There is also the highly sensitive if contentious issue of any personal effects of the pilot or crew unearthed during any excavation. At the end of the day the declaration of any personal items recovered, such as uniform parts, wallets, money, badges, rings, watches and other personal trinkets is down to you and is a measure of your own personal integrity. Personal effects if recovered should not only be declared on the paperwork but wherever possible returned to the next of kin if their whereabouts can be ascertained, and not retained in private collections. The research process should always give consideration to this issue should such a scenario arise. With both the data and resources at one's disposal today, it is not that difficult to trace relatives of former military personnel both here in the UK and elsewhere in the world. All it takes is time and a little patience. Should there be no next of kin, then maybe a local museum should be consulted. Generally, if the two avenues prove fruitless, only then might you be permitted to retain the items. In the research and contacting former RAF airmen, the logical starting point should always be the Royal Air Force Personnel Management Agency (RAF/PMA), which is based at RAF Innsworth, Gloucestershire. I have consulted with this agency on many occasions over the years and have always found them an essential component when researching former Second World War airmen and contacting their next of kin.

Researching Luftwaffe aircrew may seem a daunting prospect but is quite simple provided the rule of time and patience is observed during research. I found that when I began researching the Luftwaffe back in the early 1990s, there were few individuals in the aviation fraternity willing to divulge information and/or photographs; it appeared most that I did contact wanted to keep everything to themselves. It was the proverbial brick-wall scenario which I found very frustrating at times.

However, one individual whom I contacted quite by accident was Edwin Henry Clarke, a retired prison officer from Essex. It was Edwin who taught me many of the things that I would later employ in other research projects which would result in my books. For a couple of years or so Edwin and I worked together gathering research material primarily for the use of the German War Graves authority in Kassel, Germany. We also supplied material from our research work to the Imperial War Museums here in the UK plus archives in Germany. We also acted as a kind of UK-based liaison for the German War Graves Commission at Kassel by the way in which we supplied German families with detailed information of their relatives lost over Britain during the war. The work was of course voluntary and despite taking up much of my free time, I was also able to build a fine clientele of very useful German contacts, including translators.

From my own experience I know that the Deutsche Luftwaffenring e.V (The Air Force – Our Life) based in Bonn and the Gemeinschaft der Jagdflieger e.V (Association of German Armed Forces Airmen) in Cologne were always a good source of initial information and data. The latter organization was primarily a form of a Luftwaffe fighter pilots' association and all inquiries had to be forwarded in German and not English – a quick internet search will always clarify whether these organizations are still active and if not will generally give a link to those that still are. The Bundesarchiv based in Aachen is also a good source of data when researching German aircrew. I know that they have access to some service data particularly on Luftwaffe airmen killed while on operations over Britain. The crucial factors with these service files, if you are lucky enough to find the ones you are after and provided they exist, is that they will often indicate the places and dates of birth of the airmen concerned. Once you have the place and date of birth you can then consult with the relevant *Raathaus* of the town or city of the airmen's birth. A *Raathaus* is like our Town Hall here in the UK, and the staff there can then ascertain as to whether relatives or next of kin of the airmen are still living in the area. They will forward any correspondence regarding your research onto the relatives or next of kin, and it is then up to them to decide whether to respond to your requests. I have found this is always the best way to proceed; though it generally takes more time, it is far more personal and rewarding than using online resources and I actually like the paper trail that it creates.

When making that contact with the relatives of Luftwaffe airmen killed over the UK, it is vital that you show respect and consideration. If they refuse to give you any information, you will have to accept it as it is sometimes part and parcel of the process. If they do agree to give you information and photos, it is one of the most rewarding feelings ever. It once took me a year of research to track down the daughter of one German airman shot down and killed with three other crew in January 1943. The information and photos the lady in question was in possession of built up a complete picture of the events and aftermath of one young man's death and the effect it had upon the family. It led to a very emotional yet memorable meeting at the German Military Cemetery at Cannock Chase in the summer of 1999. I felt it is a story worth relating here as I later visited the crash site of the aircraft in question which is at Westerham in Kent.

The story begins on the freezing cold night and early hours of 17/18 January 1943. The Luftwaffe bomber group Kampfgeschwader 2 (KG2) based at Deelen in the Netherlands was tasked with flying a double mission over the city of London. It was to be the Luftwaffe's first large-scale night operation for some time and the Luftwaffe high command was confident that much damage could be inflicted upon the assigned targets which were the docks and warehouse installations in the East End area of London.

Dornier Do 217E-4 Werke Number 5591 Squadron Code U5+MR took off from Deelen with other aircraft of its group for its first sortie over London. The first raid went very well according to the Luftwaffe reports with little in the way of night fighter activity and flak was considered light – maybe the British defences had been caught off guard. The wave of German medium bombers made their attack, releasing their bombs on their targets before turning for home to land, refuel, rearm and take off for the second sortie. There was barely time for the crew to grab something to eat and have a hot cup of black coffee before making their way back to their aircraft.

Everything was going to plan as they crossed the English coast, the fires from the first raid on London were clearly visible as a red glow in the distance. Also visible in the distance were the flak and searchlights which were far livelier and threatening than on the first sortie. On course for the target, the 23-year-old pilot, Unteroffizier Joachim Schnabel, began to gently weave the aircraft through the night sky so as to make it a harder target for any night fighters and flak. Although it was a clear, freezing-cold, moonlit night none of the crew was aware that they were being stalked by RAF Wing Commander Cathcart Michael Wight-Boycott and his air interception radar operator, Flying Officer Evatt Anthony Sanders, in a 29 Squadron Bristol Beaufighter, a heavily armed twin-engine fighter equipped with an early version of air interception radar. The Beaufighter had more than proved its worth as a night fighter and was the scourge of Luftwaffe bomber crews in the Blitz of 1943. Armed with four 20mm Hispano cannon and six .303-inch Browning machine guns, its firepower was devastating against enemy bombers. Wight-Boycott noted his altitude as being 13,000 feet and his airspeed 220mph when he closed in on the dark shape in front of him but before he could open fire, he had to be sure it was 'one of theirs and not ours'. He throttled back to reduce his speed before dipping down below the dark silhouette. He opened the throttle and soon found himself positioned immediately beneath the German plane. Looking up from his cockpit through the gloom, he could now clearly see the two black crosses on the wingtips and the distinctive twin tail unit of a Dornier Do 217. This was the moment when his heart began to pound and despite the numbing, relentless cold, Wight-Boycott began to feel beads of sweat on his forehead. He throttled back again, reducing his speed until he was 300 to 400 yards astern of the enemy aircraft. Synchronizing his speed with that of the enemy bomber, he switched on the lamp for his reflector gunsight, took aim and pressed the firing button on his control stick. As the guns erupted into life, he was momentarily blinded by the flashes as his cannon and machine-gun fire struck home; the Dornier burst into flames and fell away and began to spiral down to the ground. The four-man crew would have had just seconds to escape into their parachutes provided they had not been killed by the Beaufighter salvos. As the stricken aircraft tumbled earthward, out of control, the centrifugal forces would have pinned any surviving crew to the inside of the burning aircraft, making escape impossible. The Dornier impacted the ground in a small wood up behind Pilgrim House, Westerham, Kent at 4.30 a.m. The aircraft's bomb load exploded on impact and the Dornier totally disintegrated through the combination of the impact, explosions and fire.

The four crew were Schnabel, 25-year-old Unteroffizier Richard Hartenberger, 18-year-old radio operator Gefreiter Erich Raab and 22-year-old Gefreiter Willi Schäfer. The RAF recovery team who attended the crash site at first light on 18 January 1943 began sifting through the remaining wreckage, looking for anything which might be of use to RAF intelligence. Little was discovered apart from the remains of a primitive radar-jamming device so it is possible this aircraft was also acting as a radar jammer for the Luftwaffe formation. The remains of the four crew of the Dornier were temporarily buried to one side of the impact crater, their graves marked with wooden crosses. The crew's remains would later be interred at Greatness Park cemetery, Sevenoaks, and then finally the German Military Cemetery at Cannock Chase, Staffordshire, where all four crew are interred in a single grave.

My interest in this incident transpired after the purchase of several recovered crash site relics from this aircraft which included two oxygen bottles, airframe components, engine parts and hundreds of melted lumps of aluminium engine casing. I was, however, more intrigued by the human aspects of the incident and particularly wanted to learn more about the crew of the aircraft. To get some perspective, I felt it a good idea to firstly visit the grave at the German Military Cemetery at Cannock Chase and then the actual crash site at Westerham in Kent, which was made on 10 August 1998; it turned out to be the hottest day of the year thus far and made the trip into the beautiful Kent countryside all the more inviting.

Pulling up at the bottom of the drive to Pilgrim House, it was difficult to imagine that four young Germans had met their end here. I was eager to see the crash site for myself, yet it certainly was not obvious, and it was lucky I had met up with aviation historian Peter Halliday who witnessed the aftermath of the crash back in 1943, having visited the site with some school chums. Peter had been interviewed by the *After the Battle* team and his recollections on the crash recorded in *The Blitz Then and Now* Volume III. We walked up the dirt track which ran along the left side of Pilgrim House before turning right and following a fence enclosure through a small wood where pheasants were being reared before finding the impact site directly behind Pilgrim House.

There was much evidence of digging activity as there were holes and piles of dirt that someone had not bothered to fill in. I had not come here to dig for anything but merely gain some understanding and leave a wooden poppy memorial cross to the four young men who had perished at this very spot so long ago. The site had been subject to an army dig some years previous as it was suspected that unexploded bombs might still have been present at the crash site. Following an investigation and much digging work, no unexploded ordnance was found at the site which was then declared clear. The evidence of lots of pieces of rusted bomb shrapnel would appear to concur with the original theory that all the bombs on board had exploded when the aircraft crashed into the ground. There were also many heat-exploded 13mm machine-gun bullet cases present in the soil, these having come from the Dornier's defensive armament. There are still many broken fragments of the aircraft in the ground at the site today.

Following my visit to the crash site, I made a concerted effort to contact the families or relatives of the four crew of the Dornier. This proved to be a long process of elimination which involved much letter writing to various organizations and Raathaus in Germany. The first three inquiries proved fruitless and the authorities in question were unable to find any relatives still living in the respective birth places. It was disheartening but I had one inquiry left to make and it would be this one that would make all the hard work and patience pay off. Following an inquiry to the Raathaus at Essen, the mayoral authority was able to confirm that Gefreiter Willi Schäfer, killed on 18 January 1943, had a daughter, now a Mrs Ingeborg Stiefel, who was still living in Essen and had been born the morning her father lost his life in the skies over Westerham back in January 1943. I was able to write a covering letter to Mrs Stiefel who promptly wrote back to me.

A year later we met at Cannock Chase, the first time Ingeborg had ever come to England, and it was to be her first ever visit to see her father's grave. It was a very emotional moment as you can imagine but one which would result in meeting more of the family and forming lifelong friendships. I think Willi Schäfer would have been very touched at the thought of the daughter he never knew coming to pay her respects to him and his comrades here in England. After this research project, my interest in the actual archaeological relics diminished only to be replaced by the human side, an endeavour which would after the passing of many years lead to my personal goal of becoming a professional author.

In terms of air warfare, the night air war fought in the skies over Britain and Europe was a particularly unforgiving affair as noted in the above narrative regarding the loss of Dornier 217E4 U5+MR of KG2.

German night fighter or intruder operations as they became known over Britain in the Second World War is a subject close to the heart of my co-author Julian who has through his extensive archaeological work conducted his own research into Luftwaffe intruder operations over Cambridgeshire and Hertfordshire in 1941 with a view towards examining what remaining archaeological evidence there is. I will hand over the wheel to my literary companion to reveal what is a unique account created with the grateful assistance of the following aviation historians/authors, Simon Parry, Dr Theo Boiten and Melvyn Brownless of the Aircrew Remembrance Society.

The year 1941 heralded the first serious and obvious threat of large-scale invasion of Britain for almost a thousand years; well, provided one is prepared to overlook a few smaller attempts made in between of course. Yet, none was quite as terrifying a prospect for the British people than that of being invaded by Nazi Germany; although it was not in boats nor on horseback that the initial malevolent elements were to arrive. This was an enhancement of a threat not experienced since 1917 and during the First World War, by invaders from the air. Hoping that by achieving aerial superiority and dominance of the skies above England, a landborne invasion just like the Normans before them could then be executed. Initially, these German invaders came mainly in the daylight hours, but as 1940 progressed German medium bombers such as the Heinkel He III, Dornier Do 17 and Junkers Ju 88 switched largely to night-time operations. Some of these night-time operators were not what you would call the 'usual, run of the mill Jerries'; they were intruders belonging to the newly developed German night fighter or Nachtjagd arm, with crews specifically trained for night fighter operations. The *Gruppen* or units that operated in the specific area of interest here of North Hertfordshire and Cambridgeshire, a zone known as 'Raum A' (Room A) to the Luftwaffe night fighter crews of the I, II, III and IV Staffels of NJG2 (Nachtjagdgeschwader 2/Night Fighter Group 2) operating Junkers Ju 88C2s and C4s along with a small number of Dornier Do 17z10s from the Gilze Rijen, an airfield at Deelen, Holland. The Junkers Ju 88Cs were the solid-nosed A1 or A5 airframe variants armed with combinations of up to three 20mm cannon and three 7.92mm MG 17 machine guns all firing forward, plus a single MG 15 machine gun in the rear dorsal position to defend against fighter attack from the rear. One of their main areas of operation was around the southern to mid-Cambridgeshire district, crossing the county borders into northern Hertfordshire. In this area these intruders would achieve some considerable level of success in shooting down RAF aircraft, notably Wellington bombers from No. 11 OTU (Operational Training Unit) in the Bassingbourn and outlying areas. Below is a date-sequenced account of just some of the intruder operations and incidents that occurred over Hertfordshire and Cambridgeshire in 1941:

> **9–10 April 1941**: A solitary Junkers Ju 88C night fighter made an attack upon RAF Bourn airfield. The Junkers opened fire on some buildings, also releasing several SC50 (50kg) high-explosive bombs which exploded on the runway. During the same night RAF Wellington L4253 from No. 11 OTU based at Bassingbourn was shot down by Oberleutnant (Flying Officer) Albert Schultz and his crew at 00:40 hours, the Wellington crashing onto a house in the vicinity of Ashwell in Hertfordshire. Fortunately, the occupants of the house were not in residence. With regard to the crew of the Wellington, a Sergeant Dutton plus one other crewman were recorded as being safe. It is very likely that it was Schultz's crew that bombed and strafed Bourne that same night.

25 April 1941: RAF Wellington N2912 of 11 OTU based at Bassingbourn was shot down at 00:50 hours during its landing approach by a Junkers Ju 88C night fighter piloted by Feldwebel (Flight Sergeant) Giessubel. The Wellington crashed into stationary Wellington R1404, writing both aircraft off. The crew of N2912, Sergeant P. H. Nichols (pilot) was injured, Sergeant F. N. Alstram (co-pilot) and Sergeant R. Wilson (gunner) were both killed.

2 May 1941: Six high-explosive and ten incendiary bombs fell on RAF Waterbeach airfield at 23:05 hours. The enemy aircraft which carried out this attack may well have been the one involved in a later action when a few minutes later RAF Stirling N6012 was attacked just as it had lowered its undercarriage coming into land at Oakington. The Stirling caught fire and smashed into trees at Dry Drayton. No claim was submitted by any Luftwaffe night fighter crew for this incident.

5 May 1941: RAF Sergeant Parrott was flying his No. 257 Squadron Hawker Hurricane and was in the process of landing over RAF Duxford at 01:15 hours. During his descent and unknown to him, Feldwebel Hahn in a Junkers Ju 88C was following him down before opening fire with a short burst of 20mm cannon fire, causing the Hurricane to crash near Royston, killing Sergeant Parrott. Hahn made no specific claim for this kill and it is my own opinion that he and his crew were responsible for this loss as he was operational on this night (claiming a Bristol Blenheim near Feltwell) and the previous night (claiming a Fairey Fulmar near Stoke Holly Cross). Perhaps given the navigational abilities combined with the weather conditions, some confusion had arisen in this case. Another possibility is that the German night fighter crew responsible for this incident later went missing over the North Sea on their return journey and were therefore unable to document the claim. However, it was Feldwebel Hahn who seemed to have developed a particular penchant for finding and shooting down single-engine RAF aircraft in the night skies over Britain.

6–7 May 1941: At 02:10 hours Oberleutnant Strüning and his crew in a Junkers Ju 88C4 shot down RAF Wellington R3227 belonging once again to the hard-hit No. 11 OTU from Bassinbourn. Pilot Officer McAnally was being instructed by Flying Officer Warner whilst flying the downwind leg of Bassingbourn's landing circuit. Suddenly, the Wellington was hit by cannon and machine-gun fire from both astern and slightly below. The strand of glowing tracers had been spotted by Sergeant Stuart in the tail turret of the Wellington and he was able to open fire on their attacker. Within a split second the Wellington's port wing fuel tank received hits and burst into flames. FO Warner took over the controls from his trainee and managed to turn the Wellington into the wind to make a forced landing. The landing was hard, and the aircraft broke up in a small stream and caught fire near the village of Abington Piggots. Oberleutnant Strüning would log this claim as being for a Wellington bomber shot down near Upwood. That same night Luftwaffe intruders once again targeted RAF Oakington, releasing a total of five high-explosive bombs onto the airfield.

14–15 June 1941: A Junkers Ju 88C of NJG2 flew at low level over Oakington firing its guns and dropping a single bomb which damaged offices and a parked Stirling bomber as well as killing an airman. Later, and quite possibly the same aircraft also orbited Cambridge before heading towards the small airfield at Caxton Gibbet; no aircraft were damaged in the attack.

15–16 July 1941: Tiger Moth 11 training aircraft R4968 of No. 2 EFTS (Elementary Flying Training School) had its entire tail assembly shot away over Caxton Gibbet. Fortunately, its pilot managed to bale out, landing unhurt. Unusually, the Luftwaffe crew responsible never submitted a claim for this incident. The author believes in the absence of any claim that the night fighter crew most likely responsible for this incident are those of Köster or Hahn. Given the distance, one might also conclude that this intruder that shot down the Tiger Moth is most likely the same crew that attacked Oakington aerodrome the night before. The only night fighter pilot to make any claim this night was Feldwebel Alfons Köster who claimed two Bristol Blenheims at Wyton.

18 July 1941: RAF Wellington No. X3169 from No. 11 OTU RAF was fired upon at 01:30 hours just as it was about to land at RAF Steeple Morden. Although quite badly damaged, its pilot effected a controlled landing and none of the crew was injured. Only one night fighter crew over Britain on this night would put in a claim and that was Oberleutnant Semrau for a Bristol Blenheim near Digby. With the standard navigational equipment and in some cases attempts at identification in hectic surroundings, one must consider that Semrau and his crew may have been responsible for attacking Wellington No. X3169.

> **22–23 July 1941**: Saw the dropping of seven anti-personnel SD 'Butterfly' bombs in a field to the west of Oakington. Others had fallen over the airfield causing only slight damage to a Stirling bomber; however, an airman in a tent was seriously injured by one of the exploding bombs and died from his injuries sometime later.

The night fighters of the Luftwaffe, whilst proving a considerable thorn in the side to the RAF, did not have things entirely their own way. Many of the intruders were in turn stalked by night fighter aircraft of the RAF and subsequently quite several of them were shot down. In one incident one of the intruders was lost due to over eagerness in dispatching a victim. On 22 July 1941 Leutnant Heinz Volker piloting a Junkers Ju 88C4 had poured cannon and machine-gun fire into an RAF Wellington bomber. Eager to ensure the destruction of the Wellington which was engulfed in flames, Volker pursued, hoping to get in another burst of fire only to collide with the Wellington seconds later. Both aircraft fell away, crashing into the ground outside the village of Ashwell, Hertfordshire, the crews of both friend and foe perishing. The crash site of Volkers' Ju 88 has been subject of many investigations over the years, some of which have made some interesting discoveries. Perhaps the most poignant relic recovered from the crash site was a crumpled German wound badge in bronze. The crash site itself is still littered with molten metal, broken electrical components plus heat-exploded 7.92mm MG 17 machine-gun cartridge casings. The wreckage penetrated to a depth of around three feet; the ground at the site is now a mixture of powdery burnt soil and ash full of rusted components and clinker which naturally stands out from the terrain unaffected by the crash and resulting inferno. There is considerably more to this fascinating area of the air war but space does not permit any further examination here and both Julian and I hope to provide a full analysis of this subject possibly in a second volume dedicated purely to aviation archaeology.

It should not be surprising that many American servicewomen who had arrived in England alongside their male colleagues would play a vital role in the Allied war effort. In fact, many of the young servicewomen would become the unsung heroes of the Second World War. They served as nurses in the field hospitals, mechanics in the workshops and vehicle depots and as drivers of ambulances, tanks and trucks. Some American women also volunteered to serve as ferry pilots, primarily employed by the RAF, and tasked with the delivery of fighter, bomber and trainer aircraft to the various fighter, bomber and Operational Training Units all over Britain. One such story I became aware of through aviation archaeologist/historian Jim Corbett was that of Mary Webb Nicholson, the only female American pilot to be killed in the service of the Air Transport Auxiliary in the war. This incident also happened to have a local connection to the area where we live.

Second Officer Mary Webb Nicholson was born in Greensboro, North Carolina, USA, on 12 July 1905. Even at a young age aviation appeared to be in her blood as she went on to become a highly accomplished female pilot, setting records along the way. Mary was among the earliest women to be licensed as a pilot. Her licence, from the US Department of Commerce, was numbered 9562 and was granted on 17 October 1929. Mary was a fierce advocate for the right of women to be permitted to play a greater part in the defence of freedom and democracy in the event of war and she volunteered to come to Britain and undergo training with the Air Transport Auxiliary. Subsequently, she was one of just twenty-five female US nationals selected for the task of joining the ATA to ferry military aircraft of various types from the factories to the operational RAF airfields. The idea of the ATA pilots was to free up military pilots who would otherwise have had to carry out this task themselves. When Mary arrived in England, she was based at Maidenhead, west of London, where she was billeted with a host family. She was not at all fazed by the tasks which lay ahead and her family and new friends she made in

England all spoke of how thrilled she was to have the opportunity to fly aircraft in a professional context. Mary was assigned to 12 Ferry Pilot Pool of the Air Transport Auxiliary. On 22 May 1943 she was tasked with delivering a Miles Master serial number W9029 from RAF Hull Avington in Wiltshire to RAF Tern Hill, in Shropshire. It was while en route to Tern Hill that a relatively uneventful flight took a turn for the worse. The Miles Master single-engine, two-seater advanced trainer she was flying developed a serious oil leak; it was just a matter of time before the engine overheated and seized completely with total loss of power. Mary was fully aware of the situation, but stayed calm, deciding that rather than abandoning the aircraft by baling out, she would instead attempt to land at the nearest opportunity, which arrived as she approached the sleepy, picturesque Worcestershire village of Littleworth which lies between the town of Pershore and the city of Worcester. It was at this point that the engine seized up and the propeller flew off the aircraft; she was now too low to bale out and was committed to a forced landing in a field which lay ahead of her. In the process of attempting the landing, the aircraft impacted a stone building in the field. It was a surface crash, i.e., the aircraft did not plough into the ground. Residents of the village of Littleworth along with the local farmer ran to the scene of the crash, but the aircraft was well ablaze and any attempt at rescuing Mary, who had probably been killed by the initial impact, was hopeless. It was a tragic end for such a remarkable pilot with so much experience behind her. At the time of her death Mary was 38 years of age with more experience than the fighter pilots who would have been trained in the aircraft she was delivering.

The crash site today where this brave American pilot lost her life has since been subject to some minor urban development, yet the crash site is still intact. It is situated between a group of houses and open pasture; a public footpath runs right past the spot where the aircraft hit the ground. Being a surface crash, there will be little in the way of evidence, but such was the scale of the resulting fire that small lumps of molten alloy from the aircraft are still present in the ground, though these have been scattered by the digging out of the ditch which runs beside the crash site, and of course farming activities over the years. Although I have investigated this little-known crash site, I felt it better in this case to just leave a memorial cross of remembrance to Mary at the scene as opposed to looking for bits of her aircraft. The crash site is well known to the elderly villagers of Littleworth and one of them kindly stood at the exact location where Mary's aircraft crashed for a photograph which appears in this work, courtesy of Jim Corbett who has gathered much data on this incident while conducting his own research work.

Another interesting piece of archaeology was that brought to my attention by aviation historian/archaeologist Andy 'Badger' Long, a former member of the now-defunct Severnside Aviation Society. The SAS conducted several excavations on Second World War aircraft crash sites during the 1970s and 1980s; one such crash site related to a young American airman who lost his life on 31 December 1943, a day before what would have been his twenty-first birthday. This incident was one I was unfamiliar with at the time in July 2012. It concerns Second Lieutenant Jack Tuggle Jamison who was born on 1 January 1922 in St. Louis, Missouri. Jack's family was well known as they ran the famous Jamison Mattress Corporation, a household name in the US. Like many young Americans, Jack enlisted into the US Army on 1 April 1942 and was awarded his wings on 20 May 1943. Jack soon found himself stationed in England as a pilot flying with the 22nd Photographic Reconnaissance Squadron, 7th Photographic Reconnaissance Group of the US Eighth Army Air Force. The unit was based at USAAF station 234 at Mount Farm, Oxfordshire.

On 31 December 1943 Lieutenant Jamison, army service number 0-746118, was briefed for a local photographic sortie over the Okehampton area where he would be assisting army engineers with aerial photography. His aircraft was a Lockheed P-38F-5A Lightning serial number 42-13322. This was the photo-reconnaissance version of the famous American twin-engine fighter-bomber which entered service in July 1941. The weaponry of four .50-calibre Browning machine guns and one 20mm M2 cannon was replaced by camera equipment in the nose in this version. By all intents this should have been a very simple, trouble-free operation for Jack who along with his squadron comrades were looking forward to their New Year's Eve celebration and Jack's birthday party. At 14:00 hours Jack climbed up into the cockpit of his P-38 and strapped himself in. The twin Allison engines roared into life and with his characteristic smile and thumbs-up, Jack was soon off along the grass runway and disappearing out of sight of his ground crew. The weather conditions on that day were reported as 9/10 cloud at 2,000 feet with fragmented cloud at 1,500 feet with visibility at 3,500 yards, with some slight drizzle and a westerly 15mph wind. The sortie should have taken Jack no longer than approximately an hour and a half with an ETA back at Mount Farm at around 15:30 hours.

Concerns were raised when Jack failed to return by the allotted time. By 16:30 hours and with Jack still missing, an 'Overdue Action' was taken to establish the young pilot's whereabouts. News soon reached Mount Farm that residents at Harcombe Farm in Gloucestershire had reported that an aircraft had crashed four and a half miles west of the Charmy Down airfield. One of the first senior US military personnel to arrive at the scene of the crash was George Lawson, commanding officer of the 22nd Photographic Reconnaissance Squadron. It was soon confirmed that the aircraft that had crashed at Harcombe Farm was that of Jack Jamison. The P-38 had crashed into a small pond and was completely buried. As more US Army personnel arrived at the scene, the task of recovering Jack's remains began, with George Lawson assisting in the grim task. On 8 January 1944 an investigating committee was convened to try and establish the cause of the crash as there were no immediate eyewitnesses, though a short while later two witnesses did come forward to say they had seen a twin-tailed aircraft coming out of low cloud with both of its engines spluttering as if in trouble. Despite the committee's investigation which was quite thorough, they were unable to establish the cause of the crash that resulted in the loss of the pilot. Jamison had completed ninety-one solo flying hours on the P-38 Lightning so was well accustomed to the type and was by no means a novice pilot on it. The fact that most of the vital evidence in the form of the P.38's engines and cockpit equipment, all of which were buried deep in the ground, meant that these could not be examined at the time of the crash. The ongoing concerns of planning and fighting the war and the frequency of aircraft crashes due to accidents being a regular occurrence at the time, meant little time could be set aside for these accident investigations. Jack's parents were notified of Jacks' death; when his remains were returned for burial, it was noted that Jack's mother wanted to open the casket and it took a great deal of persuasion to prevent her from doing so. This crash, like so many others, would remain a mystery until 9/10 June 1984 when the site was excavated by the Severnside Aviation Society. The recovery of the remains of the aircraft proved extremely challenging and it was the first time that a Hymac long-armed earth-moving machine was used in an aircraft excavation. As Andy 'Badger' Long explained:

> We began to find pieces of the P-38 at a depth of around fifteen feet. Some of the more significant pieces were the propeller blades. Due to the lack of damage to the propeller blades, we could ascertain that they were not rotating at any great speed at the moment of impact. Crucially, the aircraft's engine throttle controls were recovered, and these were in the 'shut off' position indicating that Lieutenant Jamison had shut off the power to both of his engines. This of course was the correct procedure in the event of a double engine failure in a P-38. The early models of the Allison engines used in the type being flown by Lieutenant Jamison were known for

> being problematic, if dangerous, and did not seem that suited to our European winter conditions. The P-38 could be tricky to handle at low levels with a loss of engine power and it is likely that Lieutenant Jamison crashed as he was attempting to find somewhere to land. Other items unearthed from the excavation which terminated at a depth of some twenty-two feet were the photographic cameras, various hydraulics and engine parts, plus structural and airframe sections.

It was thanks to the Severnside Aviation Society and their highly professional approach to the archaeological work they carried out that at least the mystery of what happened to Jack was largely solved. The key pieces of evidence in the form of the aircraft's propeller blades and the throttle controls that were not available for scrutiny at the time of the original inquiry were at last recovered, albeit many decades later.

It seems aviation mysteries can surface just about anywhere and in places you would least expect. On Sunday, 22 February 2021, I was out walking our dog in the field at the front of our cottage. The field, used primarily for the grazing of sheep, is bordered by a long-abandoned and overgrown plum orchard to the east and the new Evesham bypass to the north. It is a field we have walked over countless times yet there was something I had missed until the day in question. I noticed that there was this sheet of metal wedged beneath the wire fencing that ran the length of the old orchard. I had seen it several times before but dismissed it as probably being a piece of old shed roofing material. On this occasion I decided to take a closer look and it was at this point I noticed the characteristic rivets of the type used in aircraft construction. This was not a piece of sheet metal from the roof of a shed nor that from some antiquated piece of agricultural machinery long consigned to the local scrapyard: it was most certainly from an aircraft. I took a photograph of it in situ before removing it in order to preserve its original context.

In order to extricate this large piece of metal from beneath the fence, I had to climb over the fence into the orchard. Using a piece of tree branch, I had to dig the one section of metal out of the ground in order to free it; it took some effort and after a game of tug of war with some roots which had ensnared the one section, the piece of metal came free. The side that had been exposed was plain unpainted aluminium but when turned over it had yellow paintwork intact and was in surprisingly good condition. I propped the piece up against a tree and took a photograph of it before calling my granddaughter Freya to take the dog while I carried the piece back home. The question then remained was what aircraft did this come from. The first probable answer was the Vickers Wellington bomber that in 1943 had crashed less than a quarter of a mile away, north of the location where this piece of metal was found. This crash is well known to the locals in our village and was subject to an excavation back in the 1980s when the site was accidentally rediscovered, having been swallowed by allotments. The only problem with this otherwise perfectly feasible theory was that the rivets used were not Second World War but of a post-war type. The Vickers Wellington which had crashed back in 1943 would not have had metal panels such as the one I had found, nor would they have been painted yellow. The Wellington was mostly fabric-covered, apart from the engine panels; the section of metal I found did not match those of a Wellington bomber. So, if it had not come from the Wellington crash then where did it come from? I was unaware of any other military aircraft crashes in our immediate area either during or after the Second World War and the only way the puzzle could be solved was by conducting some good old-fashioned research which soon turned up a definitive answer.

Sifting through all post-war aircraft crash incidents on the Air Safety Network (ASN) online resource was a report for the crash of a Hunting Percival Jet Provost T.3 serial number XM423 code 'RJ' (construction number /msn PAC/W/9230) having crashed at Harvington village during the night of 30 August 1961. Harvington is another small village less than a quarter of a mile away from the village where we live, so, this had to be the one. The next port of call was the Ministry of Defence to obtain the crash report which I received via email around a week after making my inquiry. It was this report which would confirm that the piece of wreckage I had found had come from XM423. The background to the loss of this aircraft as stated in the report is:

> During the night of 30 August 1961 Pilot Officer J. Armstrong and his instructor Flight Lieutenant [later Wing Commander] I. K. McKee, AFC [Air Force Cross] took off from the Central Flying School based at RAF Little Rissington, Gloucestershire, on what should have been a routine night flying training exercise. The flight was normal up until the approach to the village of Norton near Evesham, Worcestershire, whereupon the aircraft began to experience engine problems and subsequent loss of power. The engine problems occurred so rapidly that Flight Lieutenant McKee made the decision to take over control of the aircraft and barely had time to report to the controllers at Rissington before total loss of power was experienced, forcing him to make the decision to eject both his pupil and himself from the aircraft. To attempt a crash landing in the dark under the circumstances was out of the question and both crewmen ejected safely. The aircraft struck high-voltage powerlines before crashing into the ground.

The aircraft had been delivered to the RAF Little Rissington training wing on 22 March 1960 and prior to its loss there had been no technical issues encountered with the aircraft. Another key piece to this puzzle was the yellow paintwork on the piece of wreckage I had found. The paint scheme of XM423 like others of the RAF Rissington training wing were largely metallic silver, apart from a broad yellow band around the fuselage area of the aircraft. This effectively solved the mystery but still did not answer the question of where the actual crash site was located and how this piece ended up wedged beneath the fencing of the old orchard. Consulting locals, nobody today has any memory of this crash, and nobody knows where the actual impact point was. Most of the old locals who would have known of this incident have all passed away. It is my view that this piece of metal was a piece overlooked by the recovery team at the time of the crash and may have been unearthed decades later during the construction of the Evesham bypass when it was then tossed into the orchard as just a piece of unknown scrap metal. One local resident did come forward and mentioned that back when he was a young lad, he and some of his pals found a similar large piece of silver metal which had come from the crash site which they used as a ramp for their pushbikes. Describing the location of where they had found their piece and the fact that they were later chased off by the landowner and upon their return to reclaim their 'ramp' to find it gone, appeared to concur with the research findings. A few other local contacts came forward to mention that back in the 1970s they had seen pieces of what looked to be aircraft wreckage in the form of burnt wiring and small bits of airframe stacked by a well near a farm. The well in question has long since gone and the crash site itself may now be part of the Evesham bypass and lost for good. The current owner of the orchard, Christopher Perry, could offer no idea as to how this piece of wreckage came to be on his land. What did surprise me was the total lack of local press interest in what was undoubtedly an important piece of long-forgotten local history; it is sad but as they say, it's the way of the world today unfortunately.

To round off this section, I am going to hand back to Julian who has extensively researched and documented the wartime loss of three USAAF B-17 Flying Fortress bombers lost in accidents in the skies over the village of Weston, Hertfordshire, in 1944/5. Julian's research over the years has included archaeological surveys of the sites in question, investigations which would even lead to meetings with relatives of the young American airmen who perished in these incidents in the closing stages of the war.

For most of my early life I lived in the small Hertfordshire village of Weston, a delightful rurally situated little settlement, with connections going back to Roman times and beyond (Palaeolithic hand axe found when I was 7 years old). Of course, I gleefully investigated the Roman sites available, often returning home with supermarket bags bursting with Roman pottery shards. These were mainly for 'my museum' and claimed to be 'for pot reconstructions' which never actually materialized; however, it was the history of a more recent period that really caught my attention. Back in the 1960s the village was full of military veterans from both world wars (who all seemed to own a big old creaking black-painted Raleigh bicycle), as well as many people who had worked the land before, during, between and after those cataclysmic events in our history – many of whom, apart from having the amazing skill of most amusingly pulling their huge trousers up to a position well north of their navels, were thankfully only too delighted to be able to tell a young lad all their tales. I never encountered anyone who would not talk about their experiences, although the levels of detail varied enormously. There was old Val Field who had driven tanks during the First World War and told me about his surviving a German Gotha bomber raid in 1917 on an army encampment when he was out in France, where he was one of only a few survivors. 'Blood and bits with tattered tent cloth, son, that's all that was left of many of my mates.'

There were many others too and as I eagerly listened over the following months and years to various accounts, I began to hear about the three American USAAF B-17 Flying Fortress bombers that had crashed near the village in 1944/5. One of the B-17s named *The Peacemaker* had crashed to earth due to mis-timed engines; however, the other two had been involved in a mid-air collision, killing many crewmembers and even two civilians on the ground. Some of the accounts from people, particularly those who had been young lads at the time who had gone to investigate the crash sites, were indeed truly awful. However, I was intrigued and in the late 1970s I decided to investigate and research all three aircraft and find out as much as I could. That was over forty years ago now and I have never really stopped, having no idea back then on just how fascinating this would be and the amazing people that I would meet and communicate with as a result, people who in some cases were the actual relatives of the B-17 crewmembers involved.

During World War Two Hertfordshire and Cambridgeshire saw considerable aerial activity; however, with the entry of the United States into the war in 1941, this aerial activity was to slowly increase to a never-before-seen or since level. New aircraft were making appearances in the skies over Britain, aircraft such as the P5-1 Mustang, P-38 Lightning, P-47 Thunderbolt, B-24 Liberator, and arguably the most famous of all, the B-17 Flying Fortress. 1944 would be the year all this combined activity would peak, with the build-up of armed forces prior to the Allied invasion of Europe and intensified daylight bombing raids by the USAAF on German cities. Raids deep into the heart of the Third Reich, occupied Europe and later French coastal targets, were all undertaken. Many bigger raids involved 'stacking up' as they began to assemble, form up and head off to their target. It was not uncommon at this stage of the war for some Royal Observer Corps stations to plot over 500 aircraft in the sky at one time. For many people living in the area, the noise of all these aircraft massing in the skies above would be unforgettable. Those residents living near Nuthampstead or near the huge USAAF base at Bassingbourn just over the Hertfordshire border in Cambridgeshire, would be treated to a daily chorus of four-engine heavy bombers flying overhead. So often did this take place that most people got used to it. However, what they never got used to was looking skywards later and seeing them return with feathered props, engines on fire and with sections of structure shot away, the result of a fair mauling by the defending Luftwaffe fighters and flak. Many onlookers to this daily spectacle would perhaps even cross their fingers, hoping that the smoke-streaming straggler right at the back would land safely. Tragically, this increase in activity would inevitably bring with it increases in incidents ranging from crash landings to the more catastrophic and dramatic aerial collisions. On Saturday, 12 August 1944 a B-17 named *Tomahawk Warrior* from the 398th Bomber Group collided with a B-24H Liberator over Cheshunt, killing the crews of both aircraft. Just weeks after this incident another similar tragedy occurred, involving the collision of two B-17s over the small village of Weston.

It was in the early 1970s that I first heard people in the village of Weston talking about the 'wood where the bombers came down'; I was about 10 years old when I first heard about the wartime collision of two aircraft. I cycled over to Warrens Green and parked my bike next to a hollow used by local gardeners to dump old vegetable cuttings and large stones. By pure chance I was just looking around when I spotted a large bullet with a brown-coloured patina just lying on some recently deposited earth. Picking up this treasured item, I examined it closely, noting that it had probably detonated in the fire as the B-17 exploded. Little did I realize then that thirty-five years later I would be in the same area looking at the ground, finding an exploded .50-cal cartridge case, but this time would be even more special as I would be in the company of the relatives of one of the airmen involved. The fact that my bullet had hit something at very high speed was clearly evident by its now-flattened tip, which should have been pointed. I remember thinking that it looked like the snub-wrinkled nose of a pig. I kept this first ever physical link to the crashed bombers for many years, but with the passing of time it has been lost. Asking people in the village about the incident presented some problems, as numerous variations of the incident and memories associated with it were presented to me. Firstly, it was two Douglas

Dakotas, then two Lancasters and some even said it was two Super Fortresses. Someone even mentioned that the collision was caused by a P-51 Mustang pilot who had been weaving in and out of a bomber formation, collided with one bomber which then hit another. In those days almost every 'Weston local' over 40 was able to recall the event.

In 1977, I was a beater for a shooting party and part of the drive was through the wood where one of the aircraft had crashed. I heard several of the older men mention the collision as we set course for the drive. In those days there was not much undergrowth, and I soon came across a deep depression about twenty feet across and some ten feet deep. 'Bomb hole, boy,' one of the older men said, as I stood and looked at it and the surrounding area. A curt reminder from Ron Hemmings, the head gamekeeper, that the only flying things I should be concerned with were the pheasants I was being paid to flush up and out of the wood, refocused my attention to the matter in hand.

I was now very curious and soon started asking more questions about the incident, calling on many villagers and taking notes of their recollections. However, I would not return to this wood until the summer of 1979. By this time, I had researched the incident in some depth, now knowing that the two aircraft involved were actually B-17 Flying Fortresses. I even knew the exact date and names of each crewmember, as by then I had written to an American military institution who had furnished me with some very good details. Mrs Cherry, the landowner, had even given me an example of a complete .50-cal bullet. So, now the summer of 1979 and having finished school, I decided to spend some time investigating. Walking through Weston Park, I came to the grass fields behind Warrens Green and looked at the wood with some thought. This was forbidden territory; the pheasants would be breeding now and if I got caught by Ron in these woods there would be hell to pay. However, my curiosity (reinforced by permission granted by Mrs Cherry) was stronger than my fear of the red-faced gamekeeper and slowly I shimmied under a strand of rusted barbed wire and I was in the damp midge-infested wood! I passed through some small, thin patches of bramble noting the rusted oil drums, orange nylon twine and several dead squirrels, sure signs that Ron was doing his job. I just hoped that he would not be as efficient as usual on this particular day. Despite these concerns, as earlier mentioned I did have permission which I hoped would also serve well to deflect any verbal attack from Ron if I was caught. I proceeded up the straw-strewn rise and came upon an area where the tree growth was thinner. Looking about, I spotted the bomb hole again, its dark waters now home to a pair of nesting and rather noisy moorhens. Rather ironic really, I thought, as each hatching egg involved a new birth on a site associated with so much death and destruction.

Around the bomb crater were broken trunks of pine trees and when you peeled their bark away this revealed numerous nicks, scores and scratches on the smooth surface which had been impacted by bomb casing, shrapnel splinters and internal components. All were stuck firmly, surrounded by twisted and compacted wood fibres. Further examination showed that many of the surrounding oak and ash trees also bore gashes, smashed boughs, and were distorted. Quietly I said to myself, 'So this must be where it happened.' It was summertime then just as it had been when the tragedy occurred back in 1944. Looking at the ground, I noticed numerous small pieces of contorted metal, some partially covered in moss, others just blue crumbling, powdery lumps, whilst other pieces looked to be in such good condition they could have just that moment fallen there. I noted bits of rubber and wiring and in the deeper bramble thickets considerably larger pieces of dark green-painted airframe. The larger pieces had a bubbled appearance due to the large rivets evident on their surfaces.

Over the next few years my good friend Tim Fisher and I used metal detectors in the area and unearthed some very interesting finds which included compressed and burned parachute fabric, cockpit instrument faces, a single headphone receiver, jack plugs, wiring and switches. These finds indicated clearly that we had found the area where the cockpit had impacted the ground.

The two B.17 bombers involved in the mid-air collision are as follows:

B-17G (unnamed) serial number 42-102936 390th Bombardment Group (Heavy) based at Parham, Framlingham in Suffolk.
Location: Wreckage spread over 1.5km at Weston Park.
Time: 09:05 hours.
Crew: Pilot 2nd Lieutenant Paul H. Bellamy (killed), Co-pilot 2nd Lieutenant James J. Graba (killed), Navigator 2nd Lieutenant Raymond A. Klausing (survived), Bombardier 1st Lieutenant Joseph Y. Lee (killed), Radio Operator Sergeant Irwin W. Casey (killed), Engineer/Dorsal Turret Gunner S/Sergeant Frederick O. Walsh (survived), Waist Gunner Sergeant Lotus R. Conser (survived), Ball Turret Gunner Sergeant Robert Hunter (killed), Tail Gunner Sergeant Richard A. McAteer (survived).

B-17G named *Ding Dong Daddy* serial number 42-97182 390th Bombardment Group (Heavy) based at Parham, Framlingham in Suffolk.
Location: Warrens Spring Wood at Weston.
Time: 09:05 hours.
Crew: Pilot 1st Lieutenant George E. Smith (killed), Co-pilot 2nd Lieutenant Carleton Sacco (killed), Navigator 2nd Lieutenant Robert G. Taylor (killed), Bombardier 2nd Lieutenant Herman R. Collins (killed), Radio Operator T/Sergeant Victor G. Graff (killed), Engineer/Dorsal Gunner T/Sergeant Allen J. McCasland Junior (killed), Waist Gunner S/Sergeant Martin I. Kilbride (killed), Ball Turret Gunner S/Sergeant Michael K. Kasarda (killed), Tail Gunner Corporal Gus G. Brubaker (killed).

So, the question here is what really happened on the day in question back in 1944? The following account has been made possible from a wide variety of sources and is the author's own assessment of what happened over the village of Weston on that fateful Saturday some seventy-eight years ago (at the time of this report was compiled).

At approximately 09:00 hours on Saturday, 26 August 1944 the villagers of Weston heard the familiar droning hum of bombers massing in the air above in preparation for a raid. So familiar had this sound become rarely did they even cast an eye upwards; however, this day would be different and for miles around people would stare up into the sky in horror. Thousands of feet above them a dull boom was heard and then a dreadful high-pitched screaming whine as the pitch of the engines dramatically changed.

A few minutes prior to this disturbance in the sky above, a young lad, Frank Hawkes, had stood watching a Tiger Moth aircraft perform some aerobatics over the village. Now the noise from its tiny engine was drowned out by the approaching bombers. Frank was used to this noise like everyone else but a distinct change in the noise made him look up. 'Summat's up with the Yanks,' his friend Alf said to him as they both shielded their eyes from the glare of the early morning sun. Looking up, they could see that two of the tiny silver-appearing bombers were locked together. Suddenly, now in a state of panic, they heard a booming sound as the aircraft appeared to break up in the air. Alf remarked with a concerned voice. 'Bloody hell!' before running off to get help.

An oily black smudge appeared in the sky, surrounded by hundreds of falling pieces of debris which flashed and sparkled in the sunlight. Just beneath the black smudge another B-17 could be seen spiralling earthwards minus one of its wings. By now the collision had also been seen by people as far away as Letchworth and Stevenage. Some even began to cheer, strangely believing that the aircraft were in fact German. Just after the sound of the explosion, a 5-year-old boy looked up and ran indoors, grabbing at his mother's apron strings in childlike innocence: 'Mummy, mummy there's something wrong in the sky.'

Hours prior to this incident the weather had indicated that that day would be another glorious summer's day. The runways of Parham airfield were already shimmering in the early morning heat, and as the aircrews gathered, a lone skylark trilled high above them. Each aeroplane was standing on the surrounding dispersal points, fully fuelled, bombed up and primed for readiness. Some were still having last-minute groundcrew checks, emphasized by the occasional swearword accompanying the clang of a dropped spanner. The concrete surfaces of the runways and dispersal points had that hot tarry stone aroma about them, and as each crewmember clambered aboard their respective bomber, they were met with the heady odour of hot metal, leather, oil and paint. The mission for that day was considered to be a bit of a 'milk run' (an operation considered to pose less risk than normal). Instead of a deep-penetration raid into Central Europe, it was just a routine trip over the Brest Peninsula, the targets being some German heavy artillery emplacements that had been shelling the Brest region, therefore holding up the Allied capture of the port.

The first Wright Cyclone engines spluttered into life and the base resonated to the growing, vibrating roar that carried for miles around the surrounding countryside. By 07:33 hours the 390th's aeroplanes were all airborne, engines straining with the weight of fuel and bombs. Now began the long task of waiting for all the participating groups in order to stack up over East Anglia. The cloud was quite thin on this day and from high above the crews could easily see the patchwork-quilt appearance of the English countryside. Looking around, they began to see other formations; indeed, the sky was absolutely full of aircraft. Some crews were watching the lead ship in the formation, B-17 42-102936, and noted that it appeared to fly too close under the lead squadron. This action forced the No. 4 position B-17 right into the propeller wash emanating from the lead element of three

B-17s. B-17 42-97182, *Ding Dong Daddy*, was then violently swung about by the propeller wash and forced downwards towards B-17 42-102936.

Crews watched on concerned, but to be fair the event was nothing too unusual in such heavily congested skies. Crews from other B-17s were later to state they were uncertain as to whether 182 had come down on 936 or 936 had risen too steeply below 182. However, the two aircraft began to get perilously close. '936 will you please let down a little' crackled over the intercoms. A split second later the two massive B-17s locked together, 182's propeller blades slashing through the vertical stabilizer of 936, throwing shreds of metal everywhere. Larger fragments of 936's stabilizer and fuselage now began to tear away. Terrifyingly, Frederick Walsh the top/dorsal gunner of 936 recalled looking up and seeing the propeller blade tips from 182 cutting off the barrels of his two .50-calibre machine guns. 936's wing surfaces began to disintegrate and fall away, as both aircraft tumbled over to the right-hand side and went down in a huge sheet of flames. A short while afterwards bombs began to detonate in the air and then the remains of 936 simply exploded in a brilliant white flash.

No words in any book could convey the true horror of this incident as it began to unfold. Numerous bombs were ejected from the two aircraft as they disintegrated in the sky and were now exploding all around the district as they began to hit the ground. Falling debris from the two giant aircraft, including the engines which weighed 1,184lb each, also posed a serious hazard to the village and its inhabitants below. There were many horrors witnessed that fateful day and due to the sheer scale of the incident, it was clear that any clearing-up job was going to take some time to complete.

As with all such wartime incidents as this, there were those who went out in the wake of these events looking for any souvenirs they might find. Frank Hawkes and some of his friends spotted a parachute canopy billowing out from the top of a tall conifer tree. The best tree climber was selected and then clambered up to get this precious prize. This, however, was perhaps not the best idea, as wrapped up inside it and pinned to the tree was the body of a dead airman. The lads pelted off to find the local policeman but on their way to the village there was still no escaping the horrors of what had happened as they were to find a flying boot with a foot still inside it. They stopped and dug a hole, placing the gruesome item in it where it remains to this day. The remains of *Ding Dong Daddy*'s crew were still being gathered from Warrens Spring wood for weeks afterwards, many locals stating the woodland smelt of burnt wood, oil, rubber and decaying flesh. One local ex-poacher told me it was pointless taking his ferrets into the wood to look for rabbits, as they were distracted by the numerous shreds of decaying flesh that were everywhere. Another local man, Tom Clements, thought he had discovered a really interesting keepsake when he spotted an American service-issue cap lying in a bed of nettles. Thinking it was a shame that the brass badge was missing, he turned it over but dropped it quickly – there was a large section of human skull with dark hair still attached and stuck inside the cap, glued to the material by the dry blood.

Over the years several relatives of the American airmen involved in this horrific mid-air collision have made contact with me and on two occasions have made the long journey over from the United States specially to visit the scenes of the B-17 crash sites. For the relatives of these brave young American airmen, visiting the scene where each bomber smashed into the ground is all about gaining some perspective of the events which occurred so long ago, yet whose scars are still visible to a lesser degree today.

Today the crash site continues to be covered in new alder saplings and bramble growth which obscures the blue powdery patches showing where another piece of airframe has succumbed to the corrosive passing of some seventy-eight years. Back in 2002 the wood was again cleared; this time many of the mature trees were not so lucky, and only three remained that still bore the scars and breakages attributable to the impact of *Ding Dong Daddy*. Today there are still several trees that exhibit strange growth patterns, most likely because of bomb blast, but now only one mature tree survives that bears a definite scar attributable to this incident. The large conifer where the dead airman's body and parachute were discovered was blown down in a severe gale in 2007. The bomb crater that was once so easily located has since been consumed by bramble, grass and alder saplings. The broken pines that once stood at the edge of the crater have all long fallen and now lie actually in the water-filled crater itself.

From Julian's meticulous and expert research, we can see that here can be no doubt that archaeological detritus from the crash of the two B-17s is still evident in the ground in places yet with the passing of time this too will vanish eventually, consumed by the very ground where it lies embedded. Sadly, we have only been able to merely scratch the surface with the full history of this incident as Julian's file is very extensive. Yet I hope even if in some small way this particular piece brings home the true horror of an incident, one of many to have taken place during the war and one which illustrates perfectly the risks that these brave young airmen took every single time they took off on a mission. The relics that remain from these incidents, often in the form of twisted and smashed pieces of metal, are now often the only reminders that these terrible events ever occurred; these things should always be handled and treated with the absolute respect they deserve as historical contextual relics.

14

Tale of a Tailplane

A rare piece of recovered aircraft which originated from perhaps one of the most important Soviet military aircraft of the Second World War travelled some 1,274 miles, arriving at a militaria show in Plymouth back in 2017. The piece was brought to the UK by a Polish dealer who visited the UK twice a year bringing with him a van load of items specifically to sell at the show. An old friend of mine had over the years struck up a friendship with this dealer and mentioned that he was particularly interested in aviation archaeology, so at the next militaria show in Plymouth the Polish dealer turned up with his usual van full of items but had something a little more special on board on this occasion. He gave my friend a call to arrange to meet up at the show, excitedly informing him that 'I have something very cool for you in the back of my van. Come and have a look and see if you are interested in it'. My friend was naturally very eager to get over to the show and left immediately to meet up with the Polish dealer who was already attracting a decent crowd around his stall. My friend was shown to the back of the dealer's white transit-style van. A sheet was pulled from off the piece and the dealer explained that it was a near-complete right-hand tailplane of an Ilyushin Il-2 Sturmovik attack aircraft which had been shot down by anti-aircraft fire while attacking retreating German columns fleeing through Poland in early 1945.

The tailplane looked to be a pretty impressive piece especially when removed from the back of the van and laid out on a groundsheet for my friend to view. Two separate pieces, elevator parts, were also included. This immediately caught the eyes of several other potential buyers who expressed great interest in it; the two friends watched with some amusement as they jostled each other to get a better view. Immediately, they began throwing offers at the dealer who had to tell them, 'My friend here has first refusal; if he doesn't want to buy it then we can talk and discuss price.' The four interested buyers stood back on the side-lines waiting like cats on a hot tin roof, and probably hoping my friend would not buy it. The tailplane had been retrieved from the crash site of the Il-2 in Poland and was referred to my friend as being a very rare piece which was of course fresh onto the market that day.

Then it came down to the question of price. The Polish dealer said, 'Well, I am asking for £1,000 for this piece. I had to firstly locate the wreckage which was not easy then I had to retrieve it from the ground where it had been partially buried and then bring it all the way to England by road in my van.' My friend understood that this was a fair enough price under the circumstances, thinking to himself, 'Well, if I pass on this where the hell would I find another?' Yet £1,000 was a lot of money to spend on an item he was unsure of what he was going to do with. The haggling continued a while longer and my friend managed to finally secure the tailplane for £800 cash. The two shook hands and the deal closed; the four eager bystanders walked away in disappointment, one muttering 'fuck' under his breath.

The only other problem my friend faced after his purchase was that the tailplane would not fit into the back of his car. This is something many of us have probably overlooked in the excitement of buying large pieces of militaria! Being a true gentleman, the Polish dealer offered to deliver it to my friend's door later that day after the show closed. My friend was more than just a little bit nervous at having parted with £800 and was praying that his trusted Polish friend would not do a runner with his cash and the tailplane. He need not have feared as later that afternoon the Polish dealer pulled up outside his house and helped him to unload the sizeable relic. It was still full of dried mud, some of which began to fall out from the internal sections.

Having taken it up the stairs and placing it on the floor of his spare room, he shook hands with his friend who then set off on his return journey home, promising to be back next year with more interesting items.

Nothing was ever done with the Il-2 tailplane once in my friend's possession and it remained in his spare bedroom for some years until the summer of 2020 when he decided to offer it for sale as he still had no idea as to what he would ever do with it. Having spoken with him about it over the phone a price was agreed, and I acquired the Il-2 tailplane from him. Mark Bentley of Tiger Collectibles in Bournemouth very kindly offered to deliver it for me as during a brief break in the COVID-19 travel restrictions, he had planned to check up on a holiday home he had in our locality and he would not be going far out of his way to deliver it.

Having received the piece, I began the process of removing all the dried soil that was still trapped inside which took some time to accomplish. The rest of the metal, including the green paintwork of the upper surfaces and blue of the lower, was easily cleaned with a cloth and some WD40. I noticed on the elevator section there was a hole made by a 13mm-calibre bullet indicating at some time in its life the Il-2 had been fired on by German aircraft. There was also a hole the size of a man's fist made by one of the 20mm flak rounds responsible for bringing the aircraft down as it had attacked the German columns. A part serial number was also found but no indication as to the actual serial number of the aircraft itself. Without this, finding details on who the two-man crew of the aircraft were would not be an easy task at all. One could imagine flying at treetop height into a storm of quadruple-mounted 20mm flak and in the subsequent crash the likelihood of the crew having survived would be very low indeed.

The Il-2 Sturmovik crews suffered very high losses despite the devastation they were able to wreak on the fleeing Germans with their two 23mm cannon, rockets and bomb armaments. The Germans nicknamed the Il-2 'the flying tank' as it was considered a difficult aircraft to bring down due to its good armour protection for both crew and fuel tank. Although many Il-2s fell to the guns of Luftwaffe fighters, a good proportion of losses occurred during low-level attacks in the face of heavy anti-aircraft fire, usually in the form of the mobile quad-mounted Flak 38s used by the Germans. Although the Il-2 was produced in greater quantities than any other Second World War aircraft, very few examples survive today. Only one has been restored to flying condition and a few others have been recovered from the bottoms of lakes and in dense forests where they have been resting since the end of the war.

The scarcity of relic material from these aircraft is easy to explain: if an Il-2 was shot down the Soviets wherever possible would retrieve any usable parts from the crash and put them to use as spares for other Il-2s or use them in the assembly of new aircraft. This simple yet effective philosophy of cannibalizing parts even from destroyed aircraft goes a long way to explaining why many known Il-2 crash sites in Eastern Europe and in former Third Reich territories are seemingly void of anything worthwhile archaeologically: everything still usable or of a repairable nature was taken away, refurbished and reused.

An acquaintance of mine in Poland has located the crash sites of several Il-2 aircraft, some of which are in very remote locations. All were thoroughly investigated and apart from relatively small parts, nothing of any significance was found at any of these sites. Much of what material had remained on the surface of the ground was too badly corroded to be of any use, even for a display.

The Il-2 tailplane now resides in the living room of our 200-year-old cottage where it certainly forms a conversation piece for anyone visiting us for the first time. I have learned over the years through collecting and letting things go that provided you still get enjoyment through owning these things, you do not let them go. The larger pieces recovered from Second World War crash sites are becoming very hard to find today and are thus now very expensive when they do become available. The change in the laws in Poland too have had some effect on the acquisition of once easily obtainable archaeological material from the East. It is not as easy to get these things through the Polish customs departments today as they are now considered part of Poland's historical heritage and should remain in the country where they belong and not be sold for profit to collectors in the west. One can clearly see all sides of the argument here between the dealers, the cultural heritage departments and the collectors, yet I don't think any of them will agree to agree with one another in the near future, giving sway to a noticeable increase in the illegal activity that is known as nighthawking in the relic collecting and selling business.

To explain briefly, the scourge of nighthawking is nothing new. The nighthawks are people who venture onto private or protected historical sites under the cover of darkness to metal-detect and dig for historical militaria, with the full knowledge that they are breaking the law in doing so. Some nighthawks carry out their illegal activities to swell and enhance their own private collections whilst others do so purely for profit, offering for sale most of what they unearth, often without any context on where and when the find was recovered. This is always something which should set alarm bells ringing but there are those who also invent context to add value to an otherwise ordinary item. The gangs of nighthawkers certainly have their patronage who make their activities worthwhile and so long as there is a demand for rare artefacts, there will be nighthawks happy to oblige. The threat of fines and prison sentences appear to be no deterrent as the profits outweigh the risks. I was speaking with one battlefield relic dealer a few years ago at a large militaria show. We got onto the subject of nighthawks when the dealer took a deep breath, sighed and then revealed:

> Well, I'm sorry to have to say that 90 per cent of the stuff I sell has probably been obtained illegally through nighthawking activities. In fact, much of what is for sale

> on other dealers' stalls probably originates from illegal digging and has been in circulation for years too. How do you know? Well, it's impossible to tell. When a guy gets in touch with me and tells me he has a bunch of relic SS helmets or pieces recovered from an infamous action, if I like what he has and am satisfied after close examination that the material is authentic, I won't ask too many questions and I will buy them as I have to make a living. For example, say you come to my stall and there is an item on there you have been looking for for a very long time and you want to buy it – would you pass on it if you had even the slightest suspicion that it had been illegally dug by someone you don't even know? No, of course you wouldn't walk away from it; you would buy it, wouldn't you? We collectors have that magpie nature, and many don't really care if an item has been nighthawked or not these days. As long as someone wasn't murdered for it, few actually care about this [he laughs].

This explains basically all you need to understand about nighthawking so if your mates roll up at midnight with the promise that they've got a good site to detect over but 'you've got to keep it quiet', you will have some idea that it's going to be a questionable activity and ask yourself a few moral questions before you jump in the car with them.

15

Ghosts of the 1982 Falklands War

The Falklands War will be one many Britons, particularly of the authors' generation, will have very vivid memories of. The wave of patriotism and support for the hastily assembled British naval task force which set off to reclaim a pair of British islands in the South Atlantic that few people had heard of at the time back in April of 1982 was one of those unique events in British military history. It would also prove to be a welcome political distraction for Margaret Thatcher's Conservative government of the time whose popularity with the working-class sector of British society could never have been considered amiable. When Argentine forces invaded the Falkland Islands on 2 April 1982 Thatcher and indeed her Cabinet must have sighed a sigh of collective relief. Britain was certainly in the grip of a social turmoil, the likes of which had not been experienced for many years. Thatcher's popularity was most certainly heading for decline and the reclaiming of British sovereignty in the South Atlantic was viewed as a means of perhaps redeeming both herself and her government. In this respect Argentina had done for Thatcher what Hitler had done for Winston Churchill. The Falkland Islands would have to be retaken by a task force comprising elements of the Royal Navy, Fleet Air Arm and the British Army which would have to sail 3,300 miles, taking with it all the necessary supplies and equipment with which to fight a war upon arrival.

It still beggars belief today that Royal Navy ships were sent to the Falkland Islands with woefully inadequate anti-aircraft defences. The few 40mm Bofors guns were augmented with 7.62mm machine guns of the type used by the British Army at the time. These small-calibre weapons would prove useless against the low-flying fighter jets and bombers of the Argentine air force which had the advantage of only having to fly a short distance to reach the islands: the Argentines had the home advantage over the pilots of the Royal Navy's Fleet Air Arm based on the two aircraft carriers HMS *Hermes* and *Invincible*, both of which were forced to operate miles from shore for the obvious reason of their vulnerability to Argentine air attack.

With hindsight the success of the British forces was nothing short of a miracle considering the catalogue of blunders from above, blunders which cost many lives. The Falklands War, although classed as a low-intensity war, was everything but low intensity. It was a brutal and bloody conflict. It was also subject to heavy media censorship. It is no surprise then that the British public, at least at the time, were under the impression that it was an 'easy war'; the reality was that it was anything but an easy war. The battles fought at Goose Green, Mount Tumbledown, Wireless Ridge and Mount Longdon were battles which culminated in close-quarter fighting. Hand-to-hand fighting at bayonet point was frequent, what the ordinary soldier refers to as 'gutter fighting', the kind of fighting no soldier relishes. The British forces prevailed over their Argentinian enemy due to their sheer professionalism, bravery, superior training and a lot of luck.

Victory in the Falklands was a very close-run thing indeed; in fact, it was far more a close-run thing than was previously thought. A recent anniversary documentary where many of those in command aired their opinions only serves to reinforce the fact that most of us had been fooled, not only by the media censorship of the war but by the Thatcher government too. Victory assured Thatcher and her Conservative government would enjoy another term in power, while many veterans returned home, bringing the demons of their experiences back home to their families. For some life would never be the same again; the battles with post-traumatic stress disorder which the establishment refused to recognize, the way those badly injured were hung out to dry, and good, highly experienced soldiers driven out of the army by the backward thinking of new officers coming into the battalions. The list could go on, but this would not be the real objective of this chapter so to the point we must now go.

In the wake of the Falklands War many of the areas where the battles were fought became no-go areas due to the mines which had been planted by the Argentine forces. The clear-up operation is still ongoing in certain areas of the islands yet places such as Mount Tumbledown and Mount Longdon are now accessible to those with the resources to get out to the Falklands. The archaeological record present on these battle sites is quite amazing. Historian Mike Valender spent two weeks touring the various battle sites including Tumbledown and the infamous Mount Longdon and he recalled the following on his return to England:

> My visit was somewhat a sombre affair, maybe due to the weather, but it was a depressing place, no place for heroes to lay down their lives. The Falkland Islands are bitterly cold, windswept and often wet with either rain or snow. Although the scenes of some of the bloodiest battles are now silent, the only interruption being the distant braying of sheep, the evidence of the battles is still very much there. Climbing up through the rocks and crags of Mount Longdon and Tumbledown, I traced the route taken by the attacking Scots Guards and paratroopers. Even in daylight it was eerie there; God only knows how those boys did it in near pitch darkness with an enemy waiting among the very rocks I was now weaving my way through. There is plenty of rusty shrapnel; you can tell some of the shrapnel is from mortar weapons, some of it from artillery guns. The rocks had chunks taken out of them by both bullets and shrapnel and where the Argentine positions were located, I found the odd leather high-leg combat boot possibly discarded by a wounded

> Argentine or somehow removed from a dead body. These boots were far superior quality to the ones issued to the British soldiers and were often taken off dead Argentines. Also, evident and still left on these hills are damaged anti-tank weapons and their mountings, hundreds of 7.62mm cartridge cases and even discarded water bottles and clothing remains. None of it should be taken as souvenir material. I photographed much of what I saw but chose to take nothing – to have done so would have felt like I had robbed a grave or something; it just didn't feel right to me. Before I came back home, I went to a souvenir shop in Port Stanley and bought a proper souvenir, a Falklands Island penguin mounted on a lump of Falklands rock; that was enough for me with which to remember and reflect upon my visit there.

There are also the remains of Argentine aircraft shot down in the conflict. Perhaps the most visited of these is the Argentine Air Force FMA IA-58 Pucará twin-engine attack aircraft shot down by ground fire during the conflict. The two 20mm Hispano cannon and four machine guns have all been removed and you can clearly see it has been well stripped for souvenir material over the years. There are also the remnants of Lieutenant Nick Taylor's Royal Navy Sea Harrier (XZ450) which was shot down on 4 May 1982 during an attack on Goose Green by a twin-barrelled radar-controlled 35mm Oerlikon anti-aircraft cannon. Taylor was killed as the Harrier crashed and it was reported that the nosecone of XZ450 was later found on the veranda of a property at Goose Green, having been taken as a trophy by the gun crew that shot it down. The nosecone section had apparently been signed by the gun crew. What happened to it after the Argentine surrender is not known. A substantial portion of wreckage from XZ450 is still in situ where it crashed, including an undercarriage leg. You can photograph the wreckage but nothing even down to the smallest scrap of metal should be taken as the crash site falls under the Protection of Military Remains Act and the wreckage exists today as a memorial to a British naval aviator who lost his life in the service of his country.

The local Falkland islanders will expect you to fully comply with the rules of respecting the abandoned material of war and private property and will react aggressively to anyone caught flouting them. The islanders are aware of the cultural significance of the archaeology, both visible and non-visible, on their islands. As Mike Valender said, 'The Falkland Islanders welcome real historians with honourable intentions but will not entertain "cowboys" of any form – go there if you can, trace the footsteps of those who fought there, and let the only thing you take away with you be the photographs and memories.'

16

The 1991 Gulf War & 2003 Invasion of Iraq

Iraq in its sad political and social situation is not going to be on anyone's bucket list of favourite places to visit, possibly for many decades to come. Iraq has been torn apart by war frequently in her ancient history. Largely supplied by the Soviet Union with weapons and equipment, Iraq's military soon became a force to be reckoned with. Iraq's eight-year war with Iran, fought between 22 September 1980 and 20 August 1988, following Iraq's invasion of her contentious neighbour, would prove disastrous for both sides. It is estimated that a million to twice this number were killed in the war. Iraqi forces used chemical weapons against the Iranians frequently during this protracted conflict, yet Iraq had received support from both the Soviet Union and the West who both expressed concerns at Iran's proposed expansionism in the Gulf region. However costly the Iran–Iraq War proved when it ended, it did so in stalemate with neither side accomplishing any geographical gain.

It would be two years following the end of that war when, on 2 August 1990, the Iraqi army under orders from Iraqi president, Saddam Hussein, would invade the oil-rich emirate of Kuwait in what would be a seven-month occupation of the country. Saddam Hussein had gambled on invading Kuwait, believing that no western intervention would follow due to political complexities and that he would be left with the spoils. However, this could not have been further from the reality. A multinational military force comprising elements of some thirty-six nations led by the US and Britain, fielded 956,600 personnel, including 700,000 US troops. This coalition, assembled under the banner of Operation Desert Shield, would soon give way to the military operation to liberate Kuwait by force, Operation Desert Storm. The Iraq army in Kuwait which numbered 650,000 troops was facing a formidable force determined to not only drive them out of Kuwait but annihilate them in the process if necessary. The Iraqis had also made the mistake of swelling their ranks with conscripts, many of whom were clearly unfit for any form of military service and the task of fighting a well-equipped and highly technological enemy. In fact, the only perceived threat to the coalition forces was that posed by the Iraqi Republican Guards who were considered the elite of the Iraqi army and understandably equipped with the best kit including the latest Soviet-supplied T-72 tanks. There was also the threat that Saddam in desperation might resort to the use of chemical or biological weapons (which he had used to quell Kurdish uprisings). The Iraqis certainly had these in their inventory, yet it is contentious to this day just how much of this material they possessed and whether any of it was used during Desert Storm. The endeavour to free Kuwait of the Iraqi forces began on 17 January 1991 with an air campaign focused on Iraqi military infrastructure and communications in Iraq and Kuwait. A ground offensive followed; on the eve of the ground assault British Army Major John Potter was interviewed who made the job in hand very clear: 'We will spare three kinds of people, medical orderlies, mullahs and anyone clearly indicating their wish to surrender – anyone else will be killed.'

The fighting that followed over the five weeks and four days despite some setbacks resulted in a decisive victory for the coalition forces. As the Iraqis fled Kuwait in convoys of stolen trucks and cars full of looted goods, their escape was cut off by Allied airpower. The front and rear of the fleeing Iraqi convoy which had set off along the Basra Road out of Kuwait was bombed, cutting off any escape. Many of the Iraqi soldiers fled into the desert where they were pursued by Apache attack helicopters. Coalition aircraft were literally queuing up in the skies above waiting to attack. It rapidly became a turkey shoot; such was the gravity of the footage coming in from the Basra Road that US President George Bush senior brought Operation Desert Storm to a halt. Bush, against the wishes of some of his senior commanders on the ground, had decided that the job the coalition forces had set out to do had been accomplished. Kuwait had been freed, the Iraqi army had been routed, suffering heavy casualties in the process, and the Gulf War effectively won.

Yet, Saddam Hussein would remain in power for another twelve years. During the years following Operation Desert Storm, Iraq was subject to scrutiny by United Nations weapons inspection teams who were primarily looking for WMDs, Weapons of Mass Destruction, which it was said Iraq was in possession of. It is well known that Iraq had a chemical weapons capability, mostly in its stores of artillery ammunition, and they had most certainly used these in their war with Iran, and quite possibly in Desert Storm. Yet the WMDs of the variety that British Prime Minister Tony Blair and US President George Bush junior would base their 2003 invasion of Iraq upon simply did not exist and it is clear there were more than just murky political agendas at work.

Over the years after the 1991 Gulf War, many British and US services personnel were posted to the region on tours of duty, largely to maintain a presence and deter any future aggression from Iraq. Thankfully, that aggression did not materialize, and many visiting servicemen went on their own tours of the desert, particularly around Kuwait looking for souvenirs of the 1991 war. US Navy serviceman Tim Crockett did two tours of duty in the region, the last of which was in 2001. Tim described that last tour as being 'very quiet' and somewhat pleasant with all the shopping trips to places such as Bahrain. On days off he described how he and his fellow servicemen would also go off sightseeing and how they came upon a place nicknamed 'The Tank Farm' near the Kuwaiti–Iraqi border. Tim recalled:

> The tank farm was a place we had found quite by accident, although many of the locals knew it was there.

> What had happened there is easily explained: the Iraqis had gathered a large number of their tanks and artillery there ready for deployment during the 1991 fighting. The US Air Force were called in to carry out a strike and, basically, they bombed the shit out of the place. What remains there today are wrecks of tanks and artillery and other equipment. The place was littered with live ammunition of all sizes, so you had to be careful not to mess with anything. We took photographs mostly but I did pick up a piece of bomb casing but that was about it. I guess what is still there today will be the archaeology of tomorrow as its still recent history, but it's still there as far as I'd guess unless it's all been taken away by scrap merchants.

US serviceman Sergeant Wilson J. Harvey, who worked with an EOD team, recalled how he had 'an ordnance collector's dream of a job':

> I was posted there after 1991 to assist in the clearing-up process and to train fellow army personnel on EOD methods. During my work there I found every conceivable piece of ordnance from a pistol bullet to a 1,000lb bomb. There was also a lot of stuff which had been left behind by our own forces. I was out in the desert once sweeping the area for mines and unearthed a large metal box full of British 27mm-calibre cannon shells which were used in the British Tornado aircraft. They were all in like new condition, some were armour piercing and some high explosive and potentially lethal if handled incorrectly. We took the box away and blew it up. In an old quarry we found an Iraqi 57mm anti-aircraft gun left as its crew had abandoned it. There were clips of live ammunition for the gun stacked up ready for use. Earlier we had caught

some of the local kids playing around with them; one was carrying a clip around in his arms; it was pretty crazy as the shells were all high explosives and if dropped could have gone off and killed them all. We blew those up along with the gun in situ. The biggest piece of unexploded ordnance we found partially buried in the sand was a 1,000lb high-explosive bomb which had been dropped and failed to detonate. It was out in the middle of nowhere, so we blew that up using a small initiating charge in situ. It made a fair old bang even at almost a mile's distance away and afterwards we collected some of the pieces of it. I gave much of what I had away so don't have much left now.

Through the course of my duties, I also found lots of Iraqi paperwork, much of it handwritten stuff. I found a load in an abandoned building once and you'd find it in destroyed tanks and other vehicles. I mean ancient manuscripts when found are considered as valuable archaeological material, so maybe the kind of stuff we were finding back then will be classed as the same many years from now. We also encountered the odd aircraft wreck too; most of what the Iraqi air force had was Russian built. We found a few that had been shot down or blown up on the ground; we took anything interesting for souvenirs if it wasn't too heavy. The strange thing was you'd find a wreck and then if you went back weeks later to visit it again, it would be gone. It wasn't that anyone had taken it away, just that the sands of the desert constantly shift and have a habit of covering things over after storms. After time they become completely buried and maybe years later they will be discovered again.

Quite a considerable amount of battlefield pick-up material had been brought back from the Gulf prior to the 2003 invasion of Iraq. Yet unlike most other areas of military relic collecting, Gulf War relics are not as common as that of the First or Second World Wars. This does not mean that these things are any less important, just that in the eyes of many it is too recent to be considered as history and maybe less collectable at present. I was fortunate enough to have several ex-army pals who had fought in the 1991 Gulf War and who brought back things such as exploded RPG-7 rockets, helmets, shell cases, parts from destroyed tanks and captured paperwork including ID cards. Most of it bar a few pieces have all gone now.

The 2003 invasion of Iraq orchestrated by the Bush and Blair administrations failed to receive the backing of the international community unlike the 1991 Gulf War. President George Bush junior had decided that Saddam Hussein had somehow been responsible in part for the 9/11 attacks on the US. Iraq and Saddam Hussein were in many respects a convenient scapegoat for the events of 9/11, as a member of a so-called 'Axis of Evil' which also included Iran and North Korea. With accusations that these countries were guilty of state-sponsored terrorism against the West, Iraq was in many respects the softer target of the three. Both Bush and Blair sent their military forces directly into Iraq with the sole intention of removing Saddam Hussein and his Baathist regime from power in what many now regard as an illegal war. The US-led invasion of Iraq which lasted from 20 March to 1 May 2003 achieved its objective of removing Saddam from power. He would later be discovered in hiding. He was arrested, sent for trial and hanged. As for Iraq, it would be plunged into a state of anarchy from which it could probably never recover; the domino effect the invasion had upon the region would have far-reaching political and social consequences. Iraq was not left in a better state as both Bush and Blair had promised the world and all the talk of Iraq possessing WMDs was later found to be spurious. Iraq in its current state is not a safe country for westerners and may remain so for an indefinite period.

So, in the archaeological sense the only material we currently have which serves as a record of the conflict in the archaeological sense are photographs taken by British and American service personnel. Prior to the 2003 invasion the various wrecks and relics as explained earlier were left exactly as they were after the ceasefire of 1991 and were relatively accessible to military personnel serving in the region. During this period a considerable amount of souvenir material was brought back from Iraq. However, some of this souvenir material was of a nature best left alone as some military personnel have since discovered.

The material referred to here, depleted uranium cores, was used in British and American tank ammunition and in some types of 25mm and 30mm aircraft cannon ammunition. Depleted uranium is viewed as a cheaper alternative to tungsten carbide and offered greater tactical efficiency against enemy armour. Depleted uranium is exactly as the term refers, uranium material that has a significantly reduced radioactive state. This material originates from spent nuclear fuel rods from nuclear reactors. Its use in ammunition is primarily as an armour-piercing penetrator. Depleted uranium is an extremely dense material, making it ideal for anti-armour applications and, being naturally pyrophoric, as a munition not requiring additional incendiary materials. The material used in tank and aircraft munitions is not pure uranium but alloyed with other metals before being machine processed into either sabots (for tank ammunition) or penetrators (for aircraft use). The finished penetrators used in the 30mmx173 GAU 8A Avenger round as used by the Fairchild A-10 Thunderbolt, or 'Warthog', are around two inches in length and resemble a metalworker's punch. The penetrator is enclosed in the 30mm projectile body which has a steel base and an alloy nosecone. When a depleted uranium round strikes its target, it slices through armour plate like a knife through butter. As its passes through the armour the round self-sharpens rather than becoming blunt through the impact. It also produces an incendiary effect in the form of white-hot sparks which will ignite fuel, oil, ammunition or any other flammable material in the target. Anyone within the target range will almost certainly be vapourized in their seats. So, to the point, what has depleted uranium got to do with battlefield archaeology? A huge quantity of depleted uranium was fired during Operation Desert Storm. In certain areas the desert is littered with spent depleted uranium cores, and these are classed as a military toxic and should not be handled under any circumstances. In their unfired state these rounds, as the military insist, are perfectly safe for military personnel to handle and be in proximity with.

In its fired state the true hazards were obviously less understood, until after the war when some veterans got sick with a crippling illness which was soon nicknamed 'Desert Fever' or 'Gulf War Syndrome'. One of the factors found to be a possible cause of this mystery illness was oxidized depleted uranium or uranium particles from impacted projectiles, the dust of which was in turn ingested by troops in areas where it had been used. Tanks and other military vehicles churn up a lot of dust, dust is easily ingested and you can see the feasibility of how depleted uranium particles can enter a human body where it can then pose a significant threat to health. There were recorded cases where US soldiers had picked up these fired depleted uranium penetrators. Many, having been exposed to the elements, were in a badly oxidized state and should not have been picked up under any circumstances. The military continue to claim that depleted uranium is safe. If this is so, then why was one individual who attempted to bring fired depleted uranium penetrators through an airport almost charged with smuggling nuclear materials?

It is not only contamination from depleted uranium that poses a threat in the deserts of Iraq. Tons of unexploded mines, artillery and cannon shells, bombs and grenades litter the countryside. Much of this abandoned military material is in a dangerously unstable condition. EOD teams from the US and Britain assisted in the clear-up operation at the end of Operation Desert Storm. Huge amounts of dangerous ordnance were collected, taken out into the desert and then safely destroyed. One young American EOD tech attached to the US

Marines explained, 'We will be doing this job for a very long time. The war itself was pretty short but the shit left over from it is gonna take many years to clear.'

Of course, with the 2003 US-led Invasion of Iraq, the objective to rid Iraq of its pariah president Saddam Hussein by military force was achieved, yet it failed to win the peace in the aftermath. The resulting power vacuum and subsequent insurgency which emanated from Bush and Blair's failed adventure would have ramifications reaching far into the future, not just for Iraq but the world itself.

The photographs taken at the place once known to British and American servicemen as The Tank Farm plus the photographs of abandoned unexploded ordnance outside of Kuwait will very likely be the only view we have of these things for some considerable time. The geopolitical destabilization of Iraq brought about by Blair and Bush and the dangers posed by insurgents in the region have ensured that few westerners will dare to follow in the footsteps of those who fought in Operation Desert Storm or indeed the invasion of Iraq. These relics of a more recent war will in time be consumed by the continuously moving sands of the desert and will be the battlefield archaeology of tomorrow.

17

The Trade in Archaeological Militaria

The trade in military and battlefield archaeology has witnessed a huge surge in popularity over the past twenty years or so. Not that there were not established dealers in this area of militaria prior to the 1990s when the collecting of the rusty detritus of war experienced something of a boom alongside that of the worldwide web, which in turn opened the market further, allowing anyone with the means at their disposal to become a seller or buyer of military archaeology. The advent of online auction sites increased what was rapidly becoming a very highly competitive worldwide market. Some of the old established dealers fell by the wayside, seemingly unable to compete in this suddenly flooded marketplace.

Perhaps a good example of this was the Dugup duo of Jay Howe and Paul White from Sussex. For many years the two travelled the world collecting and buying all manner of militaria but having a specialization in First and Second World War battlefield relics. They had a strong, loyal customer base, and offered their wares at fair prices often through their website where orders could be processed at the click of a button. It was a sad fact of what I can only describe as victimization by the authorities which eventually drove Jay and Paul away from what was a lucrative business. Perfectly harmless stock which included inert shells and grenades were taken from their premises and often returned to them later in a vandalized state (i.e., brass fuzes missing), making them unsaleable. This has happened to several people who have attempted to legitimately sell battlefield-recovered items. I guess in some cases it is a sign of the times, as everybody is offended by everything today.

I know of some individuals who have been hounded as Neo-Nazis just for selling Second World War German Iron Crosses. It is a sad reflection on modern society that we are no longer able to pursue an interest in what is world history as freely as we once were.

London militaria dealer Target Arms, another once-popular source of quality battlefield-recovered relics offered to collectors and historians at more than fair prices, also suddenly dropped into obscurity. For reasons unknown the proprietor decided to invest in sporting air weapons and accessories, steadily reducing his once-popular First and Second World War memorabilia lines. So why did some of these early dealers in the field suddenly fail whilst others flourished? Were there any drastic changes in the actual market or maybe a lack of understanding of what collectors wanted? I think the answer would be both yes and no for several reasons.

The Battlefield Archaeology team based in Worcestershire, who began sending out illustrated catalogues of their battlefield-recovered artefacts to collectors back in the 1990s, failed to survive due to a lack of diversity in what they were offering. Their beautifully made and labelled wooden display boxes containing equipment, buckles, buttons, cartridge cases, badges and dog tags were all very nice, yet were expensive and collectors wanted more than just these things. I myself inquired of them on several occasions, asking about particular relic items but was told that all they were able to offer were those items featured in their monthly catalogues and that was that. So, in a sense it was the normal pitfalls of any business and those who could not diversify and/or provide the types of items that collectors wanted, rapidly fell by the wayside.

Then there is the sourcing issue. In recent times the increased fascination with the First and Second World Wars has led to an increase in demand for the archaeological material associated with these two conflicts. Those dealers today who do not have the contacts inevitably lose out to the ones who do. Sourcing has become a major factor in the trade in battlefield relic items today as a lot of material is being brought into the UK from Eastern Europe. The recent changes in the laws regarding the recovery of battlefield archaeology in places such as Poland and sometimes overly biased actions of customs officials both here in the UK and in Europe have failed to stem the flow of battlefield-recovered items into the UK. Yet for some it is still very much a case of if you know 'that man that can', you're sorted.

In 2010, Relics from The Front made their debut into the world of battlefield relics. Having established good contacts both here in the UK and Europe, the business had a sound foundation on which to move forward and has succeeded online where many have failed. If you attend any of the major UK militaria shows you will find Relics from The Front and if you are as passionate about battlefield relics as what I am, you cannot help but be impressed by the scope of items they have on offer. Each item is supplied with a laminated data sheet explaining what the item is and where it was recovered. Again, the prices asked are what I consider to be very fair compared to some other dealers. Relics from The Front has been able to meet the increasing demands of collectors along with an efficient business model in which to operate. Utilizing their impressive website, which is constantly updated with new additions, sometimes daily, and attending all the major militaria shows, they have become one of the respected names in the trade with excellent service and customer feedback. Speaking with Relics from The Front's Cheryl, I asked her opinion on the market and current demand for the relics they sell. Cheryl explained:

> The market is and always has been niche, which makes it limited. The UK exiting the EU has not helped and has been further impacted by the global COVID-19 pandemic. This has driven prices high, and acquiring new items relied predominantly on travel into Europe which has not been possible until more recently. Demand remains, as collectors will always want to feed their hobby however, and there was a higher-than-normal

> demand during the initial stages of the pandemic. This demand remains steady. With regard to how Relics from The Front view the future of the business, we take it at a day at a time. It is challenging with the cost-of-living crisis. As mentioned already, collectors will always want to feed their hobby and if they collect militaria and relics, this will now be dependent on their disposable income. The factors behind our success where others may have fallen by the wayside is simple. There is the possibility that other dealers may be pricing themselves out of the market, and we do try and keep our items as cheap as possible. The research that goes into many of the items attracts buyers as does the presentation of the items as many are cleaned prior to selling. This takes time and effort but gives the buyer a good piece of history.

A good basic example of what Relics from The Front specialize in appears in the illustrative plates for this section. The items in question here is a group of recovered artefacts from the crash site of a Focke Wolf Fw 190 Werke Number 170735 'Yellow 10', piloted by Unteroffizier Horst Gabel who was shot down and killed on 15 June 1944. Gabel was a 24-year-old fresh out of flying school. At the time of his death, he had two victories to his credit and had been shot down once previously but was able to bale out. On 15 June his unit, 3/JG 1 was sent into action against an American bomber formation over Normandy. The bombers had a substantial escort fighter presence, thus the German fighter pilots intercepting them soon found themselves heavily outnumbered as the fighting began. Now 96, Pierre Goumierre witnessed this air battle from the back door of his home, a farmhouse in Normandy. Pierre recalled:

> The bombers were passing overhead, and the sky was filled with the rumble of all those engines. They were

on their way to bomb a target farther to the east, so I was told. There were a lot of aircraft filling the sky, mostly Americans. You could clearly see the long white vapour trails of the higher-flying Germans as they met the formation. They attacked the bombers from both sides, flying around them in a kind of arc, looking for the weakest spot in their defences. The tiny black specs that were flying close to the bombers were of course the American escorts. They began to fly towards the attacking Germans. You could clearly hear the sound of machine guns and cannons firing as the mass of aircraft exchanged fire with one another. Within a few seconds I saw that one aircraft was breaking away from the bomber formation with three other aircraft in pursuit. The aircraft being pursued was trailing smoke and falling from the sky at what must have been very high speed. I watched as the three pursuing aircraft pulled up and the other disappeared from view behind some trees. Seconds later there was a plume of black smoke rising into the air from where this aircraft had impacted the ground. We always used to look out for parachutes but on this occasion, there was none to be seen; the pilot whoever he was must have been still inside the aircraft when it hit the ground. At the time I can remember thinking, 'That's someone's son, father or brother in that aircraft and now he will be dead.' The crash site was not that far away, somewhere near Rabadanges from the direction of the smoke. We went to see more out of curiosity than anything else and it was then we were told the plane was a German, a Focke Wolf aircraft. There was this huge crater in the ground with a fire raging away inside due to the fuel and oil residues trapped in the ground. There was nothing left of the plane, just lots of little pieces. The pilot's remains,

> or rather what was left of him, were recovered for burial. I was told that all they could find were small pieces of flesh, remains of arms and legs and mangled flying gear. The crater made by the plane on impact was filled in with soil afterwards and left as it was.

The dates of the archaeological operation to recover the wreckage of this aircraft are unknown but are thought to have taken place over the last few years. Due to the high speed of the impact, most of the recovered material was typically small lumps of engine casing, airframe structure and skinning. The guns and their ammunition boxes were smashed, and 20mm Mauser MG 151/20 cannon shells had been widely distributed as a result. Most had their high-explosive and armour-piercing projectiles partially intact. These along with the powder charges inside the cartridge cases were removed by an EOD tech. The insides of the steel cartridge cases were then oiled to destroy the primers which were of the electrical type, indicating these cannon shells came from the magazines of the inboard 20mm MG 151/20 cannons, as these fired through the arc of the propeller blades necessitating the need for electrical priming. Several steel cannon shell belt links were also recovered along with one of the firing bolts from one of the 20mm Mauser MG 151/20 cannons. Items such as these would form a good representative display of items from this crash and were put aside with any of the other interesting finds recovered during the excavation. Relics from The Front acquired these through their European contacts and offered the three 20mm cannon shells and three shell links on their website for £35. The 20mm Mauser MG 151/20 firing bolt being a scarcer item was later sold for £45.

These pieces are the kinds of items that collectors and historians relish the most. They appeal to those who are fascinated by ammunition, Second World War military aviation in general and those who specialize in collecting items associated with a particular type of aircraft such as the Focke Wolf Fw 190 (an aircraft which has many fans here in the UK). If Relics from The Front can continue to source items such as these as the situation in the hobby and market itself evolves, then they will continue to have a secure future in these uncertain times.

The major militaria shows held every year in the UK, shows such as The War and Peace Show, Stoneleigh Military Convention, Malvern Military Show and War in the Vale, are as popular as ever with historians and collectors alike. The wealth of battlefield-recovered material which can be encountered at these shows where dealers come from all over the UK and Europe, can be overwhelming. It is perhaps always a good idea to go to these shows with some idea as to what you are looking for. Of course, adhering to this rule is easier said than done as most of us turn into 'kids in a sweet shop' the moment we enter these environments. At Stoneleigh, for example, you can buy anything from a missile down to a tunic button but beware the prices these days are not cheap for several reasons: travel expenses and the cost of a table or stall are just two of the basic overheads most dealers have to consider before they even show a profit. With the advent of the show season for 2022 now upon us, it will be interesting to see if the regular faces still attend the UK militaria show circuit and get their opinions as to whether they have managed to survive the difficult times of the past two years.

To close, we would like to say that it is amazing just how long it has taken for the awareness of the historical value and significance of battlefield recovered relics to come to the fore with the greater public and collecting community. The days where rusty relics were once confined to cardboard boxes beneath dealers' tables and literally given away as budget-basement militaria are now long gone. This is thanks to the greater understanding of our own family history today and greater media coverage given to the events of the First and Second World Wars, along with the many earlier, and later, conflicts which have shaped history. As previously mentioned, there are today more documentary-style programmes covering militaria and battlefield artefacts and archaeology than at any other time previous. Some of these programmes are very good, such as *Time Team*, *Battlefield Detectives* and *River Hunters* but others are poorly presented and amateurish. Choosing daft and overly dramatic titles such as *Nazi War Diggers* or referring to the detritus of warfare as 'treasure' is something many serious historians find disrespectful and something which places the entirety of the emphasis on monetary value as opposed to historical significance. Yes, there have been (and always will be) certain artefacts recovered in archaeological digs carried out by both professional and amateur alike where high-value items have been unearthed, items which later change hands for many thousands of pounds or more. It is sad that most of the programmes being aired today with reference to battlefield and military archaeology in general are all about the potential profits and the degree of celebrity status those presenting them might attain from getting their mugs on TV.

Speaking of celebrity status, it is also slightly amusing that only in this millennium could you find real celebrities, albeit with well-expired sell-by dates, prepared to endorse some of the second-rate rubbish masquerading as history. With the wealth of media available today it is without doubt easier than it has ever been to self-proclaim one's expertise while poncing one's ego. This trend appears to be increasing and will no doubt continue unabated until viewers grow bored of the same old insipid television being peddled by the producers of these programmes. I have recollections of when it was just the *World at War*, often aired on a Sunday evening when most people were at home, but those days are now long gone, seemingly lost in the progression we are constantly being told is so beneficial to us.

Afterword

There is little I would like to add here other than to thank Julian for all his efforts for making this volume a reality. It has been a true pleasure to work with a man whose knowledge and passion for his subject is immediately obvious. The writing of this volume has, like a few of the books which now form my backlist, presented its own unique problems, but these were overcome without any detriment to the material presented therein. I am sure Julian will agree that we both hope this volume will provide a useful text, even if only in a small way, about military archaeology and the unearthing of artefacts from wars sometimes fought many centuries ago.

The history of warfare is best illustrated not only by the photographs and testimonies of those who were there but by the physical objects which remain after those who fought are long gone. We as historians/collectors and enthusiasts have a moral duty to preserve what we can of our past which is now fast disappearing into the grey electronic fog of the modern world. We English are famous for having a magpie mentality when it comes to collecting things. There are the eccentrics among us who collect virtually anything, often unfairly referred to as 'hoarders'. Yet without these colourful people, institutions such as museums and archives would probably become void of material over time. Collecting things is the one endearing factor about being English; it's something we English have always done, and no doubt will always do, even though not all are always able to explain how or why they started. One of the few merits of living in the new millennium is the now wider availability of metal-detecting equipment to the general public and the interest in both history and archaeology is today within the reach of everyone, not just those with endless funds at their disposal; it is growing way beyond what even those learned history professors of old would have imagined many years ago.

I often reflect on what John Copper, my middle school history teacher, would have made of the historical events that have occurred since his premature passing. Time marches on and the present soon becomes the past as we hurtle constantly into the future. With the relatively new phenomenon of magnet fishing as yet another component of searching out archaeology of both the distant and recent past, it was heart-warming to see youngsters casting their lines into the River Avon just below the old railway bridge in Evesham. There were soon squeals of delight resonating from the lads as the simple, yet powerful magnet cast into the soupy waters of the Avon picked something up from the bottom of the river. Whether it was a shopping trolley or a piece of other modern junk is not the point: they were abandoning their Xboxes and bedrooms and getting out to take part in something that very quickly becomes addictive. The future of traditional and military archaeology thus appears to have a secure future as the past becomes ever precious in the present and this can only be a good thing for all those who have an association with or partake directly in these disciplines.

To round things off, I would also like to thank Jon Laffin (21/09/1922–23/09/2000), at least in spirit, for his two excellent books *Battlefield Archaeology* and *Aviation Archaeology* which I first read so long ago and were two books which provided the core inspiration for the creation of this volume.

Tim Heath
The Old Inn, Worcestershire
April 2022

This is the section for an exchange of thanks, firstly to Tim for giving me the opportunity to share some of my experiences. Sharing is a vital aspect of all research as without it there really is little point in undertaking it. So, it was with great gusto and relish that I took to the challenge of assisting Tim with this publication. However, this would never have been possible if people had not originally shared their experience and expertise in such fields allowing me to gain my own. These individuals are indeed far too numerous to mention here but they know who they are. I count myself very fortunate indeed in having been involved in such activities and as such am truly delighted at this amazing opportunity to share them. It just remains to say that while constructing this work both Tim and I 'dug up' (please forgive the intrusion of a dreadful pun) a veritable feast of work, only some of which is included here. So as has been hinted in the text there may well be other future volumes to work on but as in all such cases, the progression of those depends largely on you the reader.

Julian Evan-Hart
Braintree, Essex
April 2022

Acknowledgements

We would like to acknowledge the following for the use of material and/or contributions in the production of this work: *The Armourer* militaria magazine, *Treasure Hunting* magazine, The Imperial War Museums London, The RAF Museum Hendon, London, The National Archives, Kew, The Air Historical Branch, Peter Halliday (RIP), Richard Appleby, Melvyn Brownless, Andy 'Badger' Long, Joan Bomford, the Worcester Battle Society and Jon Laffin (RIP) whose excellent books read so long ago provided the inspiration for this one, and lastly, Cheryl of Relics from The Front for taking the time to talk about the business.

About the Authors

Tim Heath was born into a military family. His interest in military history began at the tender age of 7. His initial research focused primarily on the aircraft and weaponry of the Luftwaffe in the Second World War. He later wrote extensively for the UK's leading military history magazine, *The Armourer*. In the process he has assisted a number of UK and Europe-based military history authors with their published works. During the course of his research, he worked closely with the German War Graves Commission at Kassel, Germany, meeting with war veterans and their families. For the past thirty-five years he has specialized in German social and military history, with particular emphasis on the roles of German females in the Third Reich and beyond. His first title for Pen and Sword Books, *Hitler's Girls: Doves Amongst Eagles*, was published in 2017, followed by *In Hitler's Shadow: Post-War Germany and the Girls of the BDM, Hitler's Germany: The Birth of Extremism, Women of the Third Reich: From Camp Guards to Combatants, Hitler's Housewives: German Women on the Home Front, Hitler's Lost State: The Fall of Prussia and the Willhelm Gustloff Tragedy, Anschluss and After: Resistance Heroines in Nazi- and Russian-occupied Austria.* He lives with his partner Paula in the old Worcestershire market town of Evesham.

Julian Evan-Hart was born in 1962 at Welwyn Garden City in Hertfordshire and has always had an interest in collecting things. In 1969, aged just 7, he found a mammoth tooth in the spoil from a local roadworks. As the years progressed metal detecting would logically evolve as yet another passion and led to his being involved with the excavation of numerous wartime aircraft crash sites. In 2006, he was pivotal in helping organize the world's first archaeological excavation of a Zeppelin, an event which was later to become the subject of a BBC *Timewatch* programme. Then, somewhat differently, came an invitation to go out and detect in the deserts of Jordan looking for evidence of Lawrence of Arabia. This was followed by involvement in a *Time Team* episode searching for a 'lost Roman villa' in Cambridgeshire. He considers metal detecting to be fantastic privilege in providing the ability of handling historically important coins and artefacts and that it is essential to share such experiences. Further honouring these beliefs, he has written and contributed to over thirty books including the bestselling *Beginner's Guide to Metal Detecting*. For the last seven years he has been the editor of *Treasure Hunting* magazine and has made numerous radio and TV broadcasts. He was recently quoted as saying, 'Today metal detecting makes an incomparable contribution to worldwide history and heritage, ensuring that many of our yesterdays are found today and thus are preserved for all our tomorrows.'